Acknowledgments

We share our deepest appreciation to the contributors of this collection for their steadfast commitment to seeing this book come to life.

Debbie Byrd: I would like to thank Lafayette College for funding two undergraduate research assistants and for a research grant that allowed me to visit a number of Toronto-area women's shelters and young mom centres. I am grateful to the young parents who have shared with me their stories and views, especially Kami, Beatriz, Shante, and Alissa. You are an inspiration, as is my own mom, Elizabeth Louise Machen Byrd. To Pat and Elaine, thank you for your daily acts of kindness and for making me laugh when times are tough.

Joanne Minaker: I would like to thank my partner, Bryan Hogeveen, for inspiring me and challenging me to dig deeper and care for myself with the intensity I do for others. I'm so grateful to our family – our little fire, Ayden Bryan, our morning star, Taryk Peter, and our miracle, Maylah Grace. I am because you are. Finally, deep admiration and appreciation to my co-editors, Debbie and Andrea, for their commitment to this project and to empowering mothers. *I dedicate this work to all the care-givers and community makers who support us to belong and grow as mothers, and humans, together.*

Andrea O'Reilly: I would like to thank my partner Terry Conlin for always being there with his love and support throughout my years of young motherhood. I would also like to thank Jesse O'Reilly-Conlin for his accomplished copy editing. Thank you also to my MIRCI and Demeter family for providing the safe and sustaining "homeplace" that makes possible my maternal scholarship. I dedicate this work to my three children, Clementine, Casey, and Jesse, who have allowed and aided my own becoming as a young mother.

T0308125

Feminist Perspectives on Young Mothers, and Young Mothering

Edited by Joanne Minaker, Deborah Byrd, and Andrea O'Reilly

DEMETER

Feminist Perspectives on Young Mothers, and Young Mothering
Edited by Joanne Minaker, Deborah Byrd, and Andrea O'Reilly

Demeter Press
140 Holland Street West
P. O. Box 13022
Bradford, ON L3Z 2Y5
Tel: (905) 775-9089
Email: info@demeterpress.org
Website: www.demeterpress.org

Demeter Press logo based on the sculpture "Demeter" by Maria-Luise Bodirsky www.keramik-atelier.bodirsky.de

Printed and Bound in Canada

Front cover image: stereohype.
Front cover artwork: Michelle Pirovich
Typesetting: Michelle Pirovich

Library and Archives Canada Cataloguing in Publication
Title: Feminist perspectives on young mothers and young mothering
Edited by Deborah Lea Byrd, Joanne Minaker and Andrea O'Reilly.
Names: Byrd, Deborah Lea, 1953- editor. | Minaker, Joanne Cheryl, 1974- editor. | O'Reilly, Andrea, 1961- editor.
Description: Includes bibliographical references.
Identifiers: Canadiana 20190094605 | ISBN 9781772582086 (softcover)
Subjects: LCSH: Mothers. | LCSH: Mothers—Social conditions. | LCSH: Teenage mothers. | LCSH: Teenage mothers—Social conditions. | LCSH: Motherhood.
Classification: LCC HQ759.F46 2019 | DDC 306.874/3—dc23

MIX
Paper from
responsible sources
FSC
www.fsc.org   FSC® C004071

Contents

Introduction

Deborah Byrd, Joanne Minaker, and Andrea O'Reilly

T his is a book about being young, being a mother, and grappling with what it means to inhabit these two complex social positions and identities at the same time. The contributors to this collection, some of whom have personal experience of mothering in their teens or early twenties, approach this important topic from an intersectional feminist perspective. We acknowledge that concepts of youth and motherhood are social constructions imbued with power. These two states of being—youth and pregnancy and/or parenting—are generally viewed as being in conflict with each other in modern-day Canada, Australia, and the U.S. (the cultures examined in the essays that follow). In the contemporary dominant discourse of these countries, youth is regarded as a liminal state, a transitional period in which one gradually leaves childhood behind and enters adulthood. It is a stage of life when one experiences changes in body and mind and through experimentation, risk, and trial and error, one develops a sense of self and a core set of beliefs and values. In short, the prevailing normative expectations, despite contextual variability within these geographical regions, position adolescence or youth as a process of becoming—becoming less immature, reckless, childlike, and dependent and becoming more responsible, prudent, and proper (i.e., more socially acceptable and acculturated to prevailing ideologies and societal norms). In the first half of the twentieth century, one generally was expected to make this transition to adulthood by the late teens; in contemporary Western societies, it is often acceptable for the period of youthful self-development and self-absorption to last until the mid-to-late twenties. And when becoming a mother is considered socially acceptable or deviant is governed by age, gender, peer networks, school, culture, and community norms. Marlee Kline reminds us that patriarchal ideology constructs mothering as compulsory "only for those women considered 'fit,' and not for women who have been judged 'unfit' on the basis of their social location" (120-21). Stefanie Mollborn and Christie Sennott refer to teen pregnancy as a "cultural battleground in struggles over morality, education, and family" (1283). They write the following:

> Norms about teen pregnancy belong to a subclass of social norms called age norms ... which regulate the timing of a behaviour (such as pregnancy) in the life course and its ordering relative to other life events such as marriage. Teen pregnancy lends itself to thinking about norms in bundles because is it part of what we call a chain of behaviors that lead up to and beyond pregnancy: teen sex, contraception, pregnancy, abortion, and parenthood ... each of these behaviors is highly contested when teenagers engage in it. (1284-85)

Since mothering is generally regarded by the dominant culture as an adult task requiring (among other things) maturity, good judgment, and selflessness, to be a young mother is almost by definition to be a bad or an unfit mother. Many norm bundles coalesce to reinforce appropriate age and gendered behaviour in this instance. Consequently, mothers who are, in Pat Carlen's terms, "outwith" these gendered norms have been scorned, maligned, and stigmatized; their parenting, scrutinized and monitored, leading to hostility towards young mothers (155). The looks, intense stares, and comments are unavoidable experiences shared by many young mothers, which diminish their confidence and make them feel "uncomfortable, intimidated and distressed" (Fearnley 68). As noted, at different points in time, a normative age range has been considered appropriate and acceptable for women to have and raise babies (Fonda et al.). Although, biologically, childbearing age is roughly between the developmental ages of fifteen and thirty-five, babies are born to mothers who are younger and, of course, older. What constitutes a "young mother" is both a sociocultural construct and personally defined. How categories such as age, gender, or parent are constructed, deployed, and otherwise understood has much to do with discourse and practice, which are explained fully neither by subjective experience nor by some objective lived reality.

Young mothers—variously referred to as illegitimate, unwed, teenage, girl-mom, or "babies having babies"—are socially constructed as "other" and as those who operate outside normative boundaries of acceptable or appropriate youth and motherhood. In other words, adolescence and parenting are, in popular representations, mutually exclusive, incongruent, and incompatible. The logic appears simple: girls do not have babies, and mothers are not girls.

Young mothers who transgress age and gender norms of appropriate becoming, as defined by socially constructed values, attitudes, and ideas, tend to be represented "as at-risk girls or failed subjects whose perceived poor decision-making abilities are expressed most clearly though their 'improper' sexual choices and behavior"—behaviour that led not only to a pregnancy but to an improper decision to keep and rear the child (Hamilton et al. 1186; Phoenix). Whereas great concern has long been raised about the so-called problem of teenage or young motherhood, the problems younger mothers face or the challenges that affect their youth or mothering have not received the same level of attention. Even in 2018, the World Health Organization framed adolescent pregnancy as a problem. Although many mothers who parent earlier than expected experience pressure, coercion, and unintended pregnancy, defining "adolescent pregnancy" as a problem in need of a solution may lead to obscuring the diverse experiences of young mothers and casting young moms as deviant, at risk, and a cause for concern. The fact that young mothers often come from low-income families, choose to parent outside the institution of marriage, and are disproportionately women of colour removes them further from capitalist patriarchy's vision of the ideal mother: a "30-something, white, middle-class, able-bodied, married, and heterosexual mother situated in a nuclear family, preferably as a stay-at-home or full-time mother" (Minaker, "The Space Between" 126). In addition, the neoliberal view of young mothers is problematic because it ignores the roles and responsibilities of the social structures which shape their lives and any adverse outcomes. The social characteristics of young women may increase their likelihood of early pregnancy, such as lower socio-economic status and sole-parenting. Moreover, they "are particularly likely to exhibit caregiver depression, have histories of maltreatment in caregivers' own childhoods, live in lower-quality neighborhoods, have caregivers with less than postsecondary education, have a greater number of children and very young children in the home, and experience housing instability" (Font et. al, 278). Being involved with Child Protective Services (CPS) or experiencing foster care produces a tripling effect, as young girls in these situations "are at substantially higher risk of early motherhood than low-income girls ... who did not experience CPS involvement or foster care" (Font et al. 278). However, research by Sarah Font, Maria Cancian and Lawrence Berger reveals differences in risk of early pregnancy before, during, and after being in care, with risks being particularly high before care, and much lower after being in care (274). Placement of these young women during foster care was significant because it highlights the effects of sociodemographic disadvantages and their role in reproducing inequalities, the need for social bonds and stability, and a call for a compassionate view of motherhood.

Young women in their teens and early twenties, however, do get pregnant, have babies, and parent their children—and they often do so with great success. Recognizing, acknowledging, and making visible young women's unique, heterogeneous, and valued experiences and perspectives on motherhood are central goals of this collection. The book grew out of our (the co-editors) belief that an intersectional, empathetic, and more finely nuanced understanding of young motherhood is long overdue. Intersectional feminists acknowledge that a young woman's identity as a mother intersects with, and is complicated by, such factors as race, class, nationality, religion, and gender, among other social locations and identities. Young mothers are not a homogeneous group; they have different cultural and structural locations within interlocking systems of power and privilege. They are heterosexual, queer, and trans; they are poor, middle class, and wealthy. Some have citizenship status in the countries in which they reside; others do not. Some are beneficiaries of white privilege; others experience systemic racism on a daily basis. Some young mothers are survivors of severe childhood trauma; others grew up feeling safe and secure. Young mothers live in rural areas, in suburbia, and in large cities; they reside in areas that range from politically progressive to ultraconservative. Young mothers have different degrees of access to financial and emotional resources—from mentors, peer supports, and kin networks to resources and services provided by nonprofit organizations, government agencies, or specific communities to which they belong.

And, of course, every young mother has her own unique story to tell—a story that usually resists the dominant discourse about how young mothers almost inevitably do great harm to themselves, their children, and society at large. The young mothers and their allies who have contributed to this collection endorse what Elizabeth Aparicio, Deborah Gioia and Edward Pecukonis call a "compassionate view of mothering" that entails attuned intervention that "support[s] both mother and infant mental health and well-being" (Aparicio et al. 96). Whether written by former young mothers or by academic and/or community allies of young moms, the essays in this collection seek to identify and critique the ideologies, institutions, and public policies that so powerfully—and generally negatively—affect young mothers. We share counter-narratives that challenge, deconstruct, and resist false and demeaning generalizations about young mothers' characters and their lives. Since dominant discourses generally create and reinforce narratives that justify and uphold existing and unequal power arrangements and rarely reflect the perspectives and lived experiences of marginalized groups, we felt it important to present the voices of young mothers, which feminist scholar-activists need to hear if they are to work with young mothers to effect positive changes in public perceptions and policies. When we read the stories of young mothers, we hear tales of success and struggle, oppression and resistance, empowerment and agency. We encounter remarkable grit and determination by individual women, tributes to mentors and communities of care, and, most importantly, compelling stories about the power of a mother's love. And we hear about motherhood having a transformative effect on a young woman's life—for the good. It is an effect that inspires others.

We invite our readers to hear and learn from the often silenced stories of real and fictional young mothers, which call existing social injustices into question and push the limits of possibility for more just and caring social arrangements for mothers and children. It is this hope that brings together fourteen writers from a variety of positions, academic disciplines, social locations, communities, and ways of understanding youth and mothering. We find common ground in communicating mothers' stories, challenging dominant discourses, and reimagining social arrangements of care. Following Andrea O'Reilly's conceptualization of "mother outlaws," we offer insights into how a new understanding of young mothering can help us appreciate the maternal agency, authority, autonomy, and authenticity of many mothers in their teens and early twenties ("Mother Outlaws"). As Bryan Hogeveen and Joanne Minaker argue, "If we are to recognize the value and necessity of a broad community of care for all mothers and children, we must bridge the (material and discursive) divide that separates mothers. For the sake of all mothers and children everywhere, we must close the chasm between mothers and "Other" mothers" (20). This collection continues a feminist tradition that, in the words of Hogeveen and Minaker, respects the voices of marginalized mothers because "honouring their stories is an essential step to empower them to care for themselves and their child(ren)" (21).

The Organization of this Collection

The essays in this book complement, echo, and enrich one another. We have grouped the chapters under three broadly conceived topic headings: (1) Dominant Discourses on Young Moms and Young Mothering: Concerns and Consequences; (2) Young Mothers' Stories: Challenging the Discourse; and 3) Counter-Narratives: Communicating for Change. Since most of the chapters could reasonably be placed in two or all three categories, please feel free to read the essays in any order that suits you.

Part I: Dominant Discourses on Young Moms and Young Mothering: Concerns and Consequences

Before a brief outline of the specific chapters in this section, we wanted to provide a little more detailed account of dominant Canadian, U.S., and Australian discourses about young mothers for those who may be new to this subject. Most research on young mothers and young mothering, as well as much of the coverage in the media and the news industry, focuses on negative outcomes—for the mother, for the child, and for society at large. In terms of the mother, writers often emphasize the ways in which pregnancy and/or childbirth pose health hazards to teen mothers; they note, for example, that compared to women in their twenties and thirties, teens are more likely to experience pregnancy-induced hypertension and preeclampsia and may be at a higher risk for postpartum depression (Patel and Sen). As Mary Breheney and

Christine Stephens note, this construction of teen motherhood as a health problem, both in the popular press and in medical and nursing journals, barely disguises the implication that it is a social and moral problem as well (309). Elizabeth McDermott and Hilary Graham succinctly observe that young mothers tend to be "viewed as both an 'at risk' group within society and 'a risk' to society" (60)—a risk that must be monitored and controlled lest the disease (young mothers' violation of patriarchal, racist, and heterosexist norms) spread to other young women (Macvarish).

Other researchers draw attention to the fact that many adolescent mothers drop out of high school; very few of these dropouts (at least in the U.S.) earn a high school diploma or its equivalent by the age of twenty-three (CDC). Because of their low level of educational attainment and their participation in a capitalist labour market that continues to be profoundly sexist and racist, many teen mothers live in poverty, especially when their children are preschool age. Seeking to provide the basics for and retain custody of their children, these young and usually single mothers are vulnerable to exploitation both by abusive men and males who make a living from criminal activities.

Even more attention in the scholarly literature is devoted to negative outcomes for the children of young mothers, outcomes that are often (but problematically) attributed exclusively to the mother's youth status. Regarding health, researchers point out that many younger mothers give birth prematurely to babies with a low birth weight, that teen mothers often do not receive the early prenatal care that may detect or prevent birth defects, and that young mothers are more likely than older ones to smoke during pregnancy. However, some researchers have noted that mothers forty and over, rather than young ones, are the most likely to have infants with a low birth weight (Statistics Canada). Even more emphasis has been given to the negative educational, behavioural, and economic consequences of being raised by a single mother, especially an unmarried young mother. For example, compared to children born to married women, children born to single mothers are more likely to repeat a grade, do poorly on standardized tests, be involved with the juvenile justice system, and drop out of high school.

However, these statistics paint a partial and distorted picture. As several scholars have pointed out, when it comes to such matters as I.Q. scores and school performance, family *income* plays a much more powerful role than family structure or the age of the mother: the children of older and/or married women fare better than the children of young and/or single women primarily because the former are more economically privileged (Ludtke 31-33). Similarly, when it comes to delinquency or antisocial behaviour in children, the most powerful predictors are the quality of parental supervision and parental involvement as well as the degree of parental rejection. Marital conflict or a parent's participation in criminal activity is of medium significance, whereas the parent's age and marital status are weak predictors (Ludtke 297-298). Similarly, an analysis of data from the Early Childhood Longitudinal Study—Birth Cohort of 2001 has revealed that the age at which a young woman gives birth is only one of many factors that determine the educational success of her child (Mollborn and Dennis). Yet another study found that when it comes to differences in the cognitive test scores of teen mothers and their nonparenting peers, "the effects of childbearing are negligible" (Brien et al. 392).

In terms of analyzing the consequences of young mothering, no scholar we have encountered suggests that the life of a young mother is without major challenges and obstacles, and few would question the correlation between motherhood and the negative outcomes discussed. What much scholarship on young mothering does question is a discourse that conflates correlation and causation—a discourse that has had a detrimental impact on policy decisions that affect the lives of young mothers, especially those living near or below the poverty line and racialized women. This body of work, which generally is informed (implicitly or explicitly) by an intersectional feminist perspective, refuses to frame young motherhood as a dangerous, contagious disease that is always and forever problematic, and it refuses to blame the young woman—rejecting the notion that teen pregnancy results from the personal failings of individuals who are unmotivated, immature, irresponsible, and immoral. Instead, an intersectional feminist framing foregrounds the constraints posed by systemic oppression and challenges the dominant culture's positioning of young motherhood as "uni-directionally causing such problems as poverty, child abuse, poor health, criminality, substance abuse, or low rates of educational attainment" (Healthy Teen Network). In short, the best research on young mothering challenges the widespread assumption that adolescent pregnancy or parenting is responsible for—as opposed to a result and symptom of—a complex system of social, political and economic inequities (Furstenberg; Johns et al.; McDermott and Graham).

Despite empirical evidence to the contrary (Byrd; Jacobs and Molburn; Wildsmith et al.), young mothers—over 80 percent of whom were living in low-income households before pregnancy and mother-hood—are often regarded as personally and solely responsible for their and their children's financial or educational struggles. Rather than focusing on such systemic issues as the lack of affordable and accessible birth control, childcare, and healthcare (not to mention the gender gap in wages or the high incidence of domestic and relationship violence)— the prevailing discourse blames and shames young mothers for any challenges they and their children face (Vinson). Young mothers over time have been labelled immoral, promiscuous, immature, lazy, un-motivated, irresponsible, and self-indulgent and constructed as "erring females" (Minaker, "Sluts and Slags" 73). As popular discourse would have it, these "unworthy choice makers" can only be protagonists in disaster narratives and, thus, deserve to be maligned, surveilled, dis-ciplined and punished (Kelly 10).

The four essays in Part I demonstrate how false and demeaning stereotypes about young mothers and misperceptions about the nature of the challenges they face often prevent the media, policymakers, healthcare providers, and social service agencies from providing the kinds of supports that young mothers and their children need and deserve. In the opening chapter, "Lost in the Paperwork: Young Moms, Homelessness and Bureaucracy," Melinda Vandenbeld Giles reveals failures in a social welfare system in which bureaucratic efficiency and risk management are prioritized over identifying and meeting the material needs of mothers experiencing homelessness in Ontario. For eight years, Vandenbeld Giles has been working to better understand the daily lives of these low-income mothers and their dissatisfaction with many of the community and government resources (theoretically) available to them. She has been conducting interviews with social service coordinators and public policymakers; organizing focus groups with nurses and social workers; attending community and faith-based meetings; touring women's shelters, detox centres, and resource hubs; and listening to the stories of impoverished mothers who have escaped homelessness by living in government-subsidized motels. Vandenbeld Giles's chapter features one of these Toronto motel residents: Ada, a nineteen-year-old expectant refugee mom with a nine-month-old daughter. Through Ada's story, as well as through interviews conducted with the staff of a hospital and a charitable organization that run support programs for young and/or impoverished mothers, Vandenbeld Giles reveals that rigid bureaucratic procedures combined with ignorance about the lived realities of the mothers' lives can prevent even well-intentioned agencies from offering these mothers programs that would truly help and empower them.

In "Young Mothers and Modern Domestic Adoption: Choice or Reproductive Exploitation?" Valerie Andrews examines the processes of modern domestic adoption— that is, adoptions that are posited as being chosen by a young healthy mother but that in reality are highly coercive. Like many adoption activists, Andrews argues that the language and procedures used by contemporary adoption agencies continue to be informed by the illegal and unethical practices as well as the human rights abuses that characterized the post-World War II adoption mandate era. Although contemporary adoption processes are packaged as new and improved, Andrews demonstrates that choice, consent, and openness remain illusory and that adoption agencies still operate on the (often unspoken) assumption that a young woman, especially if she has limited financial resources, is inherently unfit to be a good mother. She identifies key historical, social, and political elements that coalesced to form the adoption mandate, and then illustrates the ways in which domestic adoption in Canada continues to function as a form of reproductive exploitation of young mothers.

In her chapter "Through the Lens: Adolescent Mothers, Stigmatization, and the Media," Jenni Sullivan describes the ways in which dominant discourses about young motherhood are created and embedded in social consciousness via popular media. She shows how both pregnancy prevention campaigns and reality television shows reinforce culturally dominant, and negative stereotypes about the parenting abilities (or lack thereof) of young women. These stigmatizing narratives are not benign—they have detrimental real-life consequences for young mothers and their children. Writing from an experiential perspective, Sullivan argues that the inclusion of positive representations of young mothers in the media may begin to alleviate entrenched social prejudices and instead support the resiliency, resourcefulness, accomplishments, and empowerment of pregnant and parenting teens.

The final chapter in Part I is Deborah Byrd's "Gimme (Age-Appropriate) Shelter: Young Mothers' Reflections on U.S. Supportive Housing Facilities for Low-Income Families with Children." This chapter is based on Byrd's visits to several U.S. and Toronto area supportive housing facilities for low-income single mothers and her analysis of websites and residents' manuals of several organizations that provide housing, case management, and/or other supports to young mothers and mothers-to-be striving to escape poverty and homelessness. Central to this chapter are Byrd's interviews with a dozen young mothers, ages seventeen to twenty-two, who at the time of the interviews were active participants in a young parent mentoring program run by a nonprofit agency that also operates a supportive housing shelter for low-income families. Byrd sought to understand why these young mothers, despite their need for affordable housing and openness to case management services, would not even consider residing in the shelter. Byrd not only addressed this subject with her interviewees but compared the rules, regulations, and language of the U.S. shelter with those of a Toronto agency which runs a successful supportive housing program for young mothers. The results were telling: the young mothers objected to residency in the U.S. shelter because the agency used a deficits-based approach to mentoring; they operated under the implicit assumption that the parents residing in its facility were likely to make irresponsible decisions if not closely monitored and regulated. The interviewees resented the assumption that young and/or poor women would not be good mothers. Based on their comments, they would have likely embraced the opportunity to reside in one of Toronto's shelters for young mothers, which tend to take an assets-based approach to mentoring and empowerment.

Part II: Young Mothers' Stories: Challenging the Dominant Discourse

Motherhood scholar Deborah Byrd argues that young mothers are "rarely invited to tell their own stories" (496). Indeed, what we know about young mothers has been narrated and constructed by dominant discourses, which, in the words of Tanya Darisi, position young motherhood "as a social problem in need of remedy" (29). Young mothers, as studied in research or portrayed in popular media, are represented "as either unworthy choice makers or as passive victims: either fully in charge of their lives or without any agency" (Kelly 10). A major challenge for young mothers, Byrd argues, "is resisting the cultural pressure to internalize the negative stereotypes of young mothers as unambitious, irresponsible, immature, immoral, and as incapable of adequately nurturing a child's cognitive, physical, emotional development" (497). Indeed, as Christine Walsh argues, "teenage mothers have become separated from the category of 'mothers' by virtue of their age and perhaps their marital status; they are constructed as a social problem" (165; Kelly; Rutman et al.; Lesser et. al.; Davis et al.).

Feminist scholarship on young motherhood challenges these negative representations of young mothers as either "victims or temptresses" both by dismantling the myths of the dominant discourse and by exploring the meaning and experience of young motherhood from the perspective of young mothers themselves. In her recent book *Embodying the Problem: The Persuasive Power of the Teen Mother* (2018), Jenna Vinson emphasizes "that young mothers [may] write counter stories of pregnancy and motherhood—stories that explicitly resist the statistics, experts, and assumptions that dehumanize 'them' as a supposed coherent category of problem people" (ix). Together, the chapters in this section make audible the voices of some of the young mothers whose stories are purposefully excluded from dominant discourses. Recounting the ways in which they combat various forms of stigmatization and oppression and seek to defy cultural constraints and expectations, the stories of young mothers are—like life itself— messy: textured and poignant, sometimes joyous, sometimes heartbreaking.

How we see ourselves matters. Our sense of self is also socially constructed in part through the meanings we give to others and by how we perceive others are viewing and judging us. Heather Jackson's personal narrative, "Teen Mom Forever Ever," illustrates this social interactionist claim, as it recounts her frustrations with the personal and institutional disrespect she experienced as a young mother-to-be and then mother. Jackson also reflects on the powerful sense of agency and empowerment she developed as she negotiated young motherhood; she emphasizes that becoming an active member of an online community through girl-mom.com played a key role in sustaining her feelings of pride, confidence, self-esteem, and accomplishment. Jackson's narrative highlights the positive impact that a supportive community can have on young mothers as they collectively navigate both adolescence and motherhood.

Parenting programs are not a panacea that make struggles with racism, poverty, or social exclusion disappear, yet when young women find support in spaces that offer authentic care and practical assistance, they can often transform their lives. In "Early Motherhood: A Turning Point in the Complex Lives of Young Mothers," Karen Felstead draws on narratives from seven young mothers who attended a young parents program in a regional city in Victoria, Australia. Accounts of substance abuse, problematic home life, complex family relationships, self-harm, interpersonal violence, and incomplete schooling characterized the young mothers' challenging lives before the pregnancy and the birth of their child. Felstead's research focuses on the discursive positioning of these young mothers and how they drew upon their narratives while negotiating their complex contemporary world and took up alternative subject positions. For all of these young women, becoming a mother was a significant and positive turning point in their lives. They moved beyond the precarious situations they had experienced and used discursive resources of responsibility, decision making, resilience, and determination. Becoming a mother empowered them; it inspired them to actively envision and construct a safe and positive future for themselves and their children.

In "Single Teen Mothers on Welfare Share 'The Missing Story of Ourselves,'" Vivyan Adair highlights the degree to which the bodies of poor teen mothers and children in the U.S. are scarred and mutilated by state mandated material deprivation and public exhibition; they work as spectacles and as patrolling images to socialize and control bodies within the body politic. Against these simple, reductive, and pejorative images, Adair presents and analyzes parts of the installation *The Missing Story of Ourselves: Poverty and the Promise of Higher Education* (2005-2009), in which she and her welfare eligible teen mother colleagues speak back, as they both embrace and push against mainstream knowledge surrounding and marking them. Although they knew that the negotiation of privileged knowledge could not erase the crises and long-term impact of their poverty, through the installation, they deployed different meanings that could transform the ways in which they were able to interrogate and reformat the discursive structures that had fixed and framed them. As Adair demonstrates, because power is diffuse, heterogeneous, and contradictory, poor, single, teen mothers struggled against the marks of degradation in their installation. They contested the marks of their bodily inscription, disrupted the use of their bodies as signs, changed the conditions of their lives, and, ultimately, survived. The process of renarration transformed the ways in which poor, single teen mothers could interrogate their own lives and the systems of power that had branded them.

As we have noted often in this introduction, the journey into new motherhood is affected by (and affects) all other aspects of one's identity. In "Becoming 'Yazzi': A Queer Story of Young Parenthood," Johanna Lewis challenges dominant expectations about the lives, journeys, and realities of young parents, as she reflects on the emergence of her queer and trans family and her unconventional pathway to parenthood. Through situated analyses of specific moments of parenting ambivalence, precarity, identity, belonging, and happily queer possibilities for building families, Lewis offers a counter-narrative to the dominant, heteronormative stories of young motherhood. Her essay opens up new considerations for researchers and care providers, and gives other young parents with non-normative experiences the opportunity to see themselves reflected in someone else's story.

Part III: Counter-Narratives: Communicating for Change

Young mothers are not morally problematic despite parables of disdain and disorder that continue to circulate in popular (and academic) discussions of young mothering. Sociocultural constructions of problematic young pregnancy and parenting are being challenged by counter-narratives from experiential and feminist lenses. By counter-narratives we are not referring to simple portrayals of teen pregnancy as cool or fun but as authentic stories that recognize the despair and the hope as well as the perils and the promises of young parenthood in a way that respects the different ways to experience youth and mothering. In other words, it means adopting a compassionate view toward young mothers who experience great adversity, but, in some ways, "are parents just like any other—nervous at first, but so in love, and gaining practice, perspective, and competence each day" (Aparicio et al. 106). Feminist research on young motherhood shows that poverty is not a straightforward cause of early motherhood, nor does being pregnant or parenting as a teenager necessarily cause poverty (Marialdo and Gutierres: Wilson; Briggs et al.). As Susan Clark explains, many "young mothers adequately perform parental duties and children of young mothers are not disadvantaged" (18; Byrd; Keyes Horwitz et al.; Ross Leadbeater and Way). However, despite the evidence shown in both the research and in young women's lived experiences of motherhood, young mothers must continually prove their fitness for parenting to the world at large, which so often judges them as bad mothers; they must also demonstrate their worthiness to social service providers who engage in the monitoring and regulation of their mothering (Weinberg; Ahola-Sidaway and Fonseca). Under such surveillance, empowered mothering may not be possible for young mothers because, as Rachel Berman et al. note, "empowered mothering generally involves engaging in acts of resistance; however, it is difficult to engage in resistance while a person (rightly) feels they are being monitored" (43). The participants in Berman et al.'s study emphasize that such resistance was made possible because of the support offered to them by the young parenting program they attended. Likewise, research by Rebecca Waller et al. on mentoring and Lisa Bunting and Colette McAuley's study on peer support both emphasize that support, particularly formal support, is essential for the empowerment of young mothers. Thus, it is not surprising that community and support are central variables for young mothers' resistance and their ability to construct alternative meanings and experiences of mothering.

Unfortunately, little attention has been paid to the positive effects that pregnancy and motherhood can have on young females. Relatively few scholars emphasize that young motherhood can be life enhancing, even lifesaving; we need more qualitative research that gives voice to the many teens who have become more academically ambitious, more responsible and more concerned with having healthy relationships and a healthy lifestyle after becoming pregnant or giving birth (Byrd and Gallagher; Lesser et al.; McGrady; McDermott and Graham). More scholarship examining how race, class, ethnicity, sexual identity, and citizenship status influence the outcomes experienced by various subgroups of teen mothers is in order. For example, whereas African American teenage girls who do not have a child are less likely to graduate from high school than their white peers, African American teen mothers are more likely than white teens to finish high school (Ludtke 77). They are also less likely to give birth prematurely or to experience infant mortality than are older African American women; the opposite is the case for whites. Similar findings about the advantages of young motherhood have been found when it comes to issues of class, which, as previously mentioned, is integrally related to issues of race. For instance, a 1995 longitudinal study by Joseph Holtz "revealed that teenage mothers tended to earn more over their lifetimes and work more steadily than women who came out of the same social and economic circumstances but delayed childbearing until they were no longer teenagers" (qtd. in Ludtke 77). Clearly, more work is needed to contest exclusionary narratives.

This final section of the book explores different ways that academic and experiential perspectives can challenge dominant discourses and how young mothers today and in the past have resisted internalizing negative stereotypes. Young mothers can use language to expose vulnerability and give a voice to a vulnerable population, denounce stereotypes, and mitigate patriarchal motherhood by implementing empowered mothering.

In "'The Nurses Looked at Me As If I Had Two Heads—Because I Was So Young': Mothering in Suburban Melbourne between the 1960s-1980s," Miranda Francis examines the rich and diverse life stories of four mothers and the ways these women reflect, as older women, on the period in their lives when they were, or were labelled by others, a "young mother." These women's accounts illuminate the continuities and changes surrounding social attitudes towards young mothers between the 1960s and 1980s in suburban Melbourne, Australia. This period of considerable social change affected private lives unevenly, which complicates the way these experiences play out in families and are remembered by individuals. As the social and legal stigma associated with being an unmarried mother began to lift in the 1970s, social disapproval shifted to a new group—teenage mothers. This chapter outlines not only how social attitudes towards young mothers have changed but also how individual families have coped with these shifts and made decisions within these frameworks. By capturing the voices of women whose family lives have been affected by these shifting mores, Francis demonstrates their lasting impact across generations and shows how powerful counter-narratives can be.

In "Reconceptualizing Vulnerability and Autonomy as a Way to Shift Dominant Narratives about Young Mothers," Erin Kuri examines how dominant conventional and patriarchal understandings of the concepts of vulnerability and autonomy are problematic for marginalized identity groups like young mothers. Situational factors such as young age, dependency on caregivers and services, and being caregivers themselves can lead to young mothers experiencing vulnerability, which can lead to exploitation, harm, and neglect. Vulnerability has traditionally been associated with weakness, passivity, and being in need of protection. For this reason, association with the term has been controversial, as it has historically led to damaging consequences for marginalized individuals and groups. In this chapter, Kuri argues for a critical feminist reconceptualization of the concept of vulnerability as entwined with autonomy. Kuri draws on the work of feminist scholars such as Judith Butler, Catriona Mackenzie, and Margaret Urban Walker to shift the narrative of what it means to be vulnerable as a human being and what it means to be a young mother in a society that positions human vulnerability as incompatible with autonomy.

Next, in her work, "Destabilizing Self-Destruction: For the Sake of Young M/others," Sunahtah Jones begins from the premise that motherhood is not a monolith. It is an inherently political series of sociocultural understandings and dynamics that are distinctly shaped by intersecting institutions of race, ethnicity, class, gender, sexual orientation, religion, and able-bodiedness. Jones points to revolutionary acts that are often performed through mothering and motherhood, as well as the impact of oppressive ideas of motherhood that ostracize mothers viewed as the "other." Jones's poetry articulates the experiences of young mothers and mothers of colour on a global scale; it prioritizes the distinctions between the oppressions of mothers within ostracized communities while acknowledging similarities between institutions of oppression that target young mothers and mothers of colour specifically.

Andrea O'Reilly's chapter, "Matrifocality, Maternal Empowerment, and Maternal Nurturance: Conceiving Empowered Young Motherhood in Miriam Toews's *Summer of My Amazing Luck*," considers how Toews's novel, a story about single young mothers living in public housing in Winnipeg, Canada, counters normative discourses. O'Reilly argues that Toews situates young motherhood as a resistant and redemptive maternal space, wherein young mothers are empowered to define and live their own meanings and practices of mothering. More specifically, the chapter explores how the young mothers create a matrifocal space at the residence they humorously name Half-a-Life and how through this community the women can achieve maternal empowerment through an empowered mothering and an empowered maternalism.

The collection closes with an invitation to acknowledge and appreciate the diverse stories of young mothering, especially those all too often obscured from view. Stephenie White offers her tale of young motherhood in a raw and beautiful piece of writing called "Young Motherhood Lost and Found." White, who is an Indigenous young mom, invites us to empathize with the plight and promise of young, marginalized mothering as a process of becoming—safe, stable, secure, and, ultimately, loved.

This collection concludes with Joanne Minaker's Afterward entitled "Becoming and Unbecoming." Minaker complements White's piece by sharing what she's learned meeting young moms and studying young marginalized mothering. Minaker calls for us to practice empathy and compassion in building relationships with youth, especially young mothers. Stephenie's story reminds us, writes Minaker, that the young mothers in this book are becoming and also unbecoming. These courageous young women are letting go of negative cultural expectations and surmounting barriers to maternal agency and autonomy, and we support them in their journey.

Conclusion

Hogeveen and Minaker write that "supportive and caring spaces hold much promise in assisting young mothers traverse the rocky shore of motherhood as they attempt to transform their lives" (22). And *Feminist Perspectives on Young Mothers* makes one important claim: young mothers and their children deserve to be heard, understood, and supported no matter their social position, geographical location, or how they came into parenthood. Despite their differences in approaches and kinds of theoretical analysis, all the authors have one theme in common: valuing and respecting young mothers and challenging negative stereotypes surrounding them. Together, we expose the problems of dominant discourse in silencing and scapegoating young mothers (and their children) and call for counter-narratives that not only challenge marginalizing discourses but promote positive change.

This book brings an intersectional representation of young mothering to the literature, and it refuses to present young mothers or young motherhood as a homogenous identity or experience. Indeed, young mothers are a complex group, and they speak with a diverse array of voices. However, not all voices are (or could be) represented in one collection. Despite a call for papers looking for global perspectives, the book is limited to Western views. As allies, but not Indigenous women ourselves, we recognize that including the voices of Indigenous young mothers is integral to truth and reconciliation, yet we have not added enough Indigenous voices here to challenge inaccurate and negative portrayals of Indigenous young moms. The one exception to this is the powerful contribution of Stephenie White, whose writing we hope will inspire other Indigenous young mothers to share their own stories. We are listening.

Future Research and Directions for Social Change

Within these pages are several issues that require more attention—from poverty to racism and from silenced stories to misunderstood lives. Fortunately, our collection shows that there are maternal warriors who are rewriting their stories each day. In all the complexity and systemic oppression surrounding young mothering, we find not only challenge but an invitation to care. We call on policymakers, practitioners, educators, community members, and academics to recognize as legitimate the experiences and narratives of younger mothers, who have been too rarely recognized as good mothers. There is still much work to do to advocate for change in theory and practice. Young mothers when truly supported can be empowered to take the lead mobilizing to create more supportive spaces from which they can become the people they desire to be and to raise their children the way they choose.

Work Cited

Ahola-Sidaway, J., and S. Fonseca. "When Schooling Is Not Enough: Support, Empowerment and Social regulation of the Teen Mother in Contemporary Canada." *Journal of the Association for Research on Mothering*, vol. 9, no. 1, 2007, pp. 53-61.

Aparicio, Elizabeth M. et al. "'I Can Get Through This and I Will Get Through This': The Unfolding Journey of Teenage Motherhood in and Beyond Foster Care." *Qualitative Social Work*, vol. 17, no. 1, 2018, pp. 96-114.

Barcelos, Chris, and Aline Gubrium. "Bodies That Tell: Embodying Teen Pregnancy Through Digital Storytelling." *Signs: Journal of Women in Culture and Society*, vol. 43, no. 4, 2018, pp. 905-927.

Berman, Rachel, et al. "Don't Look Down of Me Because I Have One: Young Mothers Empowered in a Context of Support." *Journal of the Association for Research on Mothering*, vol. 9, no. 1, 2007, pp. 42-52.

Breheney, Mary, and Christine Stephens. "Youth or Disadvantage? The Construction of Teenage Mothers in Medical Journals." *Culture, Health and Sexuality*, vol. 12, no. 3, 2010, pp. 307-22.

Brien, Michael J., et al. "Teenage Childbearing and Cognitive Development." *Journal of Population Economics*, vol. 15, no. 3, 2002, pp. 391-416.

Briggs, Gemma, et al. "Teen Mothers and Socioeconomic Status: The Chicken-Egg Debate." *Journal of the Association for Research on Mothering*, vol. 9, no. 1, 2007, pp. 62-74.

Bunting, Lisa, and Colette McAuley, "Research Review: Teenage pregnancy and motherhood: the contribution of support." *Child and Family Social Work*, vol. 9, no 2, 2004, pp. 207-15.

Byrd, Deborah. "Young Mothers and the Age-Old Problems of Sexism, Classism, Family Dysfunction and Violence." *Mothers, Mothering and Motherhood Across Cultural Difference: A Reader*, edited by Andrea O'Reilly, Demeter Press, 2014, pp. 487-506.

Byrd, Deborah, and Rachel Gallagher. "Avoiding the Doomed to Poverty Narrative: Words of Wisdom from Teenage Single Mothers." *Journal of the Association for Research on Mothering*, vol. 11, no. 2, 2009, pp. 66-84.

Carlen, Pat. *Women's Imprisonment—A Study in Social Control*. Routledge and Kegan Paul Ltd., 1993.

Carson, Anna, et al. "A Narrative Analysis of the Birth Stories of Early Age Mothers." *Sociology of Health & Illness*, vol. 39, no. 6, 2017, pp. 816-31.

Darisi, Tanya. "It Doesn't Matter if You're 15 or 45, Having a Child is a Difficult Experience: Reflexivity and Resistance in Young Mothers' Constructions of Identity." *Journal of the Association for Research on Mothering*, vol. 9, no. 1, 2, 2007, pp. 29-41.

Erni, R., and W. Phillips-Beck. "Teenage Pregnancy and Parenthood Perspectives of First Nations Women." *The International Indigenous Policy Journal*, vol. 4, no. 1, 2013, pp. 1-22.

Fearnley, Barry. "Contemporary Young Motherhood: Experiences of Hostility." *Journal of Children's Services*, vol. 13, no. 2, 2018, pp. 64-78.

Fonda, Marc, et al. "Socially Constructed Teen Motherhood: A Review." *The International Indigenous Policy Journal*, vol. 4, no. 1, 2013.

Font, Sarah A., et al. "Prevalence and Risk Factors for Early Motherhood among Low-Income, Maltreated, and Foster Youth." *Demography*, vol. 56, no. 1, 2019, pp. 261-84.

Furstenberg, Frank F. "As the Pendulum Swings: Teenage Childbearing and Social Concern." *Family Relations*, vol. 40, no. 2, 1991, pp. 127-38.

Hamilton, Patricia, et al. "At the Intersection of Idealized Youth and Marginalized Almost-Adulthood: How Girls Negotiate Young Motherhood in London, Ontario." *Journal of Youth Studies*, vol. 21, no. 9, 2018, pp. 1182-97.

Hogeveen, Bryan, and Joanne Minaker. *Criminalized Mothers/Criminalizing Mothering*. Demeter Press, 2015.

Horwitz, et al. "School-Age Mothers: Predictors of Long-Term Educational and Economic Outcomes." *Pediatrics*, vol. 87, no. 6, 1991, pp. 862-68.

Jacobs, Janet, and Stefanie Molburn. "Early Motherhood and the Disruption in Significant Attachments: Autonomy and Reconnection as a Response to Separation and Loss among African American and Latina Mothers." *Gender and Society*, vol. 6, no. 6, 2012, pp. 922-44.

Kline, Marlee. Complicating the Ideology of Motherhood: Child Welfare Law and First Nation Women." *Mothers in Law: Feminist Theory and the Legal Regulation of Motherhood*, edited by M.A. Fineman and I. Karpin, Columbia University Press. 1995, pp. 118-42.

Lesser, Janna, et al. "'Sometimes You Don't Feel Ready to Be an Adult or a Mom.' The Experience of Adolescent Pregnancy." *Journal of Child and Adolescent Psychiatric Nursing*, vol. 11, no. 1, 1998, pp. 7-16.

Ludtke, Melissa. *On Our Own: Unmarried Motherhood in America*. Alfred A. Knopf, 1997.

Macvarish, Jan. "The Effect of 'Risk-Thinking' on the Contemporary Construction of Teenage Motherhood." *Health Risk and Society*, vol. 12, no. 4, 2010, pp. 312-22.

Marialdo, L., and R. Gutierrez. *Young Parents Sexual Health Consultation Report*. 2005.

McDermott, Elizabeth, and Hilary Graham. "Resilient Young Mothering: Social Inequalities, Late Modernity, and the 'Problem' of 'Teenage' Motherhood." *Journal of Youth Studies*, vol. 8, no. 1, 2005, pp. 59-79.

McGrady, Shannon. "The Authentic Lived Experiences of Young Mothers: How Empowered Young Women Mother Within and Against the Institutions of Childhood, Gender, and Motherhood." *Journal of the Motherhood Initiative*, vol. 3, no. 2, 2012, pp. 66-83.

Minaker, Joanne. "The Space Between: Mothering in the Context of Contradiction." *Moms Gone Mad: Motherhood and Madness Oppression and Resistance*, edited by Gina Wong, Demeter Press, 2012, pp. 124-140.

Minaker, Joanne. "Sluts and Slags: Censuring the Erring Female." *Criminalizing Women: Gender and (In)justice in Neo-liberal Times*, 2nd ed., edited by Gillian Balford and Elizabeth Comack, Fernwood Publishing, 2014, pp. 73-91.

Modesto, Olivia P. "A Hermeneutic Phenomenological Study of Teen Mothers Who Graduated from an Alternative School." *The Qualitative Report*, vol. 23, no. 12, 2018, pp. 2923-935.

Mollborn, Stefanie, and Christie Sennott. "Bundles of Norms About Teen Sex and Pregnancy." *Qualitative Health Research*, vol. 25, no. 9, 2015, pp. 1283-99.

O'Reilly, A. "Introduction." *Mother Outlaws Theories and Practices of Empowered Mothering*, edited by A. O'Reilly, Canadian Scholars Press, 2004, pp. 1-28.

Patel, Payal H, and Bisakha Sen. "Teen Motherhood and Long-Term Health Consequences." *Maternal and Child Health Journal*, vol. 16, no. 5, 2012, pp. 1063-71.

Phoenix, A. *Young Mothers?* Polity Press, Cambridge, 1991.

Ross Leadbeater, Bonnie, and Niobe Way, *Growing Up Fast: Transitions to Early Adulthood of Inner-City Adolescent Mothers.* Psychology Press, 2013.

Rutman, Deb, et al. "Undeserving Mothers? Practitioners' Experiences Working with Young Mothers In/From Care." *Child and Family Social Work*, vol.7, no. 3, 2002, pp. 149-59.

Vinson, Jenna. *Embodying the Problem: The Persuasive Power of the Teen Mother.* Rutgers Press, 2018.

Waller, Rebecca, et al. "Understanding Early Contextual and Parental Risk Factors for the Development of Limited Prosocial Emotions." *Journal of Abnormal Child Psychology*, vol. 43, no. 6, 2015, pp. 1025-39.

Weinberg, Melinda. "Young Single Mothers: The Work of Proving Fitness for Parenting." *Journal of the Association for Research on Mothering*, vol. 6.2, 2004, pp. 79-89.

Wildsmith, Elizabeth, et al. "Teenage Childbearing among Youth Born to Teenage Mothers." *Youth and Society*, vol. 44, no. 2, 2012, pp. 258-83.

Wilson, Corinne. "An Inappropriate Transition to Adulthood? Teenage Pregnancy and the Discourse of Childhood in the UK." *Journal of the Association for Research on Mothering*, vol. 9, no. 1, 2007, pp. 92-100.

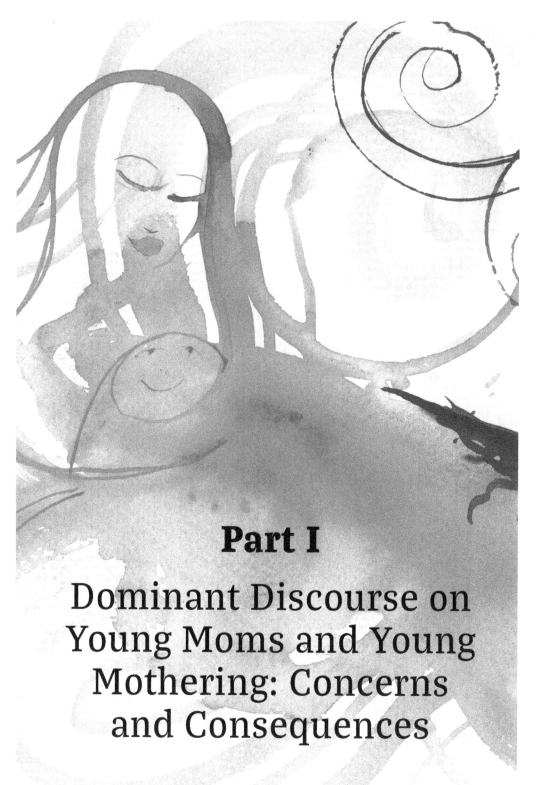

Part I

Dominant Discourse on Young Moms and Young Mothering: Concerns and Consequences

Chapter One

Lost in the Paperwork: Young Moms, Homelessness, and Bureaucracy

Melinda Vandenbeld Giles

Although all mothers are stigmatized by homelessness, young mothers experience particular stigmatization and bureaucratic difficulties particular to their age. In this chapter, I discuss the contradiction between the plethora of programs in Ontario designed specifically to assist mothers and expectant mothers under the age of twenty-five who are experiencing homelessness and the actual lack of resources for these women. With so many programs apparently available, how is it possible that when I went to visit a nineteen-year-old expectant refugee mother from Croatia with a nine-month-old baby in her Toronto motel room, she had yet to attend a single mothering program? I will discuss this contradiction by illuminating how young moms experiencing homelessness in Ontario (living in motels, shelters, on the street, or couch surfing) come to be made legible in particular ways within the Ontario welfare system. Whether their life experiences match this particular categorization is less relevant than the continued funding-driven needs of donor organizations and/or state-funding imperatives. Thus, as the chapter title indicates, the mothers become lost in the avalanche of paperwork that defines, categorizes, and dehumanizes without providing any actual financial or emotional support.

Since May 2010, I have been conducting interviews with social service coordinators and public policymakers; organizing focus groups with nurses and social workers; attending community and faith-based meetings; touring women's shelters, detox centres, women's resource hubs; and visiting families living in motels in an effort to better understand the daily lives of mothers experiencing homelessness in Ontario and those with whom they interact. For the purposes of this chapter I will include data from the time I spent with Ada (a nineteen-year-old Croatian mother) living in the Sands Motel. (I use pseudonyms for participants' names, the name of the motel, and any organizations mentioned.) As part of my social anthropology PhD fieldwork, I spent time interacting regularly with mothers living with their children in the Sands Motel in Toronto. Since Ada is the only mother in this particular group under the age of twenty-five, I specifically reference her words. I also include the time I spent at a centre for young mothers in rural Ontario, where I interviewed a support worker. And I include my participant observation data and interviews from the time I spent with a nursing team who work with women living on the streets in the Toronto region (many of whom are under twenty-five) helping them throughout their pregnancy. I also interviewed the manager and social worker for an urban hospital program that helps young moms who are experiencing homelessness achieve a healthy pregnancy. The purpose of the chapter is not to critique the programs themselves; it is to highlight a system in which the voices and lived experiences of these young moms becomes lost in the bureaucratic paperwork so that in the end all that is left is a story of "success" verified by numerical data while homelessness rates (particularly for youth) continue to rise and women with children remain without support systems.

Field Notes
24 Sept. 2014, Sands Motel

Ada opened the door hesitantly and peeked out. She had beautiful brown eyes and long dark hair. She was barefoot and wearing a simple but elegant black and white dress. She smiled and immediately welcomed me into her motel room. I introduced myself as a University of Toronto student doing some research on the motels, and she seemed very pleased to see me. I came inside, closed the door, and sat down on the only chair in the room.

I was immediately accosted by the stale air and smell of old cigarette smoke. Her baby slept on the bed. The room was small. A playpen stood in one corner, and two beds pushed together took up most of the floor space in the room. There was an open tiny closet in the corner, but there were few clothes, and it looked mostly packed with things. One door led to the bathroom. The only thing between the room and the outside was a locked door without even a deadbolt. The brown floral carpet was stained along with the mattresses. The bed sheets were dark and stained, and Ada told me the motel owner gave them a cup to put underneath the dirty bedposts to prevent bed bugs. When she lifted up the sheets, I could see the filthy dark stains on the mattress and the way the mattress itself was sunken in. There was no space to cook, no kitchen. The Sands doesn't even have a communal kitchen, so there is simply no place to make dinner. The one table stood beside the bed and was covered with KFC, pita bread, and diapers. There was a fridge on the left-hand side but not even a hot plate. I could see that in the tiny space between the playpen and the table, Ada had some cooking items, a large bowl, and some cutlery on the floor.

Ada's nine-month-old baby was asleep when I first arrived, but then she woke up, and there really wasn't anywhere for her to play. She sat in the tiny space on the dirty brown carpet under the table and in front of her playpen. I couldn't imagine what would happen if she tried to learn to walk. There was nothing outside the motel room door but a concrete parking lot. Ada and I sat and talked for a while. Her baby seemed happy most of the time we spoke and smiled when I played peek-a-boo. Ada picked up her baby, and we started laughing together as little Azra rolled on the bed making faces. Suddenly, instead of being in a pay-by-the-hour motel room, we were two women enjoying an afternoon conversation about our children.

Ada's Story

When Ada and I were talking that cold September afternoon, after a moment, I left my perch on the chair and went to pick up her baby girl. I was hesitant at first, since I didn't want to overstep my boundary as a researcher; however, it quickly became obvious that Ada was eager for human connection, since she mentioned that in an average week, she scarcely spoke to anyone except her case worker and her husband. As I played with Azra, Ada proceeded to tell me about the circumstances that brought her to the motel and how she felt about living there.

"So how long have you been living in the motel?" I asked, discreetly placing the recorder between us on the bed when Ada said she didn't mind.

"Everything here six months. Pregnancy six months, six months here."

"Oh! I didn't even realize you were pregnant!" We both laughed, and Ada nodded. Her slim figure belied any indication that she was already six months along.

"So you've been living in this motel room for six months and you're six months pregnant?" I asked to clarify. Ada said she was struggling with her English, and I didn't want to misunderstand anything. Ada nodded again.

"And how old is your daughter?"

"Nine months."

"Wow." Ada laughed again, indicating that yes, it wasn't easy having a baby and being pregnant so quickly again.

"Hi there! Oh, peek-a-boo!" I played with Azra while she cooed and gurgled. Ada and I talked a bit about what it's like to be a mom and how hard it can be looking after a baby, especially when Ada's husband was always away either working or looking for work.

"So what do you think of this motel?" I asked casually. The mood changed suddenly. Ada looked distressed and put her baby back on the floor to play.

"Big problem here. This motel, everything no good. Here have nothing. One bed. One toilet. Here cooking. We have nothing here in Canada. No refugee claim. We're going home. My home, Croatia. We have no house, no nothing."

"Your refugee claim was not accepted?"

"No. Every day you wait for document. Waiting for passport go home now. But we have no house, no nothing in Croatia. No home."

"What has it been like for you living in this motel for six months waiting for documents?"

Ada shook her head and pointed to Azra. "Ah, this child cannot eat. My social worker, she tell me, go home, Croatia. She give me 150 dollars for food, for everything. She no help me."

"How often does your social worker come by?"

"She bring me check. Eleven, twelve, five o'clock at night. I going to shopping, food. Milk for baby. Pampers. Everything's more money. Everything is my problem. My social worker tells me go home, go home. You're waiting for document. Go home. You no like giving you money. There is no program. There is nothing now."

"How old are you?"

"Nineteen."

"Did your social worker tell you about any programs for young moms?"

"I don't know. She no give me tokens. No bring me nothing. We have nothing. Every week, someone tell me go here, go there, but they give me nothing. She tell go this, come there. I say I have no tokens. You give me 150 dollars for food, pampers for baby, for milk, everything. But is fifty dollars for pampers, thirty dollars for this, four dollars for milk. Money is gone."

"So you feel like your social worker keeps asking you to go to programs and do things but doesn't give you any transit money to get there?"

"No. And we have nothing. We have no home. This is no home, this motel. We have nothing. We have no money."

Our conversation was interrupted, as the baby made gurgling noises and started to cry a bit. She could feel her mother's distress. I realized that my questions were making Ada unhappy, and I was starting to feel emotional myself, so I switched the topic and talked about my seven-year-old daughter and what it was like when she was a baby. Ada smiled again and nodded, wanting to share her own stories of mothering.

"Happy for my child. She is my child. Happy mom. She like going to shopping. Everything is this, my child. She get everything. This first my child. She's everything. My child happy. She no like sleep in bed. She like to going outside, every minute, every day. She sleeping in stroller. She no like everything in one room. She like go out."

"Does it make it hard sometimes living here?"

"Can no stress for baby. You can't stress. You go outside. Put stress outside. This child, she's everything you understand."

"This is a difficult situation."

"Ah, yes. They put in this motel. Look." Ada pointed to the small, cramped room. "Yeah, cockroaches, bedbugs in bed. She eat me. In bedroom. No helping, this motel. I tell my social worker, change this motel. She tell me, big problem to change. Everyone in this motel no like. No happy here. Other mothers, two or three children. Fight here. No camera. Nothing here. Come outside. You can look at everybody here. Come the police. Look here. One door."

"There isn't even a latch."

"No. There is nothing here. This motel, I don't know. Think Canada help me. No help. In Croatia, everything broken. People broken. Not happy here. Not happy go home. Don't know what we're doing."

"So you're in limbo?"

"Yeah. This motel, no good for child. Family here, but no home. Everybody tell me, why you come here in Canada? You lost everything." The baby started to cry, and I realized that I was creating a stressful situation. I nodded and stood up.

"Would it be okay if I come back and visit sometimes?"

"Yes, yes. Thank you very much!" Ada nodded and smiled, taking my hand in hers. I smiled back.

"So nice to see you!" I left the motel feeling forlorn and helpless. This nineteen-year-old girl had shared so much of her story with me, yet there was nothing I could do to help.

Regulation of Young Moms

As illustrated by the above narrative, the problem is not that there are no programs for young moms. Ada had even shown me a pamphlet her case worker had given her advertising a weekly drop-in program for young moms. The problem is the disconnect between these programs and the everyday realities of the mothers living in these motels. When I went to the motel and asked the mothers what sort of program would be most beneficial for them, they looked at me and laughed. They said that they were constantly being pressured to attend this or that free program or workshop. In fact, if they didn't attend, their relationship with their case workers tended to become strained. Yet according to the women, the only point of these programs was to make either their case workers look good or to make the shelter system look good. As long as just a few token moms could show up and give glowing reports, the funding could continue and the program could be considered a success. When I asked Ada why she didn't seem interested in the free program for young moms, she looked at me quizzically and explained to me that she was an excellent mother and she couldn't understand why her case worker seemed to think she needed some kind of program that would teach her to be a better mom, particularly when it would cost her the transit money to get there and she would have to take her baby in the stroller on the bus as well. All of the moms said they didn't need any more programs. What they needed was for the mould to be removed from the walls, for the motel management to deal with the bedbug and cockroach infestation, for deadbolts to be put on the doors, and for the shelter to demand from the motel owner that they be allowed to use the motel laundry machines.

In *Technologies of the Self*, Michel Foucault writes, "Technologies of the self ... permit individuals to effect by their own means or with the help of others a certain number of operations on their own bodies and souls, thoughts, conduct, and way of being, so as to transform themselves in order to attain a certain state of happiness, purity, wisdom, perfection, or immortality" (18). Foucault effectively reveals how these technologies of the self are not new; however, what is new in the current neoliberal era is the degree to which these technologies of the self have become bureaucratized. Foucault analyzes the ways in which the technologies of domination of others and technologies of the self intersect. This point of intersection Foucault identifies as governmentality (19). In *South Koreans in the Debt Crisis: The Creation of a Neoliberal Welfare Society*, Jesook Song defines the Foucauldian concept of governing or governmentality as referring to the "liberal political reasoning and technologies that are suffused throughout society by various social actors and spheres, such as NGOs, businesses, residential communities, families, schools, and individuals as well as state administrative institutes" (xii). In other words, the recommendation to attend the various parenting programs are not so much a matter of choice but rather a governing and regulatory system aimed at bringing so-called deviant young moms in line. The conversation becomes about the moms needing knowledge, with funding going toward more educational programs rather than direct funding for resources and the mitigation of poverty.

Field Notes
5 Nov. 2013, Helping Hands Organization for Young Moms

The autumn leaves crunched beneath my tires, as I turned into the parking lot of Helping Hands. At a recent conference I'd met a social worker, Alice, who counselled young moms at Helping Hands, a rural charity helping mothers under the age of twenty-five who have few supports; many of whom are homeless. Alice had mentioned how some of her clients lived in nearby motels, and many lived in the shelter or were couch surfing.

It was a perfect day for a drive into the country. Helping Hands charity is in a nondescript box building. I parked the car, gathered my things together, and arrived prepared with my ethics proposal and digital recorder. Immediately upon entering Helping Hands I felt encompassed by a warm welcoming atmosphere in sharp contrast to the shelter, which felt insular and institutional. Even though I was a half hour early, Alice came around the corner and said hello, immediately offering a tour of the office. We walked into a large comfortable room with soft couches and carpets and filled with bouncy chairs in bright blue, green, and yellow colours. Alice proceeded to describe the warm space.

"So here is the lounge where the moms can relax with their babies and have lunch. We offer several programs. Some of the moms come here all day to finish high school or attend parenting classes while the children are looked after in the childcare centre." Alice took me down the hallway to another brightly lit and cheerful room where several caregivers, babies, and moms were playing and relaxing. The room was filled with bright coloured artwork and happy children's music. "This is the childcare centre." We then went to see the clothing closet, which was impeccably organized with tiny hangers and everything arranged by size. Next, Alice showed me the food bank filled with canned goods. "The moms are free to take whatever they need."

After the tour, we settled in Alice's office, a small space painted in a cheerful green and filled with notes and books. "Sorry about the small space. I don't spend a lot of time in my office since I'm usually driving around to do outreach." I nodded, sitting down and taking my recorder out in addition to the ethics paperwork. Alice was extremely helpful and giving of information. We spoke for over an hour and her genuine concern and warmth were apparent. However, she told me about how she had to step out of her middleclass sensibility in this job and realize that these moms existed in a very different world where violence and teen pregnancies become normalized and expected. She said it was an issue of intergenerational violence and trauma, and what the girls really needed was to be educated so they could imagine a different kind of future for themselves.

I visited Helping Hands over a year before beginning my fieldwork at the motel. Reading my field notes now, after having spent time at the motel, has made me interpret my visit to Helping Hands differently. The cheerful narrative of Helping Hands and the happy young moms there contrast starkly with the moms living in the motels. There were a few happy mothers at Helping Hands, but what about all the other young moms receiving no support in this rural area north of Toronto? And even for the moms attending the workshops and programs at Helping Hands, other than providing a few canned goods and used clothing, what tangible support does this organization actually provide to eradicate the extreme everyday poverty and violence of these young girls' lives? Does educating these young moms help them escape an abusive situation whether at home or with a partner if they have nowhere to go and no monetary resources? Do these programs put food on the table other than some canned goods?

Providing childcare so the moms can study and finish high school is important, but how many moms can actually access this program? And even if they finish high school, what kinds of jobs will they be able to find? This isn't necessarily to critique the existence of these programs, but it is to point out some of the inconsistencies and normative narratives that are implicit within this charity paradigm. The primary assumption is that what these young moms need more than anything is education on how to be better mothers because (so the narrative goes) their history of intergenerational violence has left them with no role models. Regardless of whatever assistance is provided, it is given within a particular regulatory framework within which the moms must operate or not have access to the resources.

Measuring Success

In *Discipline and Punish: The Birth of the Prison,* Foucault writes, "After a century and a half of 'failures,' the prison still exists, producing the same results, and there is the greatest reluctance to dispense with it" (277). According to Foucault, this reluctance is the result of prisons effectively providing a basis for surveillance and categorization of deviant populations; therefore, prison systems prove to be an enormous success in terms of unintended consequences, even though they are a failure in terms of the initial liberal conceptions of reformation. Unfortunately, substitute "young mothers experiencing homelessness in Ontario" for "prisoners" and the striking similarities in terms of social regulation and categorization become obvious.

In the summer of 2010, I spent time working with five street nurses who were helping young homeless pregnant mothers. On a hot August afternoon, we sat around a table drinking ice water while they told me their stories. They were candid and clear about the excruciating levels of bureaucracy they were forced to deal with. As frontline workers, they were the ones at the end of the day who had to go through the reams of forms and checklists trying to sort out how to help their clients (the young moms) within this paperwork trail. As one nurse put it in reference to CAS (Children's Aid Society):

> Oh, CAS is complicated. I have a sixteen-year-old right now, but because she's sixteen, she has her own worker because she's a crown ward. While she was pregnant, she had the PAC [Children's Aid Pregnancy After-Care Worker] coming out to see her, and then when the baby was born. Now the baby has a worker and a high-risk nurse, so she's seeing four different CAS workers, one for herself and three for the baby. I don't even know who to call. No wonder these clients are so overwhelmed. They have so many workers. Why can't the worker that's for her baby be her worker? But they don't do it that way. It's confusing. So they can have multiple workers throughout their lives. And then depending on where they are living in the city, it's a different office. And if they move during the pregnancy, then they get another new worker. They can't continue with the same worker.

The manager of the nursing team told me about a hospital program a few years back that exemplifies the absurdity of funding-driven initiatives and regulatory bureaucratic requirements, which become self-referential to the point that the measure of program success becomes based on efficient bureaucratic management. The hospital program was created as a pilot project to address the issue of urban homeless teen pregnancy. It provides a stark example of how far removed measurements of success become from initial conceptualizations. The hospital program was available to inadequately housed pregnant women under the age of twenty-seven and receiving prenatal care through this particular urban hospital. The pilot project lasted from July 2005 to August 2007. The idea was to bring young homeless pregnant teens directly into the hospital system by giving them a passport that would be signed at every appointment. Many of these mothers feared CAS would take their babies away if they gave birth in a hospital (a reasonable fear since the current policy dictates CAS involvement for homeless mothers). Many mothers thought that by complying with all of the regulations pertaining to the program, this would increase their chances of maintaining custody.

However, the final evaluation report did not consider whether the program had an effect in terms of addressing the material needs of homeless pregnant youth—the purported reason for its creation. The primary research question in the report is: are young pregnant homeless women able to retain and utilize passports throughout their pregnancies? Whether or not the young mothers actually found the passport helpful was of secondary concern (Moravac et al. 13). Since the results of the research determined that 88 percent of passport users held on to their passports throughout their pregnancies, the pilot project was considered a success. This is despite the fact that 50 percent of the women residing in the shelter system at enrolment remained in the shelter system post-delivery and despite the fact that 9.2 percent of the women living in apartments at time of enrolment ended up in shelters at post-delivery (20). Nor is there even mention of how many babies were apprehended at birth, which was considered outside the boundaries of the evaluation.

This example vividly shows how far removed the reports and policy initiatives have become from the initial instigation. The purpose of the hospital program was to integrate resources to better meet the needs of young pregnant mothers. Yet just as Foucault reveals in his analysis of the prison system, despite the obvious failure of the passport program in leading to any advantages in terms of meeting the material needs of homeless young mothers, the project is nevertheless a success in terms of replicating the governing structures and divisionary mechanisms of society through which deviant populations can be more effectively labelled and documented.

Conclusion

Neoliberal policies have created an unequivocal increase in rates of homelessness, particularly for women and families (Layton 50). Although all mothers experiencing homelessness are stigmatized and labelled, the particular normative assumptions associated with young mothers who are homeless lead to even greater regulatory paradigms. The above examples only illustrate the edge of a broken system. Since the mid-1990s, the Ontario welfare state has become overburdened and overly bureaucratized by adopting a risk-assessment model that prioritizes the paperwork trail above meeting material needs. If the box can be checked off, then success is achieved. Yet what gets lost in all this paperwork are the voices of the young homeless mothers telling us what they actually need—and, importantly, that those needs are not being met.

Work Cited

Foucault, Michel. *Discipline and Punish: The Birth of the Prison.* 1975. Vintage Press, 1979.

Foucault, Michel. *Technologies of the Self: A Seminar with Michel Foucault.* Edited by Luther Martin et al. The University of Massachusetts Press, 1988.

Layton, Jack. *Homelessness: How to End the National Crisis.* Penguin Canada, 2008.

Moravac, C, et al. *Evaluation of "My Baby and Me" Infant Passport for Young Pregnant Homeless Women in South East Toronto.* Toronto Public Health, August 2009.

Song, Jesook. *South Koreans in the Debt Crisis: The Creation of a Neoliberal Welfare Society.* Duke University Press, 2009.

Chapter Two

Young Mothers and Modern Domestic Adoption: Choice or Reproductive Exploitation?

Valerie Andrews

W hile modern domestic adoption is promoted by Canadian adoption agencies as "new and improved," in actuality, contemporary adoption policies and practices reproduce those of the postwar adoption mandate. The postwar adoption mandate has been described as a "process of interrelated institutional power systems which, together with socio-cultural norms, ideals of gender heteronormativity, and emerging sociological and psychoanalytic theories, created historically unique conditions during the post-WWII decades wherein mostly white unmarried mothers were systematically and often violently, separated from their babies by means of adoption" (Andrews, *White Unwed Mother* 21).[1] Choice, consent, and openness remain illusory in contemporary adoption culture, as the separation of a young, healthy mother and her newborn baby by adoption has been embedded and normalized in Western society.[2]

This chapter examines the processes of domestic infant adoption in Canada, which is generally framed as a choice for young mothers; and identifies various social justice issues being raised by contemporary adoption activists and reformers. Precluded in this chapter is a discussion of other forms of adoption—kinship, step, transracial, transnational, and the adoption of children from child welfare agencies. Instead, this chapter focuses on the ways in which the postwar adoption mandate continues to shape and inform dominant discourse surrounding young motherhood and contemporary domestic adoption policies and practices in Canada.

As a survivor of the postwar adoption mandate for unmarried mothers, an adoption activist, and the executive director of Origins Canada, I am in a unique position to illustrate the issues of concern to adoption activists and reformers in Canada.[3] Although this chapter concentrates on critically analyzing contemporary adoption practice within the context of modern domestic adoption, I do not assume that there are no mothers who actively seek adoption or that there are no positive adoption outcomes.

Although adoption has been situated as an option for unmarried mothers in Canada since the late 1900s, prior to the 1930s, adoption was uncommon. Rarely referred to as adoption, it did not take the form that it later would. The first law in Canada for the regulation of the transfer of children by adoption was introduced in New Brunswick in 1873, followed by the passage of a similar law in Nova Scotia in 1896 (Strong-Boag 25). In 1921, the Adoption Act was enacted in Ontario (Chambers). However, adoption was still not widely prescribed for unmarried mothers. As Karen Murray points out, "despite the new adoption law, many people were convinced of the 'naturalness' of keeping a mother and child together and supported an unwed mother's right to raise her child" (273). In addition it was thought that the moral laxity of the mother would be transferred to her offspring.

Adoption as a form of child procurement and transfer changed significantly in postwar Canada. In the 1940s, during the powerful postwar climate of maternalism and the mother imperative, the white unmarried mother was cast as "psychologically ill," and adoption became the prominent social prescription for out-of-wedlock pregnancy. During the mandate era, white unmarried mothers were the primary source of newborns for heterosexual couples pursuing adoption. For example, between 1960 and 1965, total adoptions in Ontario were 32,724; adoptions from unmarried mothers[4] represented 24,222 or 74 percent of these (Andrews, *White Unwed Mother* 170). However, by the early 1970s, the supply of white newborns dropped dramatically. Many women were using the newly available contraceptive pill. Those who did become pregnant increasingly chose abortion, which was now legal, or single motherhood; the latter being supported by government allowances. Sole parenting became less stigmatized due to the sexual revolution and the second-wave feminist movement.[5] Although there is no direct comparable data for Canada, by 1988, surrender rates by unmarried mothers in the United States had fallen to approximately 2 percent (Sobol and Daly, *Statistics* 494). This is in stark contrast to surrender rates in maternity homes during the adoption mandate where unmarried mothers surrendered their babies for adoption at the rate of 85-95% (Andrews, *White Unwed Mother* 166).

Declining rates of infants available for adoption led to drastic changes in domestic adoption practices in the 1970s[6], and "as early as 1975 discussions were turning towards 'open adoption' as a way to introduce a new path in adoption in response to a 'baby population' that was 'dwindling'" (Baran qtd. in Corrigan D'Arcy 123).[7] Studies appeared in academia about surrendering mothers and the declining rates of domestic infants for adoption. An adoption literature review of ninety-one peer reviewed journals published between 1978 and 2008 revealed two main themes in articles pertaining to surrendering mothers:

> These can be viewed as two streams of research ... the first stream (forty-three articles) examines the consequence of surrender on the mother. The second stream (thirty-two articles) examines factors that may predict and/or influence rates of surrender, often stating with concern that surrender rates have declined significantly and should be increased. The latter stream contains three main sub-themes: factors (socio-demographic, educational, attitudinal, familial, or economic) that distinguish mothers who surrender their babies from mothers who keep their babies, surveys to determine what would encourage expectant mothers to consider adoption, and comparison of different agency practices and their effects on surrender rates. (Lake 25)

Lake's study reveals that approximately one third of the articles reviewed attempt to determine the ideal circumstances in which a mother might surrender her baby for adoption. Similar articles appeared in professional journals for social workers. In an article that appeared in *Child Welfare* titled "Adoption in the 1990s: Socio-demographic Determinants of Biological Parents Choosing Adoption," Victoria Chippindale-Bakker and Linda Foster identify three factors that increased the likelihood of adoption: the "biological mother chooses and meets the adoptive parents; she has minimal contact with the baby following delivery; and she has relatively long and intense postnatal involvement with the adoption center" (353). Many other studies published between 1978 and 2008 illustrate that the shrinking supply of domestic newborns was a matter of concern for social workers and others and that new strategies were needed to increase the supply of such newborns for adoption. The implications of such studies for the young mother considering adoption are manifold. In the article "Open Adoption: They Knew it Would Work," Cedar Bradley writes the following: "This raises a huge ethical issue that is not being discussed in adoption literature. If a mother's decision about surrendering her baby is being influenced by practices carefully researched and applied to increase the odds she will surrender, is it really a free-made [sic] decision? (Bradley).

Young mothers today, as during the mandate, continue to be coerced, misled, and kept unaware of their rights. Adoption activists have defined adoption coercion as:

Any form of overt or covert pressure, manipulation, convincing, force, fraud, human rights violation, or withholdings of resources resulting in a woman surrendering her baby for adoption. Adoption coercion includes any practice that is specifically designed to ensure or increase the odds that a mother will surrender her baby for adoption. (Origins Canada)

Adoption reformers argue that adoption coercion is inherent in adoption agency practices in Canada since the practices employed have been specifically designed to reflect late twentieth century studies—that is, to increase the odds of a mother surrendering her baby for adoption.

The postwar adoption mandate was the harbinger of adoption culture in Western society. By the end of the twentieth century and into the new millennium, emphasis has been increasingly placed on the needs and desires of prospective adoptive parents. The adoption market is currently driven by a demand by adopters for babies, a sentiment exemplified by Juan Miguel Petit, special rapporteur to the United Nations Rights of the Child:

Regrettably, in many cases, the emphasis has changed from the desire to provide a needy child with a home, to that of providing a needy parent with a child. As a result, a whole industry has grown, generating millions of dollars of revenues each year, seeking babies for adoption and charging prospective parents enormous fees to process paperwork ... the Special Rapporteur was alarmed to hear of certain practices within developed countries, including the use of fraud and coercion to persuade single mothers to give up their children. (United Nations)

Crisis Pregnancy and the Prolife Movement

Teen motherhood continues to be situated as a category of high-risk mothering that falls outside "good mother" ideologies. Although numbers of young mothers have continued to decline (Bielski), teen motherhood continues to be constructed as a crisis, which makes it more likely that a young mother will visit a Crisis Pregnancy Centre (CPC). Such a visit can lead to the loss of a child to adoption, as vulnerable young mothers are indoctrinated with messages suggesting that they are destined to fail as mothers; that their children would benefit most from being part of a family with more resources, and that they would "want the best" for their child, suggesting that they themselves do not represent "the best" for their babies. These coercive strategies have been used on young mothers since the 1940s.

The word "crisis" appears prominently in CPC marketing. These centres lure young expectant mothers with headlines such as "Crisis Pregnancy? We Can Help," "Pregnancy Counselling," or "Are You Experiencing an Unplanned Pregnancy?" Most often these centres are operated by prolife organizations, although the identification as such is often obscured. In Canada, there are approximately two hundred CPCs as opposed to approximately twenty-five abortion clinics (Arthur 3). An extensive study done in 2009 by Joyce Arthur for the Pro-Choice Action Network states the following:

It is important to educate women, the public, media, and government about the true CPC agenda to ensure that they are not trusted under their false pretences ... adoption is heavily promoted by CPCs. Some well-meaning healthcare professionals refer to CPCs without realizing who they are. Governments may provide funding to CPCs without being aware of the centre's religious anti-abortion and pro-adoption agenda. (18)

Certainly, the prolife movement has weighed in on adoption. Prolife campaigns with such slogans as "Adoption not Abortion" are often used outside of abortion clinics and in prolife marches.[8] The juxtaposition of adoption and abortion has been a successful campaign strategy for the prolife movement.

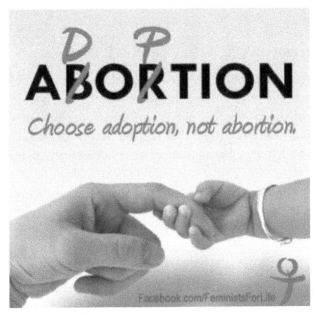

(Image retrieved from Pinterest)

Despite the position of many adoption reformers that abortion and adoption are unrelated—the former being a reproductive choice and the latter being a parenting one—wider public assertions and public policy continue to associate the two. Recent challenges in the United States to abortion rights for women suggest that adoption should be the prescription for any unplanned pregnancy. Record high adoption numbers in Alabama were recently lauded by Andrew T. Walker, director of research and senior fellow in Christian ethics at the Southern Baptist Convention. His remarks on Twitter exemplify the conflation of adoption and abortion, "I do not know what is in the water in Alabama but I want it spread throughout the rest of the U.S. Restricting abortion and increasing adoption. This is what a consistent ethic of life looks like" (@andrewtwalk). Restriction on abortion will lead to more domestic adoptions as young mothers in forced pregnancies who do not wish to parent will be subject to adoption. Adoption reformers assert that this is a form of reproductive exploitation.

In 2011, the Toronto Right to Life Association ran a series of 357 advertisements in the Toronto subway system, although the campaign concealed the sponsor of the ads.[9] The advertisements inferred that a two-parent family was preferable to a sole parent family. Women in the advertisements were referred to as "birth mother", a coercive adoption industry term. A few of the advertisements showed the image of a young, smiling woman who has surrendered her child for adoption. This type of image is misleading considering the many studies, and senate inquiries revealing the long-lasting trauma experienced by mothers separated from their children by adoption[10]. In addition, testimonials were used. Testimonials are often employed in sales and marketing strategy to illustrate to a buyer that others have been satisfied with a product or service. Testimonials of happy "birthmothers" are used extensively in adoption marketing to draw young women into adoption (Andrews, "Sales and Marketing").

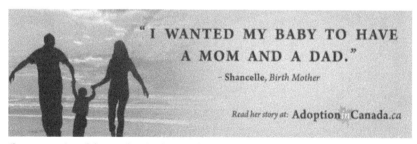

(Image retrieved from adoptionincanada.ca)

The Adoption Agency

The process of modern domestic adoption in a Canadian adoption agency is structured to ensure the completion of an adoption transaction. Considering that the paying client is the prospective adopter, a power differential emerges at the outset with respect to the expectant mother. Such power dynamics remain invisible in adoption culture. The modern domestic adoption transaction usually consists of a young mother with limited resources, adopters with resources (the paying client of the agency), and adoption agencies with marketing research and savvy sales practices designed to increase the probability of a completed adoption transaction. The newborn infant to be adopted has no power or legal representation. Although the mother, adopters, and adoptee are often referred to as an "adoption triad," many adoption activists reject such terminology due to the power inequities inherent in the adoption transaction,

> There are no 'triads,' 'mosaics,' 'circles,' or 'constellations' of adoption. These constructs exist only to dilute voice, and to promote a false equivalence of the lived experiences of those marginalized in adoption transactions to those of the adoption 'status quo'. These terms render invisible the power dynamics involved in adoption and seek to equalize the parties." (Origins Canada)

The goal of an independent adoption agency is to process adoption transactions; therefore, a steady supply of newborns is required. Adoption agencies promote the idea that adoption has changed; that contemporary mothers now have power and choice in the adoption transaction, in contrast to adoption mandate mothers. Young expectant mothers are also inundated with the notion that openness in adoption reflects a woman's exercise of her rights. For example, one Canadian adoption website states the following:

> Over the past fifty years a lot has changed with adoption that you might not know about. Long gone are the days when a woman was hidden from society until she secretly had a child, which was then whisked away and given to complete strangers. Today, adoption provides strong support and care for mothers through-out the birthing process, total control over every step of the

process, the right to have a long-term relationship with the child after the adoption; and freedom of choice over which family will receive her baby. (Adoption in Canada)

Overcoming anticipated objections is a sales and marketing method used to address objections to a product or service prior to the issues being raised by the buyer; in this case, the anticipated objection is to the practices of the past (Andrews, "Sales and Marketing"). The information provided is also false. Mothers do not have the right to a long-term postadoption relationship with their child since, open adoption agreements are not legally binding in Canada.

Open Adoption

During the decades in which the adoption mandate was at its height, the majority of adoptions were closed—that is, the parties to an adoption remained anonymous to one another. In contrast, an open adoption is one in which the identities of the parties are disclosed. In contemporary adoption culture an open adoption has also come to mean some form of postadoption contact between mother and child.

When the domestic supply of white newborns dwindled after 1970, studies found that mothers were more likely to surrender an infant if they felt empowered in the adoption process. As pointed out by David Kallen et al., "it may be that open adoption policies ... can result in greater consideration of adoption by some adolescents who currently keep and raise their babies" (312). The following is an example of openness as portrayed by one Canadian adoption agency:

> "At this stage, an openness agreement may be discussed. This arrangement will provide you with the opportunity to follow your child's growth and development over time. You may, for example, receive pictures and/or letters from the adoptive family and have scheduled visits or email contact with them." (Choices Adoption Agency, BC)

Some agencies provide mothers with forms to fill out indicating how many letters, visits, and videos per year they would like to receive from the adoptive family. This process is coercive, as young mothers fill out these forms with the belief that they are in control of openness, which entrenches the mother further in the adoption process. One mother writes about how these mothers, in fact, are not in control: "the adoptive mom PROMISED me phone calls and pics every month ... now they have changed their phone number and I get no more pics. My son is only almost 4 mos. old. They want to forget that I ever existed" (Birth Mom Support Group). The lure of open adoption then, acts a form of coercion for expectant mothers. Despite the discourse of openness in adoption culture, mothers of adoption separation have no legal rights in Canada with respect to postadoption enforcement. Furthermore, openness remains illusory since adoption records continue to be sealed or semi-sealed by the provinces, despite the ongoing work of adoption activists to enact clean legislation providing full adoption disclosure with no vetoes.[11]

Formation of Maternal Identity

Interrupting the formation of a healthy maternal identity by undermining the confidence of the young expectant mother's ability to parent has been a tactic used by adoption professionals since the adoption mandate (Andrews, *White Unwed Mother* 127). Most first-time expectant mothers, even those with resources and support, experience some challenges in forming a confident motherhood or maternal identity. Adoption agencies are aware of this and exploit the vulnerability of the young mother in an unplanned pregnancy. Early in the relationship, agencies provide the expectant mother with checklists, forms, or tasks to compare what she could give her child in contrast to what adoptive parents might provide; they also ask other types of questions designed to erode a young woman's confidence in her parenting abilities. These unethical, coercive tactics are borrowed from earlier times; social workers gave similar questionnaires to unmarried mothers during the mandate. The following are sample questions from a contemporary agency pamphlet titled "Am I Ready to be a Parent?":

> Am I willing to give up my goals for a time to take care of a child? Do I live in an environment where my decision to parent would be accepted? Do I know how to care for a child and provide for his or her needs? Do I know anything about child development?

Can I afford to financially support a child? Did you know? The estimated cost of: Diapers $20-35 per package, Car seat $60-150, Baby Equipment $1500-2000, Baby formula per week $30, Clothing per season $200-250, Baby sitting per hour $10-15, Daycare per week $250. (Adoptions From the Heart)

These types of conversations, questionnaires, and assignments damage the confidence of the young mother with limited financial resources; and entrench the idea in her mind that her baby will have a better life with someone more established than herself. This process also hinders and distorts the developing maternal identity; and instead fosters the formation of a "birthmother" identity. This is the identity endorsed by the adoption agency, since the "birthmother" identity is congruent with the completion of an adoption transaction. Andrews states that "assigning this identity to an expectant mother during pregnancy psychologically grooms the mother to produce her baby for someone else" ("Language"). The mother becomes indoctrinated with notions of "sacrifice," "bravery," "unselfishness," and "gift giving" (Andrews, *White Unwed Mother* 140). One mother writes, "Each step of the process before birth was carefully crafted to make sure that I placed my child instead of parented ... looking back, I realize that the agency made sure I was a birth mother before I walked into the hospital" (qtd. in Johnson). Another mother states that, "the only thing I was ever told was that it was best to begin separating now. To start addressing the child by the name the prospective adoptive parents picked out for him. To think of myself as a birthmother rather than a mother" (Axness 1).

Prebirth Matching

Within the first few meetings with the agency, young mothers are provided with profiles of prospective adopters to review. These profiles are competitive and many pay exorbitant fees to marketing companies to have profiles prepared so as to stand out in a sea of prospective adopters. These profiles are often accompanied by "Dear Birthmother" letters. Young pregnant women considering adoption are told the following: "Your social worker will talk with you about the type of family you want for your child. You will then be provided with profiles of approved and waiting adoptive families. A profile includes a 'Dear Birthparent' letter, written by the adoptive parents with pictures of themselves and their life" (Adoption Options). As soon as a young mother indicates a preferred profile, she is immediately drawn into an adoption transaction.

Connecting expectant mothers with adopters prior to birth is known as pre-birth matching. Adoption activists and reformers find this practice coercive, as it exploits the mother at a time when she is likely to be most vulnerable and in need of support and friendship. Mothers are not only referred to as "birthmothers" by prospective adopters, but some use the paternalistic "our birthmother" (Andrews, "Language"). Her baby becomes "our baby" and "your baby"— reminiscent of the symbolic "the baby" used during the adoption mandate era. Relationships such as these are designed to make the mother feel obliged to create a family for adopters who often have sad and compelling infertility and adoption histories; which they share with the pregnant woman prior to birth. Adoption agencies are aware of this, and they work to ensure the adoption is completed through a covenant agreement, a hospital plan, and an entrustment ceremony.

Covenant Agreement

A covenant agreement is a non-binding, non-legal, pre-birth agreement provided by some agencies and signed by both the prospective adopter(s) and the mother. The word "covenant" has religious conn-otations, and implies an unbreakable promise and moral purpose. The stated purpose of this agreement is for the parties to agree that they will carry through with arrangements made while the mother is pregnant; for the adopters, these arrangements relate to postadoption contact, and for the mother, they relate to the relinquishment of her child at birth. However, there is a major inequity in this process, since the mother is agreeing to something that will be legally binding— that is, the termination of her parental rights—whereas the adoptive parents are agreeing to something that is not legally binding—that is, the promise of future contact. This "contract" is designed specifically to further entrench an adoption outcome.

Hospital Plan

During the adoption mandate era, unmarried mothers residing in maternity homes were routinely dropped off at hospital to labour alone. Their file was labelled "MISS" or "BFA" (Baby for Adoption), which instigated hospital protocols for unmarried mothers prior to the signing of consent (Andrews, *White Unwed Mother* 101). Mandate-era protocols included the removal of the baby directly from the delivery table, known as "clean break," the segregation of unmarried mothers from married mothers, and the suppression of lactation (100).

Young mothers today are encouraged to make a hospital plan in advance of birth that mirror mandate protocols. The website *Canada Adopts* explains the importance of a hospital plan: "giving birth is a physically and emotionally challenging process ... that's why it's important to make a hospital plan in advance." This website provides young mothers with hospital protocol suggestions, including having adopters in delivery room and allowing adopters to cut the baby's cord or be the first to hold the baby. Adoption agencies are aware that the baby's birth is the most vulnerable time of the adoption transaction due to the fact that the first-time mother is unaware of the transformative nature of birth. Optimum conditions for birth are that mothers feel safe, private, and unobserved during labour and delivery (Wickam, 163). However, this rarely happens in adoption, since agencies are aware that having adopters present at delivery and in hospital increases the odds of an adoption transaction being completed. The birth of the baby is the most critical time of the adoption transaction while the mother still has custody and control. If the new mother shows any signs of indecisiveness, she is reminded by agency staff members, who also are present at the hospital, of the hospital plan she made with the agency while pregnant, and the reasons she made it; so that she does not waver.

The practice of distinct hospital protocols reproduces earlier adoption mandate-era hospital practices. The presence of prospective adopters in delivery rooms is viewed as predatory by many activists, since it is unlikely that mothers will have a stress-free delivery. The mother's ability to freely bond with her newborn immediately after birth and in the maternity ward setting through breastfeeding, bathing, changing, feeding, and use of the modern skin-to skin-bonding practice is severely compromised and the obligation to complete her task is intensified. One mother writes: "I breastfed (against agency advice) and pumped for them to feed from a bottle...my alone time with my baby was brief ... I thought about the adoptive parents standing in the lobby. I thought about how much they already loved this baby, how excited the older sibling was, and how much they had gone through to get to this point" (qtd. in Johnson). New young, healthy mothers should not be concerned with the difficulties and emotional needs of others as they relate to her newborn baby and her own motherhood.

Consent and Revocation

In Canada, a mother who enters into a domestic infant adoption agreement must sign a consent to adoption, which terminates her parental rights. Early consent has been identified as a factor that "may affect the utilization of adoption as a pregnancy resolution" (Sobol and Daly 158). Consent to adoption procedures in Canada are moving toward the United States model of early consent—that is, either prior to or within a few hours of birth; a practice considered unethical by most adoption reformers. In Alberta, a mother can sign termination of parental rights immediately after birth, once she is medically cleared (See Table 1). Most provinces allow for a revocation period—that is, the number of days after a consent is signed in which the mother may change her mind and revoke her consent. As Table 1 reveals, revocation periods vary by province. However, once a consent form is signed, it is extremely difficult for a mother to retrieve her child, especially if the child has been placed on adoption probation[12] or if an Adoption Order[13] has been made. Even though a mother may revoke her consent within the prescribed legal time frame, adoptive parents are usually reluctant to give up a baby they have come to believe is theirs. Judges in Canada and the United States have historically ruled on the side of adoptive parents against unmarried or young mothers, especially if the mother has a history of being in the care of a social service agency, such as the Children's Aid Society.

Table 1. Consent and Revocation Periods by Province and Territory

Province	Consent Not Before	Revocation Period (from Date of Signing Consent)
Newfoundland	7 Days After Birth	21 Days
PEI	14 Days	14 Days
Nova Scotia	15 Days	
New Brunswick	4 Days	30 Days
Quebec	Unknown	Unknown
Ontario	7 Days	21 Days If no Adoption Order
Manitoba	48 Hours	21 Days
Saskatchewan	72 Hours	14 Days if no Adoption Order
Alberta	Birth (Medical clearance)	10 Days
British Columbia	10 Days	30 Days
Yukon	7 Days	21 Days or application to court after 21 days
Northwest Territory	10 Days	30 Days
Nunavut	10 Days	30 Days

Source: Raw data retrieved from provincial adoption legislation

Entrustment Ceremonies

An entrustment ceremony is another practice designed to give the mother the illusion that she is in control of the adoption process (Beginnings Adoption Agency). This ceremony may take place in a hospital chapel prior to or just after the discharge of the mother and baby from hospital. Unlike mothers of the adoption mandate era when babies were whisked away directly from delivery tables, modern mothers are encouraged to take an active role in "placing" their baby. Mothers might dress the baby, choose the poetry, music, or other arrangements, and hand their baby over to the adopters. This practice often takes place within twenty-four hours of birth when the mother's oxytocin levels are extremely high, which create feelings of love, trust, and sociability. Mothers are still recovering from birth; may be on medication, or suffering from postpartum depression.

Conclusion

In the current domestic adoption climate in Canada, the ability of a young expectant mother to choose freely or to give informed consent is severely compromised, as the adoption agency relies on studies, coercive practices, savvy sales and marketing, and psychological persuasion—all of which improves the odds that an adoption transaction will take place. Jess Del Balzo and Bryony Lake write the following:

> In *The Handmaid's Tale*, Margaret Atwood depicted a futuristic society in which fertile young women were held captive and used to bear children for sterile, upper-class wives. The scenario sounds extreme, but...it is not as fictional as one might hope ... reproductive exploitation has yet to be acknowledged in mainstream society. Millions of women have been exploited for their fertility in the past 50 years and millions more will fall prey to such exploitation if measures are not taken to protect them. (1)

Like mothers from the adoption mandate era, contemporary mothers—especially young ones—continue to be impacted by adoption practices that are unethical, that constitute human rights violations, and that ultimately result in the traumatic separation of a healthy young mother and her newborn. Adoption activists seek reforms to eliminate practices synchronous with reproductive exploitation. If desired, an adoption can be arranged after a birth takes place—that is, after the young mother has had an opportunity to bond with and care for her newborn baby in the postpartum setting and in a space where she is free from all entities that may benefit from the completion of an adoption transaction.

Endnotes

1. In Canada alone, over 350,000 mothers were impacted by the mandate" (*White Unwed Mother* 22).
2. Adoption culture might be described as "the production, normalization, and invisibilization, of the exchange and consumption of a set of shared meanings that surround the transfer of infants and children by adoption from one social location to another within western contexts (Andrews).

3. Origins Canada is a federal non-profit organization in Canada supporting those separated by adoption and lobbying for adoption reform.

4. Adoptions from unmarried mothers were recorded as a separate category in Ontario.

5. See the Criminal Law Amendment Act (Canada) 1968-69, which allowed for abortions with permission of a panel of three doctors and when the mother's physical or mental health was at risk. Also see *Roe v Wade*, United States ruling on abortion in 1973, which allowed for legal abortion in the United States.

6. In Canada, the United States, the United Kingdom, and Australia.

7. In response to the declining availability of domestic supply, there was also a sharp increase in international adoption rates. See Statistics Canada.

8. The Campaign Life Coalition Press Room has stated the following: "Canadians in 237 locations across the country to hit the streets with pro-life message...participants will hold signs that read: Abortion Kills Children, Adoption the Loving Option, Abortion Hurts Women, Life the First Inalienable Right."

9. This type of advertising is increasing in Canada, following the American model. It is used extensively in the United States on highway billboards, public transit, and other types of advertising.

10. See Sobol & Daly, Lake, Origins Canada, Senate of Canada report "The shame is ours", Australia Senate Report "Former forced adoption policies and practices."

11. Adoption records remain sealed in PEI, and NS, and are partially open and subject to vetoes in NFLD, NB, PQ, ON, MAN, SASK, ALTA, and BC. Vetoes can be filed by mothers or adoptees to prevent the other party from receiving full disclosure.

12. This is when a child is placed in a prospective adoptive home to be monitored and eventually to stay.

13. An adoption order is a final order by a Judge making the adoption permanent.

Works Cited

@andrewtwalk. "I Do Not Know." *Twitter*, 21 May 2019, twitter.com/andrewtwalk/status/1130838431830020096. Accessed 13 June 2019.

Adoptions in Canada, adoptionincanada.ca/media-resources. Accessed 3 June 2019.

Adoption T-shirt image. *Pinterest*, pinterest.com/pin/244672192232680638/. Accessed 3 June 2019.

Adoption Options. "What Is the Adoption Process." Adoption Options, 2017, www.adoptionoptions.com/birthparents-the-process/. Accessed 3 June 2019.

Adoptions from the Heart. "Am I Ready to be a Parent?" Adoptions from the Heart, 2019, afth.org/know-ready-to-parent/. Accessed 13 June 2019.

Andrews, Valerie. "The Language of Adoption." *Origins Canada*, 2009, www.originscanada.org/adoption-practices/adoption-language/language-of-adoption/. Accessed 3 June 2019.

Andrews, Valerie. "Sales and Marketing in Modern Domestic Adoption." *Sleeping Giants in Adoption: Power, Privilege, Politics and Class*, 8th Biennial Adoption Initiative Conference, May, 2014, St. John's University, New York, NY.

Andrews, Valerie. *White Unwed Mother: The Adoption Mandate in Postwar Canada*. Demeter Press. 2018.

Arthur, Joyce. "Exposing Crisis Pregnancy Centres in British Columbia: A Research Project for the Pro-Choice Action Network." Prochoice Action Network, 2009, www.prochoiceactionnetworkcanada.org/Exposing-CPCs-in-BC.pdf. Accessed 3 June 2019.

Axness, Marcy. "When Does Adoption Begin?" The Decree, Journal of the American Adoption Congress, 2001, vol. 18, no. 2, pp. 8-9.

Beginnings Adoption Agency. "What Is an Entrustment Ceremony." *Beginnings Adoption Agency*, www.beginnings.ca/faq-items/what-is-an-entrustment-ceremony/. Accessed 3 June 2019.

Bielski, Zosia. "Canada's Teen Birth and Abortion Rate Drops by 36.9 per cent," *Globe and Mail*, 26 May 2010, www.theglobeandmail.com/life/parenting/canadas-teen-birth-and-abortion-rate-drops-by-369-per-cent/article571685/. Accessed 3 June 2019.

Bradley, Cedar. "Adoption Critique. Open Adoption, They Knew it would Work." *Cedar Trees*, 2010, www.cedartrees.wordpress.com /2008/08/21/open-adoption-they-knew-it-would-work/. Accessed 3 June 2019.

Campaign Life Coalition Press Room. "Canadians in 237 Locations across the Country to Hit the Streets with Pro-life Message." *Campaign Life*, 2015, www.campaignlifecoalition.com/index.php?p =Press+Room&id=164. Accessed 3 June 2019.

Chambers, Lori. *A Legal History of Adoption in Ontario, 1921-2015.* Osgoode Society for Canadian Legal History. University of Toronto Press, 2016.

Chambers, Lori. *Misconceptions: Unmarried Motherhood and the Ontario Children of Unmarried Parents Act 1921-1969.* University of Toronto Press, 2007.

Chippendale-Baker, Victoria, and Linda Foster. "Adoption in the 1990s: Sociodemographic Determinants of Biological Parents Choosing Adoption." *Child Welfare*, vol. 75, no. 4, July-August, 1996, pp. 337-55.

Choices Adoption Agency. "Domestic Adoption." *Choices Adoption*, www.choicesadoption.ca/birth-parent-domestic-adoption/. Accessed 3 June 2019.

Corrigan D'Arcy, Claudia. "Birthmothers." *Mothers, Mothering and Motherhood Across Cultural Differences: A Reader,* edited by Andrea O'Reilly, Demeter Press, 2014, pp. 119-141.

DelBalzo, Jess, and Bryony Lake. "Reproductive Exploitation". *Origins Canada*, 2019, www.originscanada.org/adoption-practices/adoption -coercion/the-adoption-industry/reproductive-exploitation/. Accessed 3 June 2019.

Johnson, Nicole. "How to Prevent Coercion in Newborn Adoption." *The Adoption Institute*, www.adoptioninstitute.org/how-to-prevent-coercion-in-newborn-adoption/. Accessed 3 June 2019.

Kallen, David J., et al. "Adolescent Mother sand Their Mothers View Adoption." *Family Relations*, vol. 39, no. 3, 1990, pp. 311-16.

Lake, Bryony. *Posttraumatic Stress Disorder in Natural Mothers.* MA Thesis. City University, 2009.

Murray, Karen Bridget. "Governing 'Unwed Mothers' in Toronto at the Turn of the Twentieth Century." *The Canadian Historical Review,* vol. 85, no. 2, 2004, pp. 253-76.

Origins Canada. "Adoption Trauma Studies." *Origins Canada,* www.originscanada.org/adoption-trauma-2/adoption-trauma-studies/. Accessed 3 June 2019.

Sobol, Michael P., and Kerry J. Daly. "Canadian Adoption Statistics: 1981-1990." *Journal of Marriage and Family,* vol. 56, no. 2, 1994, pp. 493-99.

Sobol, Michael P., and Kerry J. Daly. "The Adoption Alternative for Pregnant Adolescents: Decision Making, Consequences, and Policy Implications." *Journal of Social Issues,* vol. 48, no. 3, 1992, pp. 143-61.

Statistics Canada. "International Adoptions" *Statistics Canada,* 2016, www.statcan.gc.ca/pub/11-402-x/2012000/chap/c-e/c-e02-eng.htm. Accessed 3 June 2019.

Strong-Boag, Veronica. *Finding Families, Finding Ourselves: English Canada encounters Adoption from the Nineteenth Century to the 1990s.* Oxford University Press, 2006.

United Nations. Economic and Social Council. Rights of the Child, Commission on Human Rights. Fifty-Ninth Session, 6 Jan., 2003, www.originscanada.org/documents/G0310090.pdf. Accessed 13 June 2009.

Wickam, Sara. *Midwifery: Best Practices, Volume 5.* London, UK: Butterworth, Heinemann, and Elsevier, 2008.

Chapter Three

Through the Lens: Adolescent Mothers, Stigmatization, and the Media

Jenni Sullivan

As I nursed my tiny new baby in the days following his birth, it was easy to feel as though I'd finally arrived. Despite a pregnancy full of drama, family strife, a last-minute elopement, and several new homes, I felt grounded. After a tempest-tossed adolescence, I eagerly claimed adulthood through mothering and left behind all those troubled chapters. I was surprised, however, when mothers seemed reluctant somehow to claim me. I joined a parenting group for new mothers but could not at all relate to the other women's conversations about gardens, maternity leaves, minivans, and nursery decorations when I lived in a one-bedroom apartment with no vehicle. Strangers on the city bus often smiled and cooed at my baby but would then ask if I knew who the father was or if my child was an accident. I looked young for my age and had no shortage of strangers pointing out that I appeared too young to have a child.

Eventually, I found a group in my community for young mothers and felt I'd finally found friends I could relate to. At twenty-two, I was one of the oldest members, and most of my peers had stories to tell of encounters with strangers and/or other mothers that were even more unpleasant, cruel, and oppressive than mine. My peers spoke about the doctors and nurses who had mistreated them, the relatives who had shunned them, and the dirty looks and whispered comments they had received in public. One mother had been all but accused by another mother of having children solely for the child welfare benefits she would receive. Another had been advised by a guidance counsellor to drop out of school. I wondered about the forces driving these reactions to our pregnancies and children.

Adolescent parenting has been perceived for many years as a significant source of social nuisance. It is evident from epidemiological research that teenage mothers and their children are a statistically vulnerable population. In Canada, teenage mothers have fared worse on measures of poverty and postpartum depression, whereas outcomes for the children born to teenage parents have routinely been worse on measures of childhood health, educational attainment, behaviour, and socioeconomic status (Langille 1601). Healthcare authorities such the World Health Organization and the Canadian Pediatric Society have put forth recommendations with the goal of reducing rates of adolescent pregnancies (Leslie 243). The consensus seems clear—adolescent pregnancies are medically risky and predispose young women and their children to negative socioeconomic circumstances. Sociologists and feminist researchers, however, have attempted to unravel the assumption that adolescent parenthood is necessarily as harmful as it is perceived to be (McDermott and Graham 61; Wilson and Huntington 63; SmithBattle 237). Research demonstrates that the rates of poverty and educational attainment for teen mothers are similar to those for older mothers from similar socioeconomic backgrounds (SmithBattle 237). Studies designed to control for confounding factors have demonstrated that young age is not associated with poor pregnancy outcomes or negative future health consequences for the mother (Lawlor and Shaw 552). This means that it is likely that other factors—such as poverty and childhood trauma—predispose young women to early pregnancy and also cause the negative health and sociological outcomes that are associated with teenage parenting (Lawlor and Shaw 552; McDermott and Graham 61).

Around the time my son was born, a new reality television show called 16 and Pregnant debuted on MTV; following the experiences of several parenting teenage mothers. I enjoyed the show, which was full of drama, angry grandparents, bad boyfriends, and heartbroken young mothers. However, in time I came to be disturbed by the negative image the show projected of teenage parenthood—I realized that the show reinforced dominant social views of young mothers. In their article "The Role of the Media in the Construction of Public Belief and Social Change," Catherine Happer and Greg Philo note that media has a significant influence on which cultural discourses become established in the collective consciousness (321). Media portrayals of teenage parents often serve to reinforce stereotypes about the kind of person who becomes pregnant as a teenager and about what the outcomes for her and her children will necessarily be (Wilson and Huntington 62; SmithBattle 236). In recent public service prevention campaigns sponsored by the New York City Human Resources Association, teenage parenting is warned against in much the same way as cigarette smoking—through a poster campaign with emotionally affecting images that present having a child as an adolescent as being automatically associated with negative outcomes ("New York's Teen Pregnancy PSAs"). Similarly, the Candie's Foundation uses celebrity endorsements and negative messages about teenage parenting in order to emphasize the negative aspects of parenting ("Candie's Foundation").

In their article "16 and Pregnant: A Content Analysis of a Reality Television Program about Unplanned Teen Pregnancy," Lance et al. describe how the popular reality television program focuses on stereotypical themes, such as fighting with support people and sacrificing previously enjoyed activities (292). Portrayals of young mothers in negative poster campaigns and stereotypical depictions of teenage pregnancy on television shows reinforce the stigmatization of adolescent mothers.

Many teenagers who become pregnant claim that they have felt stigmatized by the reaction of others to their pregnancy, such as peers, strangers, and authority figures, including healthcare providers (SmithBattle 238). The stigmatization of adolescent parents has many negative consequences for young mothers and their children (Smith-Battle 238; Wiemann et al. 352.e5). Adolescent parents frequently report negative interactions with healthcare providers during pregnancy, labour, and the postpartum period (Downey and Stout 32-40; Smith et al. 6; SmithBattle 238). Stigmatization by healthcare providers may be a factor in the frequency with which adolescents hesitate to seek out prenatal care or discontinue breast-feeding (Smith et al. 6). Other negative outcomes of stigmatization include increased feelings of social isolation and depression, and decreased resiliency (Wiemann et al. 352.e5; SmithBattle 238).

In exploring the negative cultural narratives surrounding teenage parents, I found that my peers and I were subjected to a limited understanding of what our lives looked like and what we were capable of. This understanding, reinforced in the media, led me to be fearful of asking for help, as I wanted to prove that I was a good and competent mother. Many of my peers also avoided asking for needed community resources, such as breastfeeding clinics, for fear they would be seen as incapable mothers. I wanted to uncover how this stigma was perpetuated.

Media Portrayals of Teenage Parenting: Youth Pregnancy Prevention Campaigns

Teenage parents feel stigmatized not only by the glares of strangers and rude public comments but also by media reports (SmithBattle 238). Media discussing teenage parents can take the form of news stories, public health campaigns, or magazine articles. In recent years, popular media conversations on teenage parenting have expanded to include reality television series that document the lives of young mothers.

In the last decade, highly visible public service teen pregnancy prevention campaigns have emerged in North America. These campaigns use posters and social media applications to prevent teen pregnancy. The New York City human resources teen pregnancy prevention campaign, which occurred in 2013, featured advertisements showing pictures of children who are crying or look perplexed, the majority of which are children of colour ("New York's Teen Pregnancy PSAs"). The advertisements feature statements such as "Honestly, mom, chances are he won't stay with you. What will happen to me?" and "I'm twice as likely not to graduate high school because you had me as a teen" ("New York's Teen Pregnancy PSAs"). The campaign also presented dismal statistics surrounding the outcomes of teenage pregnancy and offered little hope for the future of teenage parents. The view taken in the campaign is not nuanced and does not consider socioeconomic contributions to poor outcomes for adolescent parents and their children. The campaign encourages teenagers to avoid pregnancy but at the cost of further stigmatizing teenage parents and trampling on their perceived ability to parent, have good outcomes, and parent in a way satisfying to both parent and child.

Candie's Foundation has put forth another prevention campaign whose goal is to "educate America's youth about the consequences of teen pregnancy" ("Candie's Foundation"). The Candie's Foundation's catch phrase is "you should be changing the world, not changing diapers" ("Candie's Foundation"). This is problematic because it sets up a false dichotomy suggesting teen parents cannot make a difference in the world while being parents. In "Feminist Critiques of the Public/Private Dichotomy," Carole Pateman discusses the way in which a dichotomy between public and private spheres was established (155). Pateman explains that the private sphere becomes the natural dwelling place for women, caregiving activities, and embodied sexuality, whereas the public sphere is construed as a place for men and as a place where rational thought and politics occur (156). The public-private divide is unjust, as it pigeonholes women into caregiving activities and removes their autonomy and ability to participate in politics and public activity. Candie's Foundation modernizes this dichotomy. Whereas childless adolescents are assumed to have the agency to participate fully in the public sphere, this advantage disappears upon the birth of a child when women become categorized as members of the private sphere where they perform menial caregiving tasks, which are given very little value or importance. Care of an infant is reduced to "changing diapers"—a task that is implicitly characterized as unpleasant and unfulfilling ("Candie's Foundation"). Parenting is seen as a less worthwhile task than anything else a young person could do and is viewed as all-consuming task that leaves no space for personal enrichment, public service, or the pursuit of educational or career goals.

The Candie's Foundation website also promotes a phone application called "cry baby" that purports to demonstrate the realities of teen parenthood ("Candie's Foundation Cry Baby"). The application features a picture of a crying baby accompanied by shrill crying, which the adolescent must soothe by discovering whether the baby is wet, hungry, or tired, and then must resolve the problem in a few clicks ("Candie's Foundation Cry Baby"). Although Candie's Foundation suggests that this phone application reduces the incidence of teenage pregnancy by simulating the experience of parenting an infant, there is conflicting evidence on whether teenagers believe that electronic devices meant to imitate babies provide a realistic experience. Studies on the use of robotic baby dolls that imitate newborns have had mixed results; some have demonstrated that electronic dolls such as "baby think it over" result in more negative attitudes about teenage parenthood but have little effect on real world applications, such as increased contraceptive use or delay of onset of sexual activity (Somers and Fahlman 194). One study surveying an at-risk population of Hispanic teenagers demonstrated that the teenagers came out of the experience with an even more positive view of teenage parenting (Kralewski and Stevens-Simon 3). Even if applications and robotic baby dolls are successful in discouraging teenage pregnancy, they do so at the expense of reducing motherhood to a simplistic state of exhaustion and annoyance at tending to a crying plastic doll or a bodiless phone application. The full experience of parenting is much more nuanced, not to mention pleasant and joyous—a fact recognized by the at-risk Hispanic teens who cited their personal experience with babies and young children for why the robotic baby did not change their attitudes towards young motherhood (Kralewski and Stevens-Simon 4). Celebrity endorsements are another tactic used by the Candie's Foundation. This approach can harm young mothers, as they may experience a decrease in self-esteem when their favourite celebrity role model suggests that motherhood will force them to sacrifice their goals and ambitions.

Public service campaigns attempting to reduce rates of teenage pregnancy may do so at the expense of stigmatizing adolescent parents—a population that already faces a great deal of adversity (Langille 1601). These campaigns rely on stereotypes and suggest that outcomes such as poverty, single parenthood, and poor educational attainment are necessary consequences of teen parenthood. By perpetuating a modern public-private dichotomy and reducing parenthood to a state of drudgery with little reward, The Candie's Foundation reduces motherhood itself to a state of unfulfilling menial work. This attitude can damage all mothers by suggesting that their ability to effect change in the world is hampered by having children.

Media Portrayals of Teenage Parents: Reality Television Shows

Discourses in popular media can have a significant impact on cultural attitudes surrounding many issues. The effect is particularly strong when the population has little firsthand experience with the issue at hand (Happer and Philo 321). A lack of broad perspectives can influence public attitudes negatively towards a group of people, particularly those who are vulnerable (Happer and Philo 327). News media articles about adolescent motherhood are overwhelmingly negative and tend to approach the issue from the narrow perspective of public health with an emphasis on reducing the adolescent birthrate (SmithBattle 236). These views may influence public perception of teenage parents in a manner that promotes stigmatization. Whereas news media is one way in which populations become informed about certain issues, modern reality television has introduced a new way of knowing about those who society deems "other." In recent years, reality television has produced stories about the Amish, poor Southern American families, and others who fall outside of the white middle-class Western family norm. Teenage mothers are another group existing outside this norm.

A number of scholars have investigated *16 and Pregnant* from an academic lens with the intention of uncovering whether or not the program has resulted in teenagers changing their attitudes about pregnancy or in decreasing birthrates among teenagers. A survey by The National Campaign to Prevent Teen and Unplanned Pregnancy notes that more than three quarters of surveyed teens who had viewed the popular shows credited the programs with "helping teens better understand the challenges of pregnancy and parenting" ("Teens Say Parents"). One academic study undertaken by the National Bureau of Economic Research uses viewership and demographic data to calculate changes in births to teenagers attributable to the television program and concludes that the show decreased births to teens by one third (Kearney and Levine 6). These studies suggest that the show influences young people, presumably, by painting a realistic and therefore negative picture about the reality of parenting as a teenager.

In "Toward a Sociology of Reality Television," Beth Montemuro argues that reality television shows reveal norms and ideologies of contemporary culture and may either reflect, challenge, or perpetuate current inequities based on categories such as gender, class and race (84-85). In the National Bureau of Economic Research study, the authors investigate the messages sent by the shows to viewers of *Teen Mom* and *16 and Pregnant* and note such themes as the young woman's ambivalence towards pregnancy, the poor quality of or nonexistent relationship with the baby's father, and medical and health complications (Kearney and Levine 7-8). A content analysis undertaken by researchers at the University of Michigan observes such themes as lack of support, sacrifice of previously enjoyed activities as well as educational opportunities, and surprise at the challenges of parenthood (Lance et al. 292). These themes reflect many of the stereotypical understandings of teenage pregnancy and promote the idea that pregnancy at a young age will result in negative life experiences. As one star of *Teen Mom* notes, "In every episode, someone is trying to figure out if they can pay their rent or go to school or find a job or when they're going to be able to take their next nap, because they haven't slept in 24 hours. ... In every episode, someone has their heart broken" (Sun). The stereotypical themes and emphasis on sacrifice contributes to the ideology that teenage mothering is necessarily a negative experience and that teenagers should be strongly cautioned to avoid it.

In evaluating these programs, it is important to consider whether the final product reflects the true reality of the teenagers' experiences. Reality television programs have faced criticism from viewers and critics as to whether or not they can be said to be realistic in truly capturing the motives and opinions of the cast (Montemurro 93). Critical analyses of reality television shows have examined the ways in which characters are artificially constructed through deception, scripted interactions, and creative editing (Montemurro 94). Many hours of filming produce one forty-five to sixty-minute show, which leaves a great deal of creative licence in the hands of the producer. As many situations and interactions are excluded from each episode of the show, an appraisal of what remains can provide important clues into the message or morals that the show emphasizes. In the cases of *16 and Pregnant* and *Teen Mom*, research suggests that the shows reinforce the message that teenage pregnancy is a negative experience (Kearney and Levine 7-8; Lance et al. 292). Although the goal of the television show may be noble in that it attempts to provide a voice to a largely marginalized population, the show contributes to the stigmatization of adolescent parents by perpetuating a stereotypical view of what it is like to have a child as a teenager.

The television shows *16 and Pregnant* and *Teen Mom* can be seen as a form of qualitative research, as they are supposed to reflect the views and beliefs of the teenagers themselves. However, the association of teen pregnancy with stereotypical themes such as sacrifice and un-happiness contradicts a host of qualitative research in which mothers who had children in their teenage years report positive experiences. Indeed, having a baby improved their self-esteem, strengthened their ties with their families, caused them to make positive life changes, and gave them direction and purpose as well as satisfying and rewarding experiences (Wilson and Huntington 65). In this way, these shows are not a realistic portrayal of how all or even most young parents really feel about their early motherhood experiences; rather, they reflect dominant cultural discourses and stereotypes. The use of stereotypes suggests that reality television shows concerned with teenage parents reinforce, rather than contradict, dominant cultural discourses that construct adolescent mothering as a moral and public health problem. Reality television programs, public service campaigns, and other forms of media that promote stereotypical views of adolescent mothers per-petuate stigmatization.

Consequences of Stigmatization for Adolescent Mothers

Media stigmatization of teenage parents has real life consequences for adolescent parents. Adolescent mothers report encountering hostility and judgment associated with stigmatization in a large number of settings, including schools, social services, healthcare facilities, and even in their own neighbourhoods and homes (McDermott and Graham 69). Stigmatization harms the wellbeing of young mothers in the pregnancy and postpartum period when negative portrayals of teenage parents leads to insensitive or inappropriate treatment by healthcare professionals (Downey and Stout 32-40). In 2011, The Prairie Women's Centre for Healthcare Excellence released a lengthy report investigating the labour and birth experiences of adolescent Indigenous women in Winnipeg. Although some women had positive experiences with the hospital staff who cared for them, the report notes that the majority of the young women felt that staff did a poor job of treating them in a kind and patient-centred manner (Downey and Stout 36). The young women recalled doctors who did not introduce themselves or speak at all, nurses and doctors who minimized their experiences of pain, and nurses who ignored and talked over them (Downey and Stout 38-39). Many of the young women attributed the poor treatment to their age and status as Indigenous women. One woman described a significant change in the manner in which a nurse spoke to her after discovering she was seventeen years old (Downey and Stout 41). Several of the young women complained of condescending comments and lack of willingness on the part of staff to assist in their transition to parenthood (Downey and Stout 42-43). The mistreatment of the adolescent parents in Winnipeg is augmented, as racism intersects with the stigmatization of being a young parent, which demonstrates the ways in which many healthcare providers have internalized cultural messages about young Indigenous mothers. Mistreatment from healthcare providers is not isolated to young Indigenous women in Manitoba; young mothers from a variety of backgrounds report feeling stigmatized by healthcare providers (McDermott and Graham 69). Research has attributed negative attitudes towards physicians as a major barrier to pregnant teenagers accessing prenatal care (Kinsman and Slap 151). Negative attitudes towards healthcare providers are likely caused by fear of mistreatment. As a lack of prenatal care is correlated with worse health outcomes for the mother and infant, reducing the stigmatization of healthcare providers could benefit pregnant teenagers (Kinsman and Slap 151).

Stigmatization also affects the psychological wellbeing of adolescent mothers, and it can place these mothers in vulnerable situations. In a study of 934 adolescent parents, those who reported feeling stigmatized by their pregnancies were more likely to report peer isolation, family criticism, alcohol use during pregnancy, lower self-esteem, as well as intimate partner violence (Wiemann et al. 352.e4). As the authors of the study note, stigmatization is a painful experience, and many of the issues correlated with stigmatization have further deleterious effects. For example, social isolation and loneliness, which are associated with stigmatization, lead to increased feelings of stress, anguish, and despair as well as an increased risk for mood disorders (Wiemann et al.352. e6). Adolescent mothers who experience stigmatization find it to be psychologically traumatic; they associate stigma with feelings of guilt, shame, worthlessness, and anger (SmithBattle 238). In short, stereo-typical discourses of teenage motherhood, which become culturally entrenched, are not benign. The resulting stigmatization affects the health of adolescent mothers and their children as well as their resiliency.

Preventing Stigmatization

Counter-discourses for approaching adolescent parenting are possible. It is important for healthcare providers, friends, and family to recognize that the way teenagers approach their pregnancies and early parenthood experiences may defy expectations. It is likely that based on social discourses and media representations, others would expect pregnant adolescents to experience regret and dismay and that they would assume the teen would not find as much fulfillment in mother-hood as older mothers. Whereas quantitative studies undertaken in the biomedical tradition suggest that teenage parents are likely to have negative experiences with pregnancy and early parenthood, such as increased rates of isolation, poverty, and postpartum depression compared to older mothers, qualitative research offers the opportunity to understand the lived experiences of adolescent mothers (Wilson and Huntington 65). Qualitative studies suggest that the narratives young mothers use to describe having their children involve themes of resiliency, making positive life changes, and living a meaningful life (Wilson and Huntington 65). One study suggests that many young mothers find the experience of mothering restorative in helping to resolve feelings about their own difficult family histories (Middleton 235). Healthcare providers can focus on goal setting with their young pregnant clients and incorporate positive and resilient narratives into their care.

The stigmatization of young mothers is not a necessary outcome, even if stigmatizing discourses are embedded in social consciousness. Better discourses for approaching teenage parenting involve avoiding stigmatization of those who do become pregnant, mitigating potential negative outcomes with community supports, strengthening bonds with support people, and incorporating the understanding that being an adolescent parent can be a joyful experience.

Conclusion

As the years went by, I had several more children and transitioned from a new young mother to a seasoned mother. In my mid-to-late twenties, I began to notice that reactions to my children and myself out in public were noticeably different than when I was a younger mother. People stopped asking if my kids all had the same father and instead asked if we were enjoying the nice weather. I mentored a handful of young mothers in my community, and their stories resembled my own experiences at their age. They felt mistreated and misunderstood by family, friends, and healthcare providers. Many of these young parents did face barriers, such as poverty, single motherhood, and difficulty finishing their education. These barriers were often mitigated with additional support, information, and community resources. Many of the young mothers went on to complete university degrees, and they now have successful and rewarding careers; others live happily as stay-at-home moms and live in ways they find authentic. In some cases, peer mentoring forced me to re-examine my own beliefs about young mothering. For example, when a young mother of twenty years came to talk about having another child, my instinct was to discourage her—as everyone else had done. But when I asked about her motivations, I found they were similar to those of many older mothers who are considering adding to their families. The young mother wanted to have children close in age so they would grow up together. She wanted to have kids first and then tackle her education so that she wouldn't have to take time off part way through. She had everything she needed for a baby and a lot of love to give. Why shouldn't she add to her family? Why would others look down on her if she did?

Stigmatizing narratives about young parents in the media per-petuate negative stereotypes about adolescent parents. By focusing on such themes as sacrifice of previously enjoyed activities and difficult partner relationships, public health campaigns and reality television shows reinforce dominant negative cultural ideologies about young mothers and their children. Altering societal discourses surrounding teenage parenthood could provide a new framework for understanding the phenomenon. Changing the ways in which teenage parenthood is represented by the media could broaden cultural perspectives towards young mothers. In some ways, television shows with the intention of telling the stories of young mothers represent a positive first step towards deconstructing negative social attitudes. If these shows presented a wide range young mother parenting experiences, it is possible that such a medium could become a cultural force for good. Intervening in the ways in which healthcare providers interact with young parents can provide a solid foundation for mutual understanding, which could increase young parents' knowledge and use of community and healthcare resources. As young mothers tend to be a disadvantaged population, compassionate and respectful community-based support can provide them with the tools to succeed. It is important that healthcare providers, friends, and family members become aware of the positive narratives that frame many young women's experiences of pregnancy and parenting and celebrate each woman's experiences of motherhood—at any age.

Works Cited

The Candie's Foundation. "The Candie's Foundation." *The Candie's Foundation.* 2015, www.candiesfoundation.org. Accessed 4 June 2019.

The Candie's Foundation. "Cry Baby App." The Candie's Foundation, 2015, www.candiesfoundation.org/crybaby. Accessed 4 June 2019.

Downey, Bernice, and Roberta Stout. "Young and Aboriginal: Labour and Birth Experiences of Teen Mothers in Winnipeg." *Prairie Women's Health Centre of Excellence,* 2011.

Happer, Catherine, and Greg Philo. "The Role of the Media in the Construction of Public Belief and Social Change." *Journal of Social and Political Psychology,* vol. 1, no. 1, 2013, pp. 321–336.

Kearney, Melissa, and Phill B. Levine. "Media Influences on Social Outcomes: The Impact of MTV's 16 and Pregnant on Teen Childbearing." *National Bureau of Economic Research,* vol. 105, no. 12, 2015, pp. 3597-632.

Kinsman, Sara, and Gail Slap. "Barriers to Adolescent Prenatal Care." *Journal of Adolescent Health,* vol. 13, no. 2, 1992, pp. 146-54.

Kralewski, Judith, and Catherine Stevens-Simon. "Does Mothering a Doll Change Teens′ Thoughts About Pregnancy". *Pediatrics* vol. 105, no. 3, 2000, pp. 1-5.

Lance, A., et al. "16 and Pregnant: A Content Analysis of a Reality Television Program about Unplanned Teen Pregnancy." *Contraception* vol. 8, no. 3, 2012, pp. 292.

Langille, Donals. "Teenage Pregnancy: Trends, Contributing Factors and the Physician's Role." *Canadian Medical Association Journal*, vol. 176, no. 11, 2007, pp. 1601-602.

Lawlor, Debbie, and Mary Shaw. "Too Much Too Young? Teenage Pregnancy Is Not a Public Health Problem." *International Journal of Epidemiology*, vol. 31, no. 3, 2002, pp. 552-554.

Leslie, KM. "Adolescent Pregnancy. Canadian Paediatric Society Position Statement." *Paediatric Child Health*, vol. 11, no. 4, 2006, pp. 243-46.

McDermott, Elizabeth, and Hilary Graham."Resilient Young Mothering: Social Inequalities, Late Modernity and the 'Problem' of 'Teenage' Motherhood." *Journal of Youth Studies,* vol. 8, no. 1, 2005, pp. 59-79.

Middleton, Sue. "'I Wouldn't Change Having the Children—Not at All.' Young Women's Narratives of Maternal Timing: What the UK's Teenage Pregnancy Prevention Strategy Hasn't Heard." *Sexuality Research and Social Policy*, vol. 8, no. 3, 2011, pp. 227-38.

Montemurro, Beth. "Toward a Sociology of Reality Television." *Sociology Compass*, vol. 2, no. 1, 2008, pp. 84-106.

Pateman, Carole."Feminist Critiques of the Public/Private Dichotomy." *An Introduction to Women's Studies: Gender in a Transnational World*, edited by Inderpal Grewal and Caren Kaplan, McGraw-Hill, 2006, pp. 155-59.

Smith, Paige, et al. "Early Breastfeeding Experiences of Adolescent Mothers: A Qualitative Prospective Study." *International Breastfeeding Journal*, vol. 7, no. 1, 2015, pp. 1-14.

SmithBattle, Lee. "Reducing the Stigmatization of Teen Mothers." *MCN, The American Journal of Maternal/Child Nursing*, vol, 28, no. 4, 2013, pp. 235-41.

Somers, Cheryl, and Mariane Fahlman. "Effectiveness of the 'Baby Think It Over' Teen Pregnancy Prevention Program." *Journal of School Health*, vol. 71, no. 5, 2001, pp. 188-95.

Sun, Feifei. "Teen Moms Are Taking over Reality TV. Is That a Good Thing?" *TIME*, 10 July 2011.

"Teens Say Parents Most Influence Their Decisions about Sex: New Survey Data of Teens and Adults Released." *The National Campaign to Prevent Teen and Unplanned Pregnancy*, October 2016.

World Health Organization. "Adolescent Pregnancy Fact Sheet." *World Health Organization*, 23 Feb 2018, www.who.int/mediacentre/factsheets/fs364/en/. Accessed 4 June 2019.

Wiemann, Constance, et al."Are Pregnant Adolescents Stigmatized by Pregnancy?" *Journal of Adolescent Health,* vol. 36, no. 4, 2005, pp. 352.el-352.e7.

Wilson, Helen, and Annette Huntington. "Deviant (M)others: The Construction of Teenage Motherhood in Contemporary Discourse." *Journal of Social Policy,* vol. 35, no. 1, 2005, pp. 59-76.

Chapter Four

Gimme (Age-Appropriate) Shelter: Young Mothers' Reflections on U.S. Supportive Housing Facilities for Low-Income Families with Children

Deborah Byrd

This chapter is part of a larger project that draws upon scholarly research on mentoring programs for pregnant and parenting teens; visits to several U.S. and Toronto area supportive housing facilities for low-income single mothers; and analysis of websites and manuals of several organizations that provide housing, case management, and/or other supports to young mothers and mothers-to-be who are striving to escape poverty and homelessness. Also central to this project are interviews conducted with a dozen young mothers, ages seventeen to twenty-two, who reside in my own community. I have been supporting—and learning from—these and other local young mothers since 2005, when I began teaching a community-based learning course on single motherhood—a course in which my undergraduate students and I regularly interact with and try to find ways to support young mothers enrolled in a mentoring program run by an area nonprofit.[1] A synthesis of this research reveals that as with other kinds of empowerment programs for young mothers (and for adolescents in general), the supportive housing programs that most effectively help the women achieve self-sufficiency, maintain good mental and physical health, develop good parenting skills, and gain confidence in their abilities and agency are "holistic," "wraparound" programs (see, for example, Healthy Teen Network's "A Policy Platform to Promote Health and Success Among Young Families"). Such programs not only provide safe, stable housing for six months or more, but also assist young mothers with educational and career development, life skills and empowerment training, and access to quality early childhood education (and, ideally, high-quality childcare).

This research also reveals that some U.S. supportive housing facilities for low-income single mothers may have much to learn from their Toronto area counterparts, especially when it comes to empowering young mothers who are in their teens and early twenties. Toronto has a number of residential facilities that either are designed specifically for young mothers and mothers-to-be or are attentive to that particular population's needs.[2] These facilities generally use a strengths- or assets-based approach to case management, and they often stress their commitment to participatory decision making. This means that goals and plans are developed with the mom, not imposed upon her. In addition, many of the Toronto supportive housing programs designed for or accessible to young mothers and mothers-to-be urge the woman to consider the facility her home and invite her to see herself as a member of a supportive community. Some agencies, on their websites and in manuals for residents and staff, also articulate an explicitly intersectional, antiracist, and culturally sensitive approach to case management and other support services.

By contrast, the U.S. has few supportive housing facilities designed specifically for young mothers, especially those who are legal minors. Most of the residential facilities available to impoverished young mothers in the U.S. tend to be supportive housing programs for low-income single mothers of varying ages, family sizes, and life circumstances. These U.S. shelters for homeless women with children often take a deficit or weaknesses-based approach to mentoring. Many facilities seem to operate on the assumption that the mother had developed some bad habits or character deficiencies in the past and thus her life must (at least initially) be closely monitored and controlled, from her finances to the time she can spend outside the facility.

Indeed, it is striking that teen mothers in the Toronto area often have later curfews and more opportunities for overnight stays with family and friends than do women in their thirties and forties living in U.S. supportive housing facilities. Moreover, some U.S. facilities strictly limit the mother's ability to personalize her room or apartment; rather than encouraging the woman to view her space as a home and to see herself as part of a stable community, manuals emphasize that the woman is a guest, and they say little about the ways in which she may benefit from interactions with fellow residents, including those who differ from her in age, race, religion, or ethnicity.

In a study titled "Gaining Support for Teen Families: Mapping the Perceptual Hurdles," the FrameWorks Institute found that attentiveness to adolescence as a distinctive stage of development is seldom evident in materials produced by U.S. agencies whose goal is to support and advocate for young mothers (Bales and O'Neil).[3] So it should not be surprising that U.S. mothers in their teens and early 20s—who are, after all, undergoing an age-appropriate struggle to achieve a sense of autonomy, independence, and self-reliance—are unlikely to be drawn to supportive housing programs that restrict and strictly monitor resident parents' behaviour. Such is the case even when the young mothers are in desperate need of safe, affordable housing and even when the facility admits parenting couples as well as single parents of both sexes. Significantly, the interviews I have conducted with a dozen young mothers in a small Pennsylvania city suggest that these young parents would likely find the philosophy and policies of Toronto's supportive housing facilities for young and low-income single mothers appealing. Thankfully, such strengths-based facilities that stress the importance of both autonomy and sisterhood have begun to spring up in the U.S. through such organizations as the Jeremiah Program—a highly effective empowerment program for low-income single mothers that has been expanding to cities across the U.S.[4]

This chapter begins with a discussion of a three-tiered supportive housing facility for young mothers in Toronto, then contrasts the assets-based approach to mentoring used by this facility with a deficits-based model employed at a supportive housing facility for low-income families located in a small Pennsylvania city. The chapter concludes by presenting excerpts from interviews with young single mothers in this city, who critique the local shelter's weaknesses-based approach to helping residents develop the psychological, intellectual, and material resources they need to lead healthy, satisfying, and economically self-sufficient lives in the larger community. The names of the two organizations are fictitious.

Toronto's Gilmore House

On its website, Gilmore House advertises itself as "a client-centred infant and early childhood mental health organization" that supports pregnant and parenting young women ages thirteen to twenty-five.[5] Employing an evidence-based model of support that promotes both "maternal and infant health," the Gilmore House staff tries to ensure that each young mother "has access to prenatal and post-natal care, learns how to care for [and build a secure attachment with] her baby, continues her education, and develops the skills needed to build a successful life and relationship with her baby." Some of the young and generally low-income single mothers enrolled in Gilmore House programs live in the surrounding community; others reside in one of the agency's three supportive housing facilities. Often, a young mother will move through all three tiers of housing. She typically begins in a group living, dormitory-style prenatal facility that has on-site residential counsellors; about six months after the baby's birth, she moves into an apartment in a semi-independent postnatal transitional housing facility with 24/7 supports, after which she can apply for continued support services while living in a partly furnished, two-bedroom townhouse.

The Gilmore House website explicitly identifies the philosophy governing staff interaction with clients as an assets-based approach that encourages pregnant and parenting young women to "actively participate in the design of their plan of care," a plan "designed to focus on their [the mothers'] strengths." Even though the client may be as young as thirteen years old, it is assumed that she has agency and wants to be in control of her own and her child's future. For example, the section of the website that articulates the agency's values states that staff will "*help* pregnant and parenting adolescents ... identify their needs, *and take actions* that better their lives" (my emphasis). Similarly, those who participate in the postnatal housing program are assumed to already have some knowledge of other kinds of local supports available them; the staff's goal is to "*increase* [the young mothers'] knowledge about how to access community resources" (my emphasis). Those who move into the tier three townhouses are assumed "to have well developed life skills and are able to identify children's needs and seek appropriate supports."

The Gilmore House website also stresses the agency's commitment to creating a sense of community; a core value of agency staff is to "work to build trusting and respectful relationships with our clients, staff, volunteers and other stakeholders." Strikingly, the website boldly proclaims that among the agency's core values is a pro-active, inter-sectional feminist commitment to addressing systemic oppression—both within and outside the agency:

> We respect the diversity of our community. We welcome people of different ethnic, spiritual and cultural backgrounds, sexual orientation and unique abilities and needs. We understand how racism, sexism, and oppression affect the lives of the people we serve. We are committed to ending oppression at the Centre and within the community.

The young women who reside in Gilmore House's three transitional housing facilities are required to participate in specific kinds of activities. For example, although the thirteen-to-twenty-five-year-olds in the prenatal facility work with staff to design an individualized plan of care, they "must participate in structured program activities," such as sessions on health and wellness and prenatal care as well as sessions that help them complete their secondary education (or, if that has been done, prepare for entrance into the paid labour force). Similarly, the young mothers who live for up to six months in one of the ten apartments available to postnatal program participants must put their infants in the on-site early learning childcare facility, work on enhancing their parenting and money management skills, and "attend school, work or focus on pre-employment activities." When young mothers have completed their (up to six months) townhouse residency, it is the hope of Gilmore House staff that these young women will be well prepared to "transition back into the larger community" and will have learned to effectively "advocate for themselves and their child."

In the brochure distributed to new and prospective residents, Gilmore House reveals itself to be especially attentive to the youth of the mothers-to-be residing in its prenatal housing facility. The pamphlet stresses the agency of the young woman by observing respectfully that it was her "decision to become a mother at an early age" and that it will be up to her whether she "choose[s] to live" at Gilmore House. The brochure states that agency staff will offer support "when you are open to receiving help from professionals," and it emphasizes that "pregnancy is the start of many changes" for "*all women*," not just young mothers-to-be (my emphasis). Perhaps most importantly, the Gilmore House manual explicitly counters dominant discourses about young motherhood's negative effect on both mother and child by stating in bold, green ink:

> Pregnancy may also initiate *positive* changes in your life and your decision to come to Gilmore House may be the first step. Here you can focus on your well-being, education and stability and work towards becoming a mother and feeling better about yourself. You can protect yourself from harmful relationships and conditions that make it hard for you to do things important to you.

Last but certainly not least, the brochure for new and prospective residents emphasizes that the wellbeing of the mother is of equal concern to the staff as the wellbeing of her child; indeed, Gilmore House has a special maternal infant mental health team whose "primary job is to support families' capacity for self-care (with focus on the mothers)." The brochure is replete with such statements as "care for a baby is not possible without care for a mother" and "it's important to take care of your own feelings and concerns." Self-care is especially important for mothers in their teens and early twenties, the manual emphasizes. Young mothers need and deserve to have lots of age-appropriate mentoring and support; it is natural and appropriate for them to want their own needs and feelings to be attended to, even at times prioritized. Readers are told the following when the baby first arrives: "You may feel a heavy responsibility in caring for your child, and at the same time feel lonely and not cared for. *As a young person who still needs care herself, you may ask 'If I am taking care of the baby, who will take care of me?'* It can seem unfair that the baby's needs always come first."

Pennsylvania's Bradley Centre

Unlike Gilmore House, the Bradley Centre's supportive housing program is not explicitly geared to meet the needs of pregnant and parenting young women who need mentoring as well as safe and affordable shelter. On the contrary, Bradley Centre is open to any family with minor children experiencing or facing homelessness. Indeed, Bradley Centre is unusual in being one of only two shelters in a three-county area that provides apartment-style living and case management services to a diverse array of low-income families. Most shelters in the area offer emergency or transitional shelter for single women and men, for so-called "delinquent" teens, or for single women who do not have in their care any male children over the age of fourteen.[6] In contrast, Bradley Centre is open to single mothers and fathers over the age of eighteen; to adult couples, married or unmarried, and of any sexual orientation; and to adults who are legal guardians of nieces, nephews, or grandchildren. Bradley Centre is a small, five-apartment facility: the smallest unit is suitable for a single parent with one child, whereas the largest can accommodate a family of six. Residents can live in the shelter for up to one year (in rare instances, a few months longer). If they successfully complete case management requirements during their stay, the agency operating the facility continues to offer support services for a year as well as assists the family in finding affordable housing in the local area.

Although most of the parents who reside at Bradley Centre are in their mid-twenties to early forties, young mothers over the age of eighteen can apply (and have successfully applied) for residency in the facility. In fact, the agency that operates Bradley Centre also runs a teen parent mentoring program in collaboration with the local public high school, and participants in that program who apply for an apartment have priority over all other prospective residents except women exiting temporary housing facilities for battered women. But with a couple of exceptions, the mothers in the young parent program have exhibited absolutely no interest in living at Bradley Centre. Even when they are struggling to pay their rent in the private housing market, have just been evicted, or have been couch surfing for several months, they recoil at the idea of applying for residency at the shelter. As will become clear in the final section of this chapter, what the young mothers I interviewed find most objectionable is the centre's use of a deficit-based approach to supporting residents. As with many U.S.

shelters, Bradley Centre seems to operate on the premise that its residents have not in the past made responsible use of their time and money, set sufficiently ambitious educational or career goals for themselves, or appropriately nurtured and cared for their children. As a result, many aspects of the residents' lives are closely monitored and controlled, from their use of their earnings to the hours they may spend outside the facility. The young mothers I interviewed find this degree of regulation and surveillance (and implicit distrust of the parents' good judgment) offensive. Many believe that they have already demonstrated their ability to successfully balance their obligations as students, parents, and (in most cases) participants in the paid labour force. Having access to both mentoring and subsidized housing certainly appeals to these young mothers, but only if their past accomplishments are acknowledged and their desire to make independent decisions (and learn from their mistakes) are respected.

An examination of Bradley Centre's program manual for residents reveals the presence of conflicting discourses. For example, the sections about the shelter's mission and its core values and goals articulate respect for the parents' autonomy, agency, and self-knowledge. Residents are told that the shelter operates on the principle that "every person has the right to be treated with dignity and respect" and that upon acceptance, "*they* must create a development plan for their household" (my emphasis). However, a few pages later, the manual states that the agency reserves "the right to develop and implement individualized service planning strategies that target, promote, and preserve family unification, reunification, self-sufficiency and community assimilation/tenure." In other words, control over one's development plan is provisional; the staff members reserve the right to design the plan with little or no input from the parent. Moreover, the manual presents a rather extensive list of rules that prospective residents must agree to abide by, some of which imply that at least some parents will be prone to make bad choices.

The degree of restriction varies; residents who prove over time that they are capable of making wise decisions are subject to fewer and looser regulations than newcomers or those on probation for violating a rule. It is telling that level one—the level for newcomers—is called the probationary level; one begins one's residence on probation and must demonstrate obedience to all rules for three months before graduating to the "traditional" level. Good behaviour for a longer period of time entitles one to move to the third tier and be subject to "progressive" rules and regulations. When one violates any rule, one is demoted to a lower level. As the following paragraphs reveal, so many aspects of the parents' lives are closely monitored and assessed that it could be difficult for a young mother (or any parent) to reach or remain at the progressive tier.

Curfews

Upon entering the shelter, all parents, whatever their age and whether or not they are coupled, have a 10:00 p.m. curfew and must make sure any school-age children are in the building by 8:00 p.m. each night. If parents abide by all program rules for three months, their curfew is extended to 11:00 p.m. and their school-age children can stay out until 9:00 p.m. on Fridays and Saturdays. The 11:00 p.m. curfew remains in place at the highest (progressive) level, but now the parent has the option of staying out past curfew one weekend a month. A progressive-level parent also can request permission for the family to have an overnight or weekend outside the shelter as long as the request is made five or more days in advance. With this exception, no parents are permitted to leave the premises after curfew unless they have nighttime work hours. And all parents must sign a daily attendance sheet to prove that they were in residence that particular day.

Room Checks

At the probationary and traditional levels, agency staff members inspect each apartment once a week at random, unannounced times. At the progressive level, the weekly room checks still occur but are now scheduled. During these visits, the staff members not only can assess the cleanliness and orderliness of the apartment but can open and inspect all drawers, closets, and cabinets.

Financial Programing Obligations

To ensure that residents who are in the paid labour force have accur-ately reported their work hours and attendance record, parents must submit to the caseworker copies of both their work schedule and all pay stubs. In addition, the residents' manual states that all parents "are subject to and legally bound to all financial programming obligations as defined by" the agency.[7] One obligation is required participation "in budgeting preparation / counseling sessions scheduled in accordance with the frequency and receipt of income (i.e., weekly, bi-weekly, monthly, etc.)" Families also are required to deposit 20 percent of each paycheck into an escrow account "in efforts to encourage [them] to start saving for future needs and resources." These monies are fully refunded to families when they leave the shelter, minus any funds needed to cover damage to an apartment or its furnishings.

Apartment Furnishings

In part because of past incidences with bed bugs, the agency provides linens, window treatments, rugs, and furniture for all apartments. Each apartment also has a television. When a family moves in, the only items they are permitted to bring with them are clothing, cookware, dishes, personal hygiene items, cleaning supplies, and a few books and toys for the children. Electronics, including personal computers and video game systems, are forbidden. Without prior authorization from the caseworker, one cannot personalize one's apartment by bringing into the shelter knickknacks, framed pictures, a grandma's lamp, or a crib one received as a baby shower gift. The agency has adopted this policy because some families enter the shelter with absolutely no personal possessions; the agency wants residents to be on the same playing field when it comes to apartment décor and furnishings. This is a sound reason for the regulation, but it does mean that a young mother cannot personalize her apartment or bring into it household items of sentimental value or items she may have scrimped and saved to purchase.

Shelter-Sponsored Programs

Unless parents are ill, at work, or have an important previously scheduled appointment, they "are required to participate in all avenues of service provision and classes" offered or arranged by agency staff. These include mandatory attendance of programs on such matters as budgeting, parenting, nutrition, job preparation, and the development of various life skills.

Fostering a Sense of Community among Residents

On the first page of the Bradley Centre program manual, under the heading "Statement of Philosophy," residents are told that agency staff members "envision a community that empowers all of its members with good physical, mental, emotional and spiritual health and provides access to an excellent education, meaningful work, decent housing and culturally relevant life enrichment activities." But this emphasis on the importance of families feeling part of a welcoming, supportive community is somewhat undercut by the prevalent reference to shelter residents as "guests." For sound legal reasons (to avoid tenants' rights claims), the agency must explicitly state that the contract parents sign is a "Guest Agreement ... *it is not a lease.*" Perhaps because the U.S. is such a litigious society, the agency is not content with stating this distinction once; instead, it uses the term "guest" repeatedly throughout the manual, which may make it difficult for parents to envision their Bradley Centre apartment as their home or think of their fellow residents as members of a stable, close-knit community.

Before turning to interviews in which young mothers critique Bradley Centre's deficits-based approach to empowering its residents, I want to stress that this facility provides truly useful services and supports to homeless families with children. Some of the rules and regulations are in the manual because they are required by government funding sources; others are there to ensure equity in the furnishings available to each family or to make sure families save enough money for the rent and utilities down payments they will need to make when they transition into the private housing market. Some rules, like the banning of electronic game systems, are at least well intentioned, since the children who live in the shelter are often struggling academically and in the case of elementary school students are generally behind one or more grade levels in reading and/or math.

The close monitoring of residents' behaviour is no doubt also based on the agency's long history of working with and seeking to empower parents who have experienced many traumas and challenges in their lives and who have, indeed, not always made the best choices for themselves and/or their children. Some of the parents come to Bradley Centre directly after being released from prison or from a drug rehabilitation centre. Others have recently regained custody of children who had been removed from their care by social services. Still others are survivors of domestic violence, sexual assault, or the sudden (and sometimes violent) death of a partner or parent. I am not a social service provider; it may well be the case that mandated attendance of shelter-sponsored workshops and the need to adhere to numerous rules benefit and lead to the empowerment of parents who have survived such experiences.[8] What I do know is that such regulation and surveillance are very objectionable to the young mothers I interviewed —young mothers who already had chosen to seek advice, instruction, and mentoring from adults by participating, some for two or three years, in the agency's empowerment program for pregnant and parenting teens.

Supportive Housing Programs: The Perspective of Young Mothers

As mentioned earlier, the mothers I interviewed ranged in age from seventeen to twenty-two; one was a high school junior, three were high school seniors, and the others were recent high school graduates. Through my community-based learning course and through my membership on the board of the agency that operates both the teen parent empowerment program and the Bradley Centre, I had gotten to know these twelve young mothers quite well over a three-year period. We had built relationships of mutual respect and trust, and they were quite willing to let me and one of my undergraduate research students conduct audio-recorded, semi-structured interviews in which we not only asked their opinions about the Bradley Centre's facilities and policies but also asked them to identify what they would consider key components of a supportive housing facility that would benefit and be attractive to young mothers. We interviewed the mothers individually for between sixty and ninety minutes. The group was racially and ethnically diverse: four mothers self-identified as white, four as Hispanic, two as Black, and two as multiracial. Most were living in the home of a family member at the time of their interview. Two were living in their own apartments with their children, one with and one without a partner. One young mother was moving from the apartment of one friend to another because she could not find affordable housing; her daughter was living with the three-year-old's paternal grandmother.

What this group of young mothers liked most about Bradley Centre is the fact that each family has its own kitchen, bathroom, and furnished apartment; most nearby shelters for women and children have dormitory-style facilities with a common kitchen, bathroom, and living room. "If it was just me then I would be okay with only having a bedroom but not when I'm living with my child," remarked one young mother. "I need the privacy," said another. "Sometimes you want to watch TV alone." A third mother noted that "sharing space could cause conflict and tension because some moms are messy and others are neat." The idea of sharing a kitchen or bathroom with other families was particularly objectionable to most of the young mothers. One said emphatically: "Really bad would be sharing a kitchen and all sharing a bathroom because I don't know if these people are dirty or if they take care of themselves. I don't know if they're disgusting. Also with the kitchen I buy certain things for my child and if it's eaten I'm going to be really mad." Other mothers were more succinct, making remarks like "a shared kitchen—is it gonna stay clean? I doubt it" or exclaiming "I hate sharing bathrooms—yuck!"

Views were more mixed about Bradley Centre's limits on the amount and kind of personal belongings one is permitted to bring into the facility. Some of the young mothers found this policy extremely objectionable. "Bringing your own belongings is how you feel comfortable," said one mother; another remarked, "I don't have a lot but my daughter has a lot furniture-wise and if I wouldn't be able to bring that I'd be pretty upset." A third stated the following: "I work hard for what I have, so even if there was someone else that had more stuff than me I wouldn't have bad feelings about it. I'm proud of what I have because I worked for it, and they worked for what they have." The mother who most objected to the policy was a young woman who had actually tried living in the shelter with her fiancé and their one-year-old son. Although these parents were only in the eleventh and twelfth grade, they already had been living independently in the community (admittedly, with great difficulty making ends meet) for almost two years. The mother had this to say: "I have all this stuff at home, and I can't bring it with me? Especially my son's crib? Furniture is important. I have all of this stuff set up in my home and because of the way life hits you, you have to move and you can't take anything with you? That's like starting all over again. No way."

However, some of the young mothers were not at all troubled by the shelter's restrictions on personal belongings. Significantly, these were the mothers who had the fewest possessions and the most housing insecurity. "It would be easier if they provided everything because I don't have much," said the mother who was currently couch surfing.

Two other mothers were openly critical of young parents, especially couples, who would refuse to live in a shelter if they could not bring previously purchased items with them. "Honestly," said one of these mothers, "if those teens were able to bring so much to the shelter, honestly, you really don't need to be there because it's for people that don't have much. So it would bother me because there are probably people out there that don't have nothing that could use the space and you're just taking it up for low rent."

The other young mother spoke with even more passion about shelters giving priority to single mothers with very low incomes and few possessions:

> As for bringing in a bunch of things, if they're bringing like couches and flat-screen TVs and stuff like that, they don't need to be there. It's for people who are less fortunate. If you can't even make rent for a one-bedroom apartment, if you can't make that at all and are nowhere near close to it or you're just reaching it, I think you should be allowed to move in there, especially if you're a single parent.... I think single moms should be the first ones to get in because if you're a couple and you can't bring in $600 a month for rent then something's wrong with you.

When asked to share their views on curfews, the mothers were unanimous in believing that curfews should be imposed only if parents began engaging in risky, irresponsible behaviour that endangered their children. As young parents, they were accustomed to managing their own time, to occasionally going out late at night, and to leaving their child with a partner, trusted friend, or family member. They viewed themselves as responsible parents and found it both unfair and insulting that the agency seemed to assume otherwise. Here are some of the comments that demonstrate their concerns about the meaning and implications of curfews:

- The only time I have to hang out is at night because I get out of work at 11:00 p.m. If you're not having problems, then why have a curfew?

- A curfew is a killer for me. Night time is when I get away (take a walk, go grocery shopping). It's a deal breaker.... If you're eighteen and up, like an adult, you should be able to come and go as you please. You [shelter staff] have to admit you're dealing with people that are young that want to go out, hang out with friends, party. You don't want to take that away from them. There should only be some sort of repercussions if you overdo it.

- If the shelter has to have a curfew, it's gotta have a little lateness to it. But honestly speaking, I'm a mom; I'm gonna be in before curfew anyway. Why would I have my daughter out so late? I think the curfew part is kind of dumb. The way I see it is when you get a certain age you're supposed to be responsible for yourself and if you have one, your child.

- I think if that's how they're running this shelter, treating young moms just like kids; I mean they're not giving them a chance to try on their own. They're taking them under their wing and not letting them grow up.

For most of the mothers interviewed, not having total control over their finances and paychecks was almost as troublesome as nightly curfews. Most did not mind the requirement that they put 20 percent of their earnings in escrow; they seemed to believe they might not have the discipline to save a decent amount of money on their own. One young mother remarked: "If they have control over some of your paycheck then okay but if they have control over all of it I wouldn't be okay with that. If it was something like you have to put a half or a quarter in the bank every time, that'd be good. Like every time you get paid, you have to put at least a quarter of it in the bank." Most also said they would benefit from money management classes. One mother made the following comment: "It's ok when you're sitting down with the caseworker and you guys are going through the money management together. But it's another thing when you bust your ass all week and then somebody tells you this is how you have to spend your money. They can give suggestions as long as they're not telling me what to do."

What really bothered the young mothers was being required to attend money management programs. Their reasoning was similar to their thinking about mandatory curfews: "They [Bradley Centre staff members] shouldn't just assume that everyone screws up." "I think financial counseling is good," remarked one mother, "but if they were to have a program like that they could make it optional. If you wanted, you could take it in full or just part or whatever. Some people might take it just to have the security to know that they're already doing a good job." And it was the view of the interviewees that when a young mother moves into the shelter, the staff should assume that she will do a good job of managing her family's finances. Only if she fails to do so, the mothers argued, should the caseworker step in and require (as opposed to strongly recommend) money management classes. Proclaimed one mother: "They [the shelter staff] should be confident that you will be able to handle your money on your own.... If someone's not responsible and they see that, then they should step in." This idea was echoed by another mother: "I feel if I'm there at the shelter, that's proof I'm responsible.... I wouldn't fall behind [on my bills] cause my priorities come first, whatever I need to do comes first. If I pay my bills and put money into savings then there really shouldn't be a problem. I should be putting it into savings myself, but I guess I could get used to having them do it for me." Another mother argued that it would be more useful and empowering if putting a portion of each paycheck into an escrow or savings account was handled by the parent, not the agency:

> If I lived at the shelter I would put a certain amount [of every paycheck] in the bank in savings instead of blowing it. Let people learn because by them [the agency staff] taking the responsibility away, they [shelter residents] are never going to learn how to save. All they're getting used to is part of their paycheck getting taken away and taken away and taken away and when they do get out on their own, what's going to happen is they're going to go nuts with that money! Because they haven't really learned to manage it on their own.

One young mother went into great detail about how much time and thought she and her boyfriend put into managing their money:

> My boyfriend and I have sat down and said okay, we spend a lot of money on take out. Instead we have a budget now; every other week it's acceptable to get Chinese. We each have allowances now. His paycheck comes in and we pay all of our bills and then split the rest of what's left over. I can choose to spend it or save it. We sit down and say "do we really need this?" I save money where I can, but I still want to have fun, like go to the movies.

I'm twenty-one. Just because I had a baby doesn't mean I have to be cut from all the fun stuff that I would be doing. Life has smacked us around to the point where now we're saying, "God, we didn't have much saved." So now we're like let's start saving and stop the unnecessary spending. We've learned to watch what we spend but still get what we want.

As the young mothers' observations show, a deficit- or weaknesses-based approach to supporting residents of a transitional housing facility did not match with this group of young mothers' belief that on the whole, they had been behaving quite responsibly as students, wage earners, and parents of young children. Several had removed themselves from toxic home environments or ended relationships with abusive partners. All were devoted to their children; they wanted to spend as much time as they could with their infants and toddlers and were eager to learn how to best foster their children's curiosity and intellectual growth. These young mothers were concerned about hygiene and nutrition, and they did not leave their children in the care of irresponsible others so they could party the night away.

Those mothers who were still in high school were on track to graduate on time; most who had already graduated were enrolled part-time in postsecondary degree programs or were hoping to resume their education in the near future. Although two of the young mothers currently were unemployed, it was not through lack of desire or effort. One could not find safe, affordable childcare that would allow her to enter the paid labour force without subjecting her son to possible harm, whereas the other was limited to searching for jobs within walking distance because she could not afford bus fare, much less car payments. With one exception (the young couple who admitted they could have done a better job saving money by, for example, ordering fewer takeout meals), these young mothers believed they had been spending their meagre earnings wisely. Their problem was not mismanaging money; it was not having enough money to manage.

These young mothers were justifiably proud of their accomplishments. But they also knew they faced many obstacles and challenges, most of them structural rather than individual in nature. Many would have loved to live in safe, affordable housing, paying a minimal amount of rent (a small percentage of their income based on a sliding scale). Most if not all would have welcomed mentoring and would have taken advantage of programs on such subjects as money management, child development, and educational and career-goal planning. What they could not tolerate was the assumption that would make bad choices if they were not closely regulated and monitored; they felt both insulted and infantilized by the terms of Bradley Centre's guest agreement.

These young women also wanted their status as young mothers to be acknowledged. They viewed themselves as more responsible than their nonparenting peers. But as with those peers, they believed that they should be accorded the right to make, and learn from, the mistakes young people inevitably make as they solidify their sense of identity and agency and make the transition from adolescence to adulthood. For the women I interviewed, Bradley Centre's approach to supporting young mothers too closely resembles the dominant cultural narrative that associates young motherhood with the "immoral cultural values, poor decision-making, misguided mindsets, apathy and personal failings" of individual young women ("An American Frame: Teen Pregnancy and Parenting"). About this, they are quite right. What these young U.S. mothers longed for (and deserve) is the kind of assets-based approach to empowerment that characterizes many Toronto area supportive housing programs for mothers in their teens and early twenties. These facilities certainly have rules and regulations by which the residents must abide. But they also use language and engage in practices that regularly and explicitly acknowledge young mothers' strengths and accomplishments—their "capacity for self-care" and self-sufficiency as well as their ability "to take actions that better their [own and their children's] lives" (Gilmore House brochure). This is the kind of empowerment programing that the Healthy Teen Network calls for—that is, programing attentive to the ways in which adolescence, as a distinctive stage of development, intersects with a young woman's identity as a mother.

Endnotes

1. For more information about my community-based learning course and my collaboration with a local non-profit's teen parent mentoring program, see Deborah Byrd and Rachel Gallagher, "Avoiding the 'Doomed to Poverty' Narrative."

2. Among the Toronto area agencies that offer support to young and/ or low-income single mothers are Best Start Resource Centre, Humewood House/1900 Shepherd, Jessie's Centre/June Callwood Centre for Young Women, Massey Centre for Women, Queen West Shout Clinic, Robertson House, Rosalie Hall, St. Michael's Hospital's "My Baby and Me" Infant Passport program for Young Pregnant Homeless Women, WoodGreen's Homeward Bound program, and Young Parents No Fixed Address. Some of these agencies operate supportive housing facilities; others offer other kinds of supports to young and/or low-income women, including young street-involved women.

3. For an excellent study of ways in which mentoring and empower-ment programs for teens, including young mothers, could be improved to address systemic and cultural as well as individual challenges, see "Building Opportunity."

4. The Jeremiah program attributes the success of its participants in escaping intergenerational poverty to a combination of "high expectations for determined young women" and "holistic supports," among them assistance in completing a college degree, access to safe and affordable housing, quality early childhood education, empowerment and life skills training, and a supportive community in which the young mothers in the Jeremiah sisterhood take the journey towards self-actualization and self-sufficiency together.

5. Gilmore House also provides supports for families and caregivers in the local community, but a discussion of those programs is beyond the scope of this chapter.

6. Among the residential facilities that are open to young mothers or mothers-to-be in this part of Pennsylvania (in some cases only to those eighteen and older) are Birth Haven, Community Action Committee of the Lehigh Valley's 6th Street Shelters, The Neigh-borhood Centre's Roofover Shelter, Overington House, and Third Street Alliance for Women and Children. Other local shelters serve nonparenting homeless youth or nonparenting adults.

7. Unless otherwise noted, all subsequent quotations are from the Bradley Centre's residents manual.

8. As a long-time board member of the agency that runs Bradley Centre, I have over the years heard many reliable accounts of families who had to be ejected from the shelter because the parents had extremely unsanitary apartments, were skipping school or work, were letting male visitors roam the shelter unaccompanied, or were using or selling illegal drugs. Many low-income families have benefited tremendously from having access to the centre's safe, affordable housing and supportive, knowledgeable caseworkers—but quite a few have not. Ensuring the safety and viability of the shelter as well as providing structure for residents who might need it—without disciplining and punishing those who do not—are challenges the agency is currently wrestling with.

Works Cited

"A Policy Platform to Promote Health and Success among Young Families." *Healthy Teen Network*, 2009, www.healthyteennetwork. org/wp-content/uploads/2015/07/YFPolicyPlatform.pdf. Accessed 15 June 2019.

"About Jeremiah Program." *Jeremiah Program*, 2017, jeremiahprogram. org/about-us/. Accessed 10 June 2019.

Bales, Susan Nall, and Moira O'Neil. "An American Frame: Teen Pregnancy and Parenting. Healthy Teen Network." *Healthy Teen Network*, 2010, www.healthyteennetwork.org/wp-content/uploads /2014/10/An_American_Frame_Teen-Pregnancy-and-Parenting. pdf. Accessed 15 June 2019.

"Building Opportunity into Adolescence: Mapping the Gaps between Expert and Public Understandings of Adolescent Development." *The Frameworks Institute*, 2018, http://frameworksinstitute.org/ assets/files/adolescence_youth/adolescent_development_mtg_ report_2018.pdf. Accessed 15 June 2019.

Byrd, Deborah Byrd, and Rachel Gallagher."Avoiding the 'Doomed to Poverty' Narrative: Words of Wisdom from Teenage Single Mothers." *Journal of the Association for Research on Mothering*, vol. 11, no. 2, 2009, pp. 66-84.

"What is Our Approach to Capacity Building?" Healthy Teen Network. https://www.healthyteennetwork.org/capacity/approach. Accessed 15 June 2019.

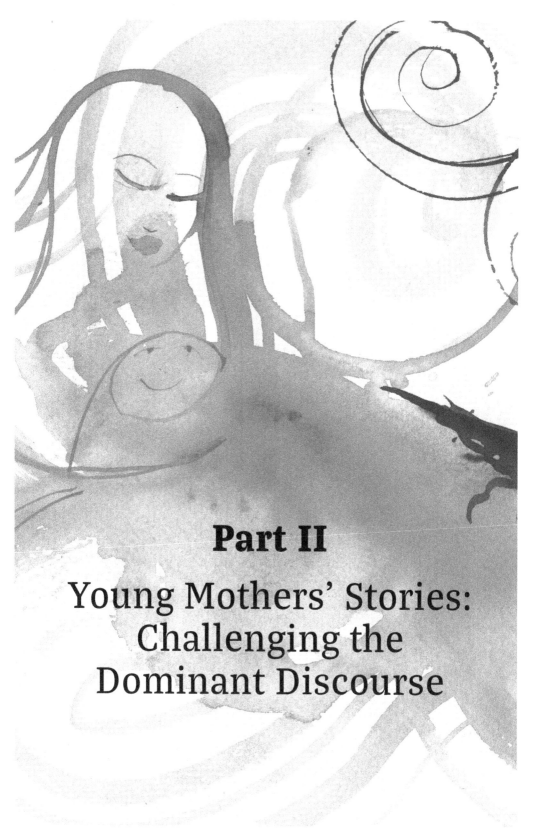

Part II

Young Mothers' Stories: Challenging the Dominant Discourse

Chapter Five

Teen Mom Forever Ever

Heather Jackson

I was a teen mother; I got pregnant when I was eighteen years old and a senior in high school. For five years, I had an off and on relationship with my daughter's father, who is a year younger than I am. We broke up for the first time when I was about twenty weeks pregnant, so I began motherhood without a partner. I permanently ended the relationship—which was characterized by infidelity and emotional, mental, sexual, and physical abuse—when my daughter was four years old. I've been a single mother ever since.

Although I am now a thirty-something single mother of a teenager, the fact that I began motherhood as a teen still continues to affect me. Many years ago, most people felt I was too young to be the mother of an infant; now they think I'm too young to be the mother of a teenager. After all this time, people continue to ask me if my daughter and I are sisters and when I say "No, I'm her mom," they respond: "What? Aren't you like, twenty-five?" or "Wait ... What? She's your daughter?!" Or servers at restaurants, clearly assuming that my daughter and I are sisters or friends who are close in age, will ask us "Are you paying together or separate?" Yes, in some ways it's nice to look younger than one's age in a world that values youth. But the experience is more frustrating than it is pleasing because sometimes people do not take me seriously as a mother or continue to treat me as if I am too young to make particular decisions. I also feel frustrated because I cannot imagine making comments about a woman's perceived age to a mother I don't know.

Young and single motherhood have, at times, been difficult for me and my daughter; we have experienced mental health crises and frightening times of financial instability and food insecurity. We have been on and off public assistance while I worked various jobs and went to college and graduate school. But as challenging as my and my daughter's lives have been, being a teen mom also drove me to do things that I don't think I would have done if I'd never become a teen mother. Teen motherhood empowered me, made me more self-aware, taught me to trust and have confidence in myself, and led me to embrace feminist values and communities. As I hope this chapter will show, we need to acknowledge the difficulties of being a teen mom, but we also need to hear stories about the ways in which teen mothers can become positive agents of change through the experience of loving and caring for a child. In the pages that follow, I provide a brief overview of research on the negative and positive consequences of teen mother-hood; I then share my story in more detail. I emphasize that supporting and being supported by other young mothers can play an important role in making young motherhood a positive, a motivational, and an empowering experience. Finally, I will also discuss the impact the feminist young mother website and community girl-mom.com has had on me and how this website has informed my mothering and feminism. Through this website, I realized that support and nonjudgmental relationships are so pivotal for teen mothers. Girl-mom empowered me to view my teen motherhood as a positive force in my life and enabled me to use my experience to empower myself, my daughter, and other teen mothers.

Negative Consequences of Teen Pregnancy

Being a mother is hard; whatever her age, race, class, sexual identity, or life situation, a mother needs—and deserves—help and support. Because such support is rarely available for teen mothers in the U.S., the outcomes of pregnancy for teen mothers and their children can be bleak, especially in the case of racialized and low-income young women and their children. For example, compared to their nonparenting peers, teen mothers are less likely to obtain a high school diploma or GED by age thirty; not surprisingly, they earn approximately $3,500 less a year than women who become mothers later in life (Healthy People 2020). Teen mothers often drop out of high school due to lack of safe, affordable childcare. Few high schools have on-site daycare facilities, even though studies show that having such a facility greatly increases teen mothers' graduation rates. School-based daycares also are beneficial to the children of teen mothers, who (due to the likelihood of their living in poverty) tend to have lower levels of cognitive attainment and more behavioural issues than do children from more well-to-do homes (Healthy People 2020). In one study, 90 percent of the children at a high school childcare centre were up to date on their health visits; in another study, teen mothers' children who had access to an on-site daycare were assessed to be within normal developmental ranges in cognition, fine and gross motor skills, language acquisition, and ability for self care (Williams and Sadler; Sadler et al.).

When discussing negative educational or health outcomes for teen mothers and/or their children, it is essential to note that many of these outcomes are primarily the result of the mother's poverty rather than her age or marital status (Geronimus and Korenman). Most teen mothers in the U.S. come from households and neighbourhoods where incomes and levels of educational attainment are low, and because of systemic racism, they are disproportionately young women of colour (Penmann-Aguilar et al.; Almgren and Yamashiro). Children who grow up in the foster system are also more likely to become teen mothers (Boonstra). In other words, negative outcomes of teen motherhood result from a complex web of structural oppressions and are not due solely—or in many cases, even primarily—to the young age of the mother.Rather than blame teen mothers for not always being able to successfully or quickly achieve a good education and/or economic self-sufficiency, we need to address such structural injustices as poverty, income inequality, racism, an inadequate foster care system, denial of the prevalence of family violence, and lack of quality, affordable childcare for all mothers.

Positive Consequences of Teen Pregnancy

In the U.S., the dominant cultural stereotype of a teen mother is that of a poor, ignorant, immature, sexually promiscuous, and unambitious young woman who is perfectly content to rely upon the welfare system to support her and her child. However, a growing body of research reveals that teen motherhood has a positive effect on many young women's lives. For example, Frank Furstenberg and Albert Crawford found that many of the teen mothers in their study experienced psychological benefits from overcoming obstacles related to parenting. The world is not perfect, and sometimes struggling to overcome challenges—such as caring for a newborn—allows a young woman to feel motivated and move forwards in her life. Struggling through painful and difficult experiences also can transform a young mother into an activist and/or create space for a young mother to both rely upon and help other people.

In another study, Clare Seamark and Pamela Lings interviewed nine women who had their first child as teenagers. The women discussed how being a teen parent changed their in a positive way, helping them to figure out what they wanted to do with their lives and whether that entailed going to college or getting a good paying job. One mother in their study remarked, "Looking back now, I'm really glad I had them when I did have them (814)." Another mother added the following:

> I wish I'd waited until I'd got my career underway, or until I'd found a partner that we'd planned it with, and that could [have] maybe given us a better start. But at the same time if I hadn't had [the] baby I might not have chosen the career that I wanted to be in. I think maybe he [my son] has given me a bit of a push, to sort my life out into what I want to do and where I want to go. So I think there's a lot of positive things come out of it as well. (Seamark and Lings, 814)

These mothers did not regret their decisions to have their babies young. The second mother indicates that although her life might have been a bit easier if she had started motherhood later, being a teen mom pushed her into reflecting on what she wanted out of life and what she needed to do to achieve those goals. Similarly, Simon Duncan et al. found that the teen mothers in their study were far from being immature and unmotivated young women content to live off taxpayer dollars; instead, their pregnancy made them feel stronger and more determined to make positive choices for themselves and their children.

Lee SmithBattle followed several teen mothers over eight years and found that motherhood made them more mature and provided a positive catalyst for change. Many of the mothers felt motherhood helped them get over their difficult past. The mothers also felt mothering anchored them and helped them discover more about who they are. Jo Bell et al. have also found that motherhood can increase a teen's self-esteem, positively influence her life, and provide a sense of stability and security.

The above research studies demonstrate that difficult as it may be, teen motherhood is not necessarily a debilitating, disempowering experience. Instead, it can help a young woman feel grounded, can enhance a young woman's self-confidence and self-esteem, and can inspire a young woman to set goals to work towards. For the teen mothers in these studies, motherhood provided them with a way to move forwards with their lives and gave them a grounding experience. Even when having to deal with poverty, racism, and sexism and having to juggle childcare, school, and work, these teen mothers still found motherhood to be a positive and an empowering experience.

My Teen Motherhood: Then

I was born and grew up in North Dakota, a conservative state. My mother and stepfather assumed I would wait until marriage to have sex; it was an unspoken rule that no one talked about. There was no comprehensive sex education at my school, and my parents certainly did not tell me anything about condoms, birth control, abortion, communication, or consent. Not many of my friends were having sex; however, my younger sister was. Eventually, we went together up the hill from the high school to the Family Planning Clinic and got birth control, secretly, every month.

Shortly after my eighteenth birthday, I met my baby-daddy and fell super in love. He was the first person I had sex with. I took the pills I got from the Family Planning Clinic everyday after school when I arrived at my after school job at McDonald's, and I never missed a single one. But a month after having sex for the first time, I got pregnant.

Initially terrified and in denial, I finally decided to take a pregnancy test. I knew the test would be positive. I just knew it. And it was. I sat there with my sister and her girlfriend, staring down at the stick. To make the matter more confusing and scary, my boyfriend and I had broken up because he had cheated on me and had started selling and doing drugs (again); he was now dating someone else. When I called him to tell him about taking a pregnancy test, he told me he did not want to hear about it. I told him to "fuck off" and proceeded to tell him the results anyway. He said nothing; he just listened to me freak out, and then hung up the phone.

I hid my pregnancy from everyone. I held in my puke during gym, band, and art class only to run to the bathroom to throw up in the toilet, sometimes puking in the trash bins as fellow students bustled to their next class. I missed gym class a few times but never had to make the class up as we usually had to; perhaps my gym teacher knew about my pregnancy and was showing me compassion.

I considered adoption and abortion. I did not know how and where to get an abortion or even how to find that information. (Note: there is still only one abortion clinic in North Dakota.) I looked up adoption agencies and called them. One person from an agency told me to enroll in Medicaid, which I did. I did not know about Medicaid until that person told me. I went to an adoption agency and browsed photos of couples wanting to adopt a child. I remember thinking how much better parents these couples would be. They were stable and had an education and resources (I assumed). I was the opposite. How could I provide a decent life for the growing fetus inside me? I had a difficult time deciding who would raise my child: strangers who were presumably (or as I often thought then,) better suited ... or me? If I put my child up for adoption, I also would have to decide whether the adoption was going to be closed or open. These were overwhelming choices for me to make at the age of eighteen, but I also feel these choices would be difficult for any woman at any age considering adoption.

I gave birth to my daughter on September 25, 2001. I started contractions the night before, but I was so unprepared. I thought that maybe I was just hungry, so I ordered pizza. The contractions became more regular. The morning of twenty-fifth, after going to the bathroom and seeing the mucus plug on the toilet paper, I called my baby-daddy, who was at his girlfriend's house, telling him I needed to go to the hospital. His mother dropped me off at the ER. I walked through the doors and told the nurses I was in labour and needed to know where to go. They looked at me very suspiciously and said, "third floor."

I took the elevator up to the third floor and told the staff I was in labour. They panicked and got a birthing room ready and had me change. I was not in much pain, mostly uncomfortable. My baby-daddy eventually came to the room and was rapping Ol' Dirty Bastard.

My midwife finally got there, and I mostly remember pushing a few times, saying "owie," and looking at my daughter when she was on my chest and being freaked out that she could recognize my voice.

Shortly after the delivery, the hospital staff gave me a Depo-Provera shot (a form of birth control) without asking my permission. I remember being in the recovery room, and a nurse walked in with a shot and an informational sheet and told me to turn over and then put the shot in my hip. The message was unspoken but clear: girls your age should not be mothers. Others on the staff communicated this idea more explicitly, encouraging me to put my daughter up for adoption or into foster care. Many told me how hard my life was going to be from here on out if I decided to keep my baby. The hospital chaplain came to talk to me and stated that my baby-daddy and I were being selfish to keep the baby and that I should put her up for adoption. However, my mom, stepdad, and dad said they would help me if I kept the baby. And one wonderful nurse told me that she had been a teen mother and still was able to become a nurse, even though it was hard. I had not really developed a bond with my daughter, but I could not bear the thought of signing her over to someone else. The way her eyes had looked at me after the hospital staff placed her on my stomach when she was born was burned into me. She knew I was her mom. With much emotion, murkiness, and confusion, I chose to keep her.

Discovering Girl-Mom

This section is about an online community called Girl-Mom, which informed my feminism as well as helped me find a way to find the positives of being a teenage mother. It was a website run by teen and young mothers for young and teen mothers. The goal of the website was to help teen mothers feel less isolated, build community, provide support, and use their experiences as a catalyst for activism and change.

A little over a year after giving birth, I moved to Minneapolis, MN, with my daughter and her dad. (We had gotten back together when our daughter was a baby.) Shortly after settling in, I began attending community college, and one evening, in what would turn out to be a pivotal moment in my life, I was in a local bookstore and came across a book called *You Look Too Young to Be a Mom*. I grabbed it because that comment had been made to me many, many times. I flipped through the book and realized how strongly I identified with the mothers and their stories. I bought the book and started reading it right away. In her bio, one of the authors talked about a website called girl-mom.com. I decided to check out the website and discovered an amazing leftist, feminist forum run by young moms for young moms. I immediately signed up for an account and introduced myself. The members were young mothers and allies of young parents. They were all so supportive and nonjudgmental, challenging and thoughtful. Sometimes people became a bit defensive during discussions, but we all cared about each other and knew that things may get a bit tense sometimes as we tried to help each other figure things out.

Girl-mom.com was started by Allison Crews, who sadly died in 2005 at the age of twenty-two. I joined in 2003 and later become a moderator and then a site administrator. I stepped down as site administrator when I was in my third year of college, as I did not have enough time to dedicate to the site as I wished I had. The website still exists, but sadly, is not nearly as active as it used to be. The website still provides access to the articles many of us wrote over the years. We wrote about how to tell parents about the pregnancy, how to apply for financial aid for college, how to deal with body image issues, how to apply for public assistance, and more. We had forums and discussions on birth control, social justice topics, child development, relationships, resources, school, work, and tons more. The website provided us young moms with an opportunity to share motherhood information, experiences, tips, and questions as well as an opportunity to share other interests. The site was a space where we could be ourselves. We also had private forums where members shared photos of their children or posted intense and difficult experiences they were going through. Sometimes we would call each other, even if we did not live close, to help each other through a difficult time. I remember talking to other young mothers about mental health, sexuality, and baby-daddy issues, and to other young mothers who felt on the brink of losing it. Girl-mom was there when I was up all night trying to get my toddler to sleep. I remember posting a thread about how frustrated I was feeling one night because my daughter would not sleep. She would constantly get up, and I would put her back in her bed, and then she would immediately run out of her room. Girl-moms gave me tips for coping with this and countless other moments of mothering madness.

We were—and still are—a family. Some of the girl-moms lived in Minneapolis, and I met all of them. Some of them were involved in RAMBL (Radical and Anarchist Mom and Baby League) and I was lovingly invited to join. We had potlucks, spent holidays together, went to protests, and developed intense, loving friendships. We traded childcare so we could afford to go out for drinks, go to shows, go on dates, and simply have nights to ourselves. We did not charge each other money, and we kept each other's children overnight. Many years later, I am still friends with all of them. One of the last texts from one of them was "I am proud of you." Our intimate conversations, love, and support for one another helped me navigate young single motherhood in a way I will never forget.

Girl-mom also helped me with my decision to breakup with my daughter's father. Many of the members had a livejournal.com account, which was another way we all connected. I remember nights where I would be crying and typing in my livejournal account and the private forums of girl-mom about how my baby-daddy was behaving. Even though we lived together, he was an absentee partner and father. He slept most of the day, and there were periods when I would not see him for days at a time because he was out drinking or doing drugs. He was cheating on me, and he became increasingly manipulative and abusive. But for a long time, I could not see the situation in the way everyone else could. Thankfully, I felt close and supported enough to be open and honest about what I was experiencing with him. The girl-moms were equally direct and honest with me, but in a kind and supportive and encouraging way. They helped me understand how unhealthy and dangerous the relationship was and made me realize that my daughter may begin to believe that having an abusive partner and parent was an okay thing. My girl-mom community gave me the courage to end the relationship and ensure my own and my daughter's safety.

Girl-mom taught me how important it is to participate in sustaining communities of care and support, and it brought my feminism to the surface and helped me learn how to act upon it in the private and public realms. The community provided the radical and feminist parenting ideals that helped me raise a daughter who is a strong, loving, and confident young woman, and to also helped me understand that making the scary decision to become a teen mother was the act of an empowered young woman. I had chosen to become responsible for another person in this world, and I was going to do everything in my power to make sure she had a good life. I wanted her to teach her about consent, safe sex, good communication, and healthy relationships. I wanted to teach her about where and how to look for help from others, especially other women. I wanted her to love herself and to have a healthy sense of self as well as high self-esteem. My parents did not teach me these things; I navigated much of this territory with my girl-moms.

Being a teen and single parent has made me a positive role model for my daughter. I have raised her without any help from men, which, by definition, helps to resist patriarchy. Of course, I have had help from my father, stepfather, and partners, but the bulk of raising and providing for my daughter has been borne by me. My daughter has been able to grow up with an independent woman who was able to figure out so much with little income and being on public assistance, but who still made sure our needs were met.

Finding girl-mom was such an important and pivotal moment in my life. The passion and activism of the mothers made me more passionate and excited about being a mother. Girl-mom helped me feel less alone and isolated because I knew other women were out there having experiences similar to mine. It also showed me that teen moms need love and nonjudgmental support. We can go far with it, just like the teen mothers in the research studies previously cited.

My Teen Motherhood: Now

Today, I am in my thirties. My daughter is going to be graduating high school in a couple of years and will be off to college. We still get asked: "Are you two sisters?" We are about the same size, and we share some clothes; I know I look young for my age. But those comments do get annoying, and sometimes I feel as if my parenting abilities are still being questioned. I am younger than most of the parents of my daughter's friends and classmates. In fact, some parents are my parents' age.

Many people around my age are just getting married and/or having children. I did the opposite. I had my baby, then went to college, and now I am working. I do not really define myself by a professional career, however. Although I do work as a professional, I mostly am focused on making sure my daughter makes it to college and I am free to live my life on my own terms. I do not want my career defining me, as a person. I want it to be a part of me, not who I am. These are values I teach my daughter.

Dating has been interesting. I have had a few long-term relationships since I broke up with my baby-daddy. My daughter likes most people I date, but she is definitely more interested in herself, her friends, and her own dating life than in mine. Dating with a teen has its challenges because some people find it shocking that I have a child the age I do, whereas other times it is easier because I do not have a clingy six-year-old screaming for me to not leave when I am going out on a date. I would take her current attitude towards my partners over her younger attitude any day.

My daughter and I are so close. She tells me everything. We kind of grew up together. Some researchers would say we are in the same generation. We trust each other. We have fun times together, and we feel comfortable around each other. I have noticed we compromise on our hangout time together. We do not have all the same interests, but we have some, and meet at that. We watch silly YouTube videos, see bands or movies we both like, and go on walks.

I have been clear about supporting what she wants to do. She does not have to stay close to home when she goes to college; she can go, be free, and be herself in the world. That's all that I have wanted for her over the years. I am still coming to terms with the fact that I will not have her in my life the way that I have and that scares me. What am I going to do? I got pregnant in high school and had her right after high school graduation. For my entire legal adult life, she and I have been involved with one another in a close, direct way. Of course, she will still be in my life, but she will not be with me in the same way she is now.

Conclusion

Being a teen mother was not the worst thing to happen to me. In fact, I felt empowered by my decision to keep and raise my daughter. Being a mother solidified my feminism; it led me to a supportive online feminist community (girl-mom) and helped me make a better life for myself and my daughter. With the support of other young mothers, I was able to leave my daughter's abusive father. I went to college and graduate school, and we moved across the country for a better (and more exciting) life. Although teen mothering sometimes has negative consequences, they have more to do with structural issues—such as capitalism, sexism, racism, and income inequality—than with the mindset and actions of teen moms themselves. Being a teen mom has affected me well into my thirties, as some people still regard me as too young to have a child my daughter's age. But structural inequalities have affected me a whole lot more. Thanks to support networks like girl-mom, I am happy and positive about the choice I made to have and raise my daughter. I feel that being a young mother has made me more of the person I am supposed to be and has made me a positive and healthy role model for my daughter. I hope future research will combat negative stereotypes of teen mothers by presenting the voices of more individuals who have found young motherhood (challenging as it can be) to be a rewarding and empowering experience. And I hope our society will begin to reduce the incidence of negative outcomes of young motherhood by providing teen mothers with the supports they both need and deserve, such as childcare in high schools, access to communities of care, and the means of getting out of poverty.

Works Cited

Almgren, Guy, and G. Yamashiro. "Beyond Welfare or Work: Teen mothers, Household Subsistence Strategies, and Child Development Outcomes." *Journal of Sociology and Social Welfare*, vol. XXIX, no. 3, 2002, pp. 125-49.

Bell, J., et al. *Living on the Edge: Sexual behavior and Young Parenthood in Seaside and Rural Areas*. Teenage Pregnancy Unit, 2004.

Boonstra, Heather D. "Teen Pregnancy among Women in Foster Care: A Primer." *Guttmacher Policy Review*, vol. 14, no. 2, 2011, pp. 8-19.

Duncan, Simon, et al. *Teenage Pregnancy: What's The Problem?* Critical Social Policy, vol. 27, no. 3, 2007 pp. 307-334.

Furstenberg, Frank, and Albert Crawford. "Family Support: Helping Teenage Mothers to Cope." *Family Planning Perspectives*, vol. 10, 1978, pp. 322-33.

Healthy People 2020. "Teen Pregnancy Prevention Initiative." *Healthy People*, www.healthypeople.gov/2020/tools-resources/evidence-based-resource/teen-pregnancy-prevention-resource-center-evidence. Accessed June 10, 2019.

Geronimus, A, and S. Korenman. "Maternal Youth or Family Background? On the Health Disadvantages of Infants with Teenage Mothers." *American Journal of Epidemiology*, vol. 137, no. 22, 1993, pp. 213-25.

Penmann-Aguilar, A.M., et al. "Socioeconomic Disadvantage as a Social Determinant of Teen Childbearing in the U.S." *Public Health Reports*, vol. 123, no. 1, 2013, pp. 5-22.

Seamark, Clare. "Design or Accident? The Natural History of Teenage Pregnancy." *Journal of Royal Society of Medicine*, vol. 94, no. 6, 2001, pp. 282-85.

Seamark, Clare, and Pamela Lings. "Positive Experiences of Teenage Motherhood: A Qualitative Study." *British Journal of General Practice*, vol. 54, no. 508, pp. 813-18.

SmithBattle L. "Reducing the Stigmatization of Teen Mothers." *MCN: The American Journal of Maternal/Child Nursing*, vol. 38, no. 4, 2013, pp. 242-43.

Williams, E., and L. Sadler. "Effects of an Urban High School-Based Child Care Center on Self-Selected Adolescent Parents and their Children." *Journal of School Health*, vol. 71, no. 2, 2001, pp. 47-52.

Chapter Six

Early Motherhood: A Turning Point in the Complex Lives of Young Mothers

Karen Felstead

"We can now be lazy because we don't have to work ... we're just slutting around ... don't know how to use protection."—Ruby

Introduction

Young mothers' stories of motherhood are often invisible within the broader contexts of society, and young mothers may themselves be negatively affected by and unable to resist dominant cultural narratives circulated about them. Early motherhood manifests itself as a problem and social concern in academic literature policy and public discourses (Arai; Breheny and Stephens). Much of it invariably details the negative outcomes faced by young mothers, including poor parenting skills, health issues, welfare dependency, and lower educational attainment with little opportunity for future employability, which exacerbates their likelihood of living in poverty (Keegan and Corliss). Community judgment invariably considers young mothers irresponsible and unmotivated (SmithBattle) because they allow themselves to become pregnant to access welfare payments. These discourses about young mothers may be difficult to untangle, as young mother identities are complex and varied, but understanding the often, invisible subjugated narratives of young mothers creates new visible subject positions that warrant a voice.

After a brief discussion of the currency of these dominant, often constraining, discourses within the Australian context, this chapter considers how young mothers negotiate their complex social world through the development, circulation, and affirmation of counter-narrative accounts of their lives and identities. This is achieved through the reading of narrative accounts generated from individual participant-centred interviews with seven young mothers, aged fifteen to nineteen at the birth of their first child. The mothers attend, or had attended, a Young Parents Program (YPP) that operates in a large regional city, situated west of Melbourne in Victoria, Australia. Drawing upon a Foucauldian framework examining the discursive construction and operation of power/knowledge and subjectivity, as well as a discursive analysis of these young mother narrative accounts, this chapter seeks to illustrate points of resistance emerging from their narratives. In particular, it focuses on how accounts of becoming a mother are a significant turning point in young mothers' lives and identity narratives. Preliminary findings indicate that despite a challenging past with accounts of drug taking, problematic home life, partner abuse, self-harm and incomplete schooling, motherhood has changed the young mothers' views about their lives as they seek a different and more positive future for their children.

Background

Concerns about young mothers increased in the first part of the twenty-first century despite declining birth rates (Wilson and Huntington). There was a perception that rates were high (Duncan), although Australian data from the last decade indicate that rates have decreased. In 2008, 12,932 babies were born to young mothers (aged fifteen to nineteen) in Australia, whereas in 2012, the number of babies born to young mothers had reduced to 11,420 (ABS Media Release, 24 October 2013). By 2015, births to young mothers under the age of nineteen had further declined to 8,574 births (ABS Media Release, 8 November 2016).

Young mothers are not a homogenous group (Wilson and Huntington; Hanna). Geographically, they are situated in a wide range of locations—from capital and regional cities to small rural towns—which may determine the kinds of housing and support systems available. Emotional and economic support from families is available for some young mothers, whereas other young mothers are alienated from their mothers, family, and their children's fathers. Opportunities to remain at or return to school or the workforce depend on support that is available, including access to childcare. Community support programs, such as a YPP, in the local area may not be accessible, due to transport issues or a lack of information about available services. Young mothers are also subject to more intense public scrutiny, as dominant discourses about young mothers construct them as welfare dependent with no aspirations for the future. They are deemed to lack responsibility because of their early pregnancy and are deemed unable to make decisions about their lives.

Mothers identified as "problem mothers ... find themselves at the intersection of expectations surrounding both professional expertise and normal mothering" (Croghan and Miell 446). Under significant pressure to be good mothers, young mothers are deemed responsible for their children's development and future. The social construct of good mothering practices is used to critique parenting practices (Macleod) of all mothers and those who do not demonstrate the expected mothering practices "are positioned as the deviant 'other' and considered to be unfit to parent" (Wilson and Huntington 61). As Susan Goodwin and Kate Huppatz argue, "the good mother is also recognised as institutionalised in social arrangements and social prac-tices, and hence operating beyond the belief systems or choices of individual women" (2). Young mothers, in particular, are positioned in dominant cultural narratives as unable to parent adequately and as lacking responsibility. They cannot make decisions about their lives and have no aspirations for the future.

Theoretical Focus and Methodology

This study draws on a Foucauldian framework of discourse to "understand complex relationships involving social interactions, structures, systems and everyday lives (Souto-Manning, 160) of young mothers. The individual, in this case, the young mother is constructed or produced through the formation of knowledge and power structures (Foucault). Discourses have the power to communicate and shape realities of the young mothers' worlds, and in particular, how power is exercised at a local level to constitute young mother subjectivities.

Young mothers—aged between fourteen and nineteen when their first pregnancy was confirmed—were invited to participate in the research, and seven young mothers agreed to be interviewed. The young mothers were all Australian and had lived in socioeconomically disadvantaged areas located in the regional city where they lived. All participants had attended the YPP during the early years of motherhood or were still actively involved. The Young Parents Program referred to in this study was located in a large regional city, west of Melbourne in Victoria, Australia. Once ethical clearance had been granted, permission was sought from the program coordinator, Tim, to visit the site and invite young mothers from the program to participate in the research. Individual interviews were arranged with each participant, and the interviews were conducted in a private office in the same location where the program was conducted, which provided a safe space for the participants while they remained close to their child/children who were cared for in another room. Interviews were recorded and the audio recording was transcribed verbatim. Preliminary interview questions related to the age of the participants (at the time of the interview), the age when the participants became pregnant with first child, their living arrangements, their children's names, the relationship with father of the child, and their mobile phone number. For anonymity, these aspects were recorded in field notes and were not included in the audio recording. Individual written narratives were created from the transcripts and returned to the young mothers to review before the second interview. Four of the young mothers agreed to second interviews. Three participants were no longer available for follow-up interviews as they had moved away from the area or were working fulltime. The second interview provided an opportunity for the participants to add, change, or remove comments made in the first interview. The researcher also asked further questions to clarify and expand the participants' responses. The young mothers chose their pseudonyms to protect themselves, their children, and their extended families. The specific location of the YPP was also not named to protect the young mothers and their families.

The second interviews were also transcribed, and details were added to the narratives. Data analysis software (NVivo) was used to code the narratives. Connections and relationships were identified and grouped into broader themes. As well as relating the problematic events in their lives, the "narratives also express(ed) emotions, thoughts, and interpretations" (Chase 656). Each young mother took a leading role in shaping herself, her experience, and reality, as she recounted her life before and after the birth of her baby.

The Young Mothers

All the young mothers—Lynne (nineteen), Tara (sixteen), May (nineteen), Ruby (eighteen), Cassandra (eighteen), Elly (fourteen), and Amanda (sixteen)—had experienced problematic events in their lives, and none had completed their secondary education. May lived with the father of her child, whereas Elly, had no contact with the father of the first child but was in a long-term relationship with a new partner who helped care for the first baby and they had proceeded to have three more children. The other young mothers had little or no contact with the father of their child. Tara experienced a miscarriage prior to the birth of Alyssa and related this to the frightening events where other people she mixed with would overdose on drugs. Each young mother's life had already begun to arguably unravel at the seams before their pregnancies were confirmed. All the participants had left home because of difficult family relationships; they all had lived in unsafe surroundings, and, in most cases, they had all engaged in risky behaviours before their pregnancies were confirmed, including the regular consumption of a range of drugs, Ruby, Elly and Amanda were also subjected to abusive behaviour and interpersonal violence by the father of their child and other members of their complex family groups. During the interviews, May and Amanda disclosed worrying self-harm attempts related to prior emotional traumas they had experienced. Lynne revealed information about her mental health issues prior to becoming pregnant and the ongoing care she required during the early months after her son was born. Housing difficulties for Ruby meant she couch surfed, and at one stage, she lived in a shed with her boyfriend. Each narrative outlined troubling and problematic circumstances that the young mothers had to contend with and find solutions.

All young mothers were surprised about their pregnancy confirmation, and they had not planned their pregnancies. They all acknowledged the range of emotions they experienced when the pregnancy was confirmed, facing questions about the future with or without the baby. Although some young mothers received advice and pressure from health professionals to terminate the pregnancy, they were quite distressed by the idea and wanted to have the baby. Both Ruby and Elly experienced pressure from the father of the child, often through violent outbursts, to terminate the pregnancy but both chose to remove themselves from the volatile situations and continue with the pregnancy. In most cases, after overcoming the initial shock of the pregnancy announcement, the young mothers' families provided support during the pregnancy and after the birth of the baby. Interestingly, none of the young mothers mentioned that they had received advice about adoption from the family or health professionals before or once the baby was born.

Baby: A Significant Turning Point

The complex nature of the young mothers' journeys into and through early motherhood was revealed in their narratives, yet despite the difficulties they faced, they demonstrated resilience and determination with a desire to make a better future for their children. Becoming a mother was a significant turning point for each young mother. Elly referred to it as the "lightbulb moment," when she realized that she could not put her baby through the abuse and drug taking: "I said enough is enough. I can't do this. I can't put my baby through this ... It was just a lightbulb that clicked. I just sat there and I—I sat there and looked—I could pretty much see my future if I was still here." Lynne recounted that if she had not become pregnant, she might have gone to jail. However, having Mason changed how she would live her life and she sought professional help:

Well, I knew I couldn't do drugs anymore. Like I was still using weed, but I got off the 'ice' [Crystal methamphetamine], and then it took me a while to get off the weed. I stopped the 'ice' pretty much as soon as I found out I was pregnant but the weed it took a few months. I got a drug and alcohol worker. I would probably still be on drugs ... I was getting in trouble with the cops a lot up there, so I'd probably be in jail by now.

Tara expressed that she did not know where she would be now if she had not had her daughter: "I was in a pretty bad state before I fell pregnant ... I was not, like mentally wise, I was not good." Tara was not a drug user, as she wanted full control of her actions, but she was involved with people who did take drugs. At the time, Tara felt a sense of belonging with this group; however, after her pregnancy was confirmed, Tara separated herself from the group. Tara talked about choosing a better lifestyle and thinking about her future, and although she still worried about the future, it was less of a concern now than before she had her daughter, Alyssa. Ruby could not imagine a future without Keegan and did not want him to experience the type of life she had experienced. Early in her pregnancy, Ruby took on a second job to pay for her driving lessons, and after Keegan was born, she purchased a car and found a new independent living space. Ruby indicated that she might not have considered alternative ways of living if she had not had Keegan. Cassandra stated that if she had not become pregnant with Rose, she would have finished school and commenced fulltime employment. However, as Cassandra wanted to care for Rose, she was not thinking about further study now. Earning money was important, so Cassandra continued with her part-time job with promotions and opportunities for full-time work at her current place of employment when Rose was older. Each young mother made positive choices about the future based on how their life was situated and how they could enrich the lives of themselves and their children.

Both May and Amanda shared more troubling accounts of what life might have been like if they had not had their child. May suggested that if she had not had Nicole, she would be "probably dead in a gutter." She continued: "I was on so many drugs before her it wasn't funny. So yeah, I would have been literally fucked up if it wasn't for Nicole." Amanda echoed similar sentiments to May in her response regarding her life without her son, Toby. She stated the following:

"[I'd] probably be dead or in jail. Honestly, I think with all the drugs I was doing before ... probably could have got me in a lot of trouble. I was very suicidal before I had Toby." Having her son was a life-changing event for Amanda: "He did, he changed my life. I couldn't even imagine life without Toby. I don't even want to imagine it. I feel like he's all I have. I need to try and do what's best for him." Early motherhood changed how both young mothers viewed the world.

Points of Resistance: Returning to Learning

Prior to attending the YPP, the young mothers all reported they had been unable to stay in school to complete their secondary education. Some felt excluded and stigmatized by other students, and other young mothers highlighted barriers to school attendance once they were pregnant. Tara experienced physical barriers when she found she could not use the stairs later in the pregnancy. Emotional barriers, including exclusion and victimization by other students, took their toll on Cassandra, and she felt she could not remain at school. Other young mothers reported that school staff members were not supportive, and they were asked to leave much earlier in their schooling or once they were pregnant. Ruby became pregnant in the months leading up to completing school, but because she missed four weeks close to the end of the school year, she was asked not to return.

All the young mothers commenced at the YPP either during their pregnancy or within the first three months of giving birth. The program was designed to support young mothers in the community by providing an individualized and flexible program in a supportive environment that focused on parenting, childcare, and vocational learning. At the YPP, the young mothers could complete the Victorian Certificate of Applied Learning (VCAL),[1] which would open up opportunities for further study. In particular, Elly had only completed the first year of secondary school before leaving, and although she was sent to other alternative education centres, she did not continue schooling, as she admitted her behaviour was disruptive. Elly went on to complete most of her schooling at the YPP, and she completed a hospitality course. May had only completed the second year of secondary school before being excluded for disruptive and risk-taking behaviour at several schools, including at an alternative one. However, once May attended the YPP and started learning again, her views about education changed, and she wanted to be able to read so she could assist her daughter, Nicole, in the future.

Attending the YPP was viewed as a significant turning point in each of the young mothers' lives. All the young mothers had attended the program for varying periods of time. When each young mother was asked why she came to the program, each answer invariably centred on finishing schooling and receiving support and advice from the staff members in the program. Five young mothers—Lynne, Tara, May, Ruby, and Cassandra—who had not reached the age of twenty-one, were still attending the program, whereas Elly and Amanda had left the program as they had reached 21 years of age. The young mothers talked about the program in a positive light. They could attend the program because qualified carers cared for their children while they were involved in different aspects of the program. Lynne reiterated that she liked school as well as the teachers, who could help her complete her education. She was good at English and liked math, and she studied most evenings. Ruby had completed the literacy and numeracy VCAL while attending the program, and her portfolio of evidence[2] was used as an example of excellence at the VCAL Board.

Aspirations for the Future

Each young mother had aspirations for the future. It was clear that the participants had considered how they wanted their future to be for themselves and their children. May outlined plans to go to university with the hope of being a social worker or youth worker. However, she conceded that she would need to get herself on track first. May believed she could help other people because she would "kind of know how they feel." She had some knowledge of a pathway program for university but indicated she knew she would need a good score to gain admittance.

Elly mentioned that she did not have her car license yet for a range of reasons, and she called this "a work in progress", planning to gain her license within a year. She wanted to be a motor mechanic, so needed to know how to drive. Elly had also considered becoming a midwife, particularly for young mothers. She wanted to model midwives who had been supportive during her pregnancies.

Before her pregnancy, Ruby had volunteered at a soup bus for homeless people for four years. She indicated that she had some under-standing of what life was like for other people in the community. Ruby did not want her son to experience the same life she had experienced growing up, so finishing her secondary education and moving on to a business course was very important to her. Ruby had a license, but at the time of the first interview, she did not own a car, so she walked to the program every day during her pregnancy. Also, despite having an emergency Caesarean section after a very long and difficult labour, Ruby returned to YPP five days after giving birth. After Keegan was born, Ruby was able to purchase a car, move out of her family home, and live with her sister where she could set routines, be independent, and have more space. After indicating her interest and aspiration to take up studies in Business, Ruby was given the opportunity to sit on a board of directors for a regional banking corporation as part of the bank's community engagement program to build capacity and community involvement.

Amanda had expressed an interest in working in the funeral in-dustry, which had been her goal for several years. However, she found it difficult to commence work, as the funeral agencies in the area she lived were mostly family owned. Amanda offered her services volun-tarily at one funeral organization and learned many aspects of the industry, and she was not deterred in her goal. However, Amanda could not take a mortuary course, as she did not meet the criteria, which required her to be employed by a funeral agency. She had also been advised that she was too young. Moreover, the cost of the course was too great, so she decided to remain working in her current employment.

The young mothers in this study all indicated aspirations for the future and drew on discursive resources of responsibility and deter-mination to transform their lives. Through interviewing young women in economically deprived areas of England, Alison Rolfe shows how her participants drew on "discursive resources around responsibility" (311) and the concept of responsibility was also highlighted in this study as the young mothers made responsible decisions about the security and welfare of their child. For example, once her son was born, Ruby was determined that she would only allow the father of the child to see his son if he agreed to drug tests. Ruby stated that if he could not control his drug habit, he could not visit or see the baby. Tara also considered the welfare of her child and stated that the relationship with the father of her daughter would only be renewed after he had received professional support for his mental health issues. For Amanda, escaping the trauma of the interpersonal violence she had experienced, and navigating the court system, she was able to take out an intervention order[3] against the father of her child. Despite the process being a complex undertaking at the time, Amanda was determined to create a safe and secure environment for her son. For Lynne and Elly, the father of the child had no access visits, but both young mothers had new supportive partners who had taken on the responsibility of raising the baby, even though the child was not their offspring. For Cassandra, independent living was the only option for the safety and welfare for herself and her child, but as a young mother, navigating the rental market required extensive work. Negotiations with real estate agencies were problematic, and on several occasions, she was refused the opportunity to rent a property. Finally, Cassandra was accepted as a tenant, but she then had to negotiate access to the utilities (electricity, water and gas) before she could move in. She drew on her internal resources of determination to persevere and advocate for herself and her son.

Conclusion

The findings in this study challenge the assumption that becoming a young mother has only negative outcomes. Becoming a young mother was a significant turning point for the participants in this research. In his research about the effects of early motherhood on the mother's short and long-term health behaviours, Jason Fletcher suggests that early motherhood may alter the "priorities of young women toward pursuing fewer risky and unhealthy activities (217). This finding was evident in the narratives in this study. The young mothers who had engaged in risk-taking behaviours made immediate changes to their lifestyle; they made decisions about how they wanted to live their lives. The young mothers who had taken drugs made positive changes to their health by removing the influences of peers who took illicit drugs and by no longer consuming drugs themselves. They envisaged a future that was different from their own experiences before becoming a mother. Clare Seamark and Pamela Lings have also found that young mothers understood motherhood as a "turning point" (818), as they were motivated to care and provide for their children.

Although the young mothers related that both pregnancy and early motherhood were challenging, they all drew on the discursive resources of a better future for themselves and their children. Despite facing a range of complexities in their lives, they took an active role in constructing their lives as young mothers who could make decisions about how to stay safe and about what was important for themselves and their children.

Arguably, one of the most important aspects of this research was that the young mothers became more visible in their narratives. I was continually reminded that their lives shifted, sometimes precariously, through complex and problematic events. The stories they shared had contradictory elements; at times, life was better after the birth of their baby, but then their stories circled back to troubling aspects, such as broken relationships, abusive partners, and difficulty with housing agencies. However, at the time of the interviews, all of the young mothers had moved beyond their broken relationships, abusive partners, and risk-taking behaviour. They were able to draw on external resources through the YPP and the community of young mothers in that network. They used their internal resilience and determination to negotiate their worlds and live their lives differently and with happiness. As Cassandra says about her life with her daughter Rose, "We're both happy. We've got a happy family and life".

Ethics

The Human Research Ethics Committee (of the author's institution) approved this research prior to the commencement of the interviews. Some of the young mothers were below the age of eighteen at the time of the interview. However, given that the participants were already in a parenting role, living independently, negotiating their living and work-related environments, and managing their finances they were deemed as being in a position to understand the implications of giving consent to participate in this research.

Acknowledgments

A very special thank you to the young mothers—Lynne, Tara, May, Ruby, Cassandra, Elly, and Amanda—who willingly shared their stories of motherhood. Their narratives emphasized the significant turning point having a child was in their lives and how they envisioned a different future for themselves and their children. Also, thank you to Tim, the coordinator of the Young Parents Program, who provided a safe space for the young mothers to talk about their lives.

Endnotes

1. The Victorian Certificate of Applied Learning (VCAL) is an active learning option for students in year eleven and twelve. The VCAL provides practical work-related experience, as well as literacy, numeracy, and personal life skills. Like the Victorian Certificate of Education (VCE), the VCAL is an accredited secondary certificate.

2. A portfolio of evidence demonstrates that the student has completed the learning and assessment tasks. It shows the successful completion of the learning outcomes as decreed by the Victorian Curriculum and Assessment Authority.

3. In the state of Victoria, an intervention order is an order made by a magistrate under the Family Violence Protection Act 2008 or the Personal Safety Intervention Orders Act 2010. There are two types of orders. One intervention order helps to protect a person from a family member who is violent, and the second order helps to protect a person from someone other than a family member who makes them feel unsafe.

Works Cited

Arai, Lisa. "Low Expectations, Sexual Attitudes and Knowledge: Explaining Teenage Pregnancy and Fertility in English Communities. Insights from Qualitative Research." *The Sociological Review* vol. 51, no. 2, 2003, pp. 199-217.

Australian Bureau of Statistics. "Number of Teenage Mothers Lowest in a Decade." *ABS*, 24 Oct. 2013, www.abs.gov.au/ausstats/abs@. nsf/lookup/3301.0Media%20Release12012. Accessed 11 June 2019.

Australian Bureau of Statistics. "Teenage Fertility Rate Lowest on Record." *ABS*, 8 Nov. 2016, www.abs.gov.au/ausstats/abs@.nsf/lookup/3301.0Media%20Release12015. Accessed 11 June 2019.

Breheny, Mary, and Christine Stephens. "Irreconcilable Differences: Health Professionals' Constructions of Adolescence and Motherhood." *Social Science & Medicine*, vol. 64, no. 1, 2007, pp. 112-24.

Chase, Susan. "Narrative Inquiry: Multiple Lenses, Approaches, Voices." *The Sage Handbook of Qualitative Research*, edited by N.K. Denzin, Sage Publications Inc., 2005, pp. 651-79.

Croghan, Rosaleen, and Dorothy Miell. "Strategies of Resistance: 'Bad' Mothers Dispute the Evidence." *Feminism & Psychology*, vol. 8, no. 4, 1998, pp. 445-65.

Duncan, Simon. "What's the Problem with Teenage Parents? And What's the Problem with Policy?" *Critical Social Policy*, vol. 27, no. 3, 2007, pp. 307-34.

Fletcher, Jason. "The Effects of Teenage Childbearing on the Short- and Long-Term Health Behaviors of Mothers." *Journal of Population Economics,* vol. 25, no.1, 2012, pp. 201-18.

Foucault, Michel, and Colin Gordon. *Power/Knowledge: Selected Interviews and Other Writings, 1972-1977.* Pantheon Books, 1980.

Goodwin, Susan, and Kate Huppatz. *The Good Mother: Contemporary Motherhoods in Australia.* Sydney University Press, 2010.

Hanna, Barbara. "Negotiating Motherhood: The Struggles of Teenage Mothers." *Journal of Advanced Nursing* vol. 34, no. 4, 2001, pp. 456-64.

Keegan, Marcia, and Michael Corliss. "The Labour Force Participation of Young Mothers Versus Older Mothers." *Australian Journal of Labour Economics* vol. 11, no. 2, 2008, pp. 149-61.

Rolfe, Alison. "'You've Got to Grow up When You've Got a Kid': Marginalized Young Women's Accounts of Motherhood.: *Journal of Community & Applied Social Psychology,* vol. 18, no.4, 2008, pp. 299-314.

Seamark, Clare J., and Pamela Lings. "Positive Experiences of Teenage Motherhood: A Qualitative Study." *The British Journal of General Practice: The Journal of the Royal College of General Practitioners,* vol. 54, no. 508, 2004, pp. 813-18.

SmithBattle, Lee. "Reducing the Stigmatization of Teen Mothers." *MCN, The American Journal of Maternal/Child Nursing,* vol. 38, no.4, 2013, pp. 241-43.

Souto-Manning, Mariana. "Critical Narrative Analysis: The Interplay of Critical Discourse and Narrative Analyses." *International Journal of Qualitative Studies in Education,* vol. 27, no. 2, 2014, pp. 159-80.

Wilson, Helen, and Annette Huntington. "Deviant (M)Others: The Construction of Teenage Motherhood in Contemporary Discourse." *Journal of Social Policy,* vol. 35, no. 1, 2006, pp. 59-76.

Chapter Seven

Single Teen Mothers on Welfare Share "The Missing Story of Ourselves"

Vivyan Adair

"My kids and I been chopped up and spit out just like when I was a kid. My rotten teeth, my kids twisted feet. My son's dull skin and blank stare. My oldest girl's stooped posture and the way she can't look no one in the eye no more. This all says we got nothing and we deserve what we got. On the street good families look at us and see right away what they'd be if they don't follow the rules. They're scared too, real scared."—Welfare recipient and homeless family advocate. (qtd. Adair, "Branded with Infamy" 451)

I begin with the words of a twenty-two-year-old welfare recipient and single mother of three. Although officially she has only a tenth-grade education, she expertly reads and articulates a complex theory of power, bodily inscription, and socialization that arose directly from the material conditions of her own life. She sees what many far more so-called educated scholars and citizens fail to recognize: that the bodies of poor women and their children in the U.S. have been produced and positioned as texts that facilitate the mandates of an increasingly didactic, profoundly brutal, and mean-spirited regime. The clarity and power of this young mother's vision challenges feminists to consider and critique our commitment both to decoding displays of heavy-handed social inscription and to detextualizing them, as we work to end experiences of pain, humiliation, and suffering directed specifically towards poor, young, and unmarried mothers and their children in an era of punishing welfare and post welfare reform.

At the Intersection of the Textual and the Corporeal

My own very young mother—with four children under the age of eight by the time she was twenty-four—was kind and loving and probably irreparably hurt and damaged. She taught, nurtured, and loved us ferociously as she struggled and utterly failed to keep us fed, sheltered, and safe. We clung desperately to her fragile dignity, wisdom, grace, and laughter against all the forces of a cruel and indifferent world. She was crushed by the weight of my brothers and sister and me. We were bent and broken and taken from her, with scars that never faded; with injuries, infections and ailments for which we found neither respite nor repair; with feet mangled by cheap, used Salvation Army shoes; and with the gnawing void of hunger clawing at our tender backs, indignities, and humiliations for which I still can find no words.

With access to neither medical insurance nor care, when my already fragile, toddling sister's forehead was split open by a car door slammed in frustration, we had to pin her tiny body to the ground as my mother sewed the angry gash together on her own, practicing the meticulous dressmaker's stitches for which she had received such acclaim and so little reward. My sister somehow endured, but she registered the pain, the terror, and the trauma with a brand, a stigmata, and a sign of our lack—an angry and frightening scar that visually cleaved her forehead in two for the remainder of her life.

In our school cafeteria as "free lunchers," we were reminded with a large and colourful sign to line up last. In that same auditorium each fall, we were coerced up onto a makeshift stage with the promise of first dibs on free milk. There, our pristine school nurse sat upright and sucked air through her teeth as she donned surgical gloves to check the hair of poor children for lice. I burned and choked and raged with shame, as my far more "decent" working-class colleagues and friends, in colour-coordinated Sears sweater sets and matching tartan knee-high socks, averted their eyes from our reluctant genuflections while delicately spooning their mac and cheese and sipping their Tree Top juice from small Dixie cups.

Living in our car between evictions and with access to only public bathrooms, I developed a series of painful urinary tract infections, for which we could afford no medical attention. When my teachers wouldn't let me go to the bathroom every hour or so—insisting that I was just being willful—I would wet my pants in class. Our schoolmates guffawed at our gap-jawed and duct taped shoes, our crooked and ill-serviced teeth and the way we stank, as teachers excoriated us for our inability to concentrate in school, our refusal to come to class prepared with proper school supplies, and our unethical behaviour when we tried to take more than our share of free lunches. Whenever backpacks or library books went missing, we were publicly interrogated and sent home to think about our offenses, often accompanied by notes that reminded my young mother that living off taxpayer's dollars and being a "generational freeloader" meant she should be working twice as hard to make up for the discipline that allegedly walked out the door with my father. And when we occasionally cried foul and lashed out, our behavior was used to justify even more elaborate punishment that exacerbated the effects of our growing anomie.

On my seventeenth birthday, I awoke in a shelter for battered women. I had four missing teeth, a broken clavicle, and bruised ribs. In the small cot next to me lay my infant daughter, still traumatized by the brutalization we had suffered at the hands of her own father. With scant education, with no family support, with few resources and no job—and mired in the pain, anomie and shame of being marked as a battered, impoverished single mother and welfare recipient in an era of increasingly punitive poverty reform—I had little reason for hope.

That morning, we boarded a public bus to find our way to the welfare office where I had hoped to secure support with which we might begin to rebuild our lives. I recall that as we soberly boarded, passengers recoiled, reacting to my still vaguely blood-stained clothing, unwashed hair, and emaciated, bruised, and deformed face. I am quite sure that even my beloved and beautiful child startled them with her blank and oddly aged gaze. At the Department of Health and Human Services, I was met with similar looks of disdain mingled with uneasy pity. Only my caseworker was clear and unequivocal: it would take at least two weeks to reopen my case and process my request for assistance; I would have to reveal the legal paternity of my child; I could not apply for food stamps unless I had a rent receipt for a "proper home" in my own name (which of course I did not have); and state issued medical coupons would only cover the repair of my one missing front tooth. The others—a bicuspid and two molars—he explained with unintended irony, were not considered medically necessary for somebody "feeding at the public trough."

I was ashamed and humiliated. In that moment however, I understood quite clearly that as when we were children, our bodies were being written and read like texts and that this reading of the bodies of poor teen mothers and their children determined I would walk through the world with inadequate clothing, missing teeth, a distanced and shell-shocked child, and a presence that would continue to both evoke and justify fear and punishment. In that moment, I began to appreciate the complexity of the circuit through which bodies are represented and understood in ways that reflect and reify dominant ideology. Ideology, in turn, determines, shapes, and reinforces public policy, and public policy leaves its marks on the bodies of poor mothers and their children who are then interpreted endlessly as broken, scarred, dangerous, and illegitimate "others" in need of further public and material control (Adair, "Branded with Infamy" 455).

As children, our disheveled and unkempt bodies and decaying teeth had been produced and read as signs of our inferiority, stupidity, and undeservedness. As a young welfare mom, my mutilated, broken body was positioned and read as a sign of my inner chaos, immaturity, selfishness, illegality, and indecency. In order to pay my rent and to purchase diapers, I sold plasma at two or three different clinics on a monthly basis until I became so anemic that they refused to buy it from me. I kept on going back to the man who continued to berate and batter me, after being denied welfare support. I exposed myself to all manner of danger, disease, and irrevocable disgust by trading my worn, used body for a little rent relief or a ride.

Poverty becomes a vicious cycle that is written on our bodies and intimately connected with our being in the world. The food banks we gratefully drag our exhausted children to on weekends hand out bags of rancid candy bars, hot dogs that have passed their expiration dates, stale broken pasta, and occasionally a bag of wrinkled apples. We know—to the bone—that we are worth no more. Our emaciated or bloated and always abject bodies are then read as a sign of our lack of discipline and proof that we have failed to care and work and obey as we should have. Perhaps, I remember a plump and chipper public health nurse once chiding, arms akimbo, I should put down the Cheetos and join a gym so that I might find a nice man to support me.

The bodies of poor women and children, scarred and mutilated by state mandated material deprivation and public exhibition, work as spectacles and as patrolling images socializing and controlling bodies within the body politic. Public and widely publicized narratives purport to write the story of poor teen mothers and their unruly children in an arena in which only their wayward bodies have been positioned to speak. They promise to tell the story of the poor in ways that allow Americans to maintain a belief in both an economic system based on exploitation and an ideology that claims that good, deserving, and rights-bearing citizens are all beyond exploitation.

In this dichotomous, hierarchical frame, the poor teen mother is juxtaposed against a logic of normative subjectivity as undeserving and as the embodiment of dependency, disorder, laziness, and sexual chaos. She is positioned as greedy, cunning, rash, and untrustworthy and as a threat to inviolate male authority in and out of the home. When poor teen welfare mothers are positioned and reified as unstable and dangerous, their figures are temporarily immobilized and made to yield meaning as a space of chaos and disorder that must be brought under control and transformed through public displays of discipline and punishment, for the sake of the nation. In the process prolific overlapping stereotypes of poor single teen mothers flatten out complexities to produce trite, unavailing stories of poverty. As welfare scholar Halloway Sparks notes: "The image of welfare mothers as poor, unwed, out of control teenagers who are inept, irresponsible and producing babies for monetary gain is alluring ... these stereotypes reduce complexity and channel our fears toward an easy target. Stereotypes of incapable, ignorant and evil unmarried teen mothers are used to justify social policy" (212).

Resisting the Text

I left the shelter with little help or hope the following fall to join thousands of other poor women around the nation in going back to school. I did so initially simply to earn the skills and credentials that would allow my infant daughter and me to survive. Yet in school, I was supported and challenged by dedicated, able and patient instructors who encouraged me to transform my life through the pathway of higher education. My passage was guided by teachers whose classrooms became places where I was able to build bridges connecting my own knowledge of self and others to crucial new knowledge, skills, and methodologies. Dedicated faculty created exciting, engaging exercises and orchestrated intensely challenging discussions that enabled me to devour a vast range of knowledge and to use my newfound skills to re-envision my gifts, strengths, and responsibilities to the world around me.

While in school, I studied, attended classes, worked, and cared for my daughter. I gratefully received minimal *Aid to Families with Dependent Children* ("welfare") grants, food stamps, and Medicaid. I continued to sell my plasma at blood banks and engaged in paid medical experiments to pay rent and to buy diapers, baby food, and books for classes. And I learned and grew. Little by little the larger social, creative, political, and material world exposed itself to me in ways that were resonant and urgent, inviting me to negotiate, analyze, and reframe experiences, identities, histories, pathways, and questions that had previously seemed inaccessible. The process was invigorating, restorative, and life altering.

My journey continued with the support of other poor single mothers reading and rewriting their own lives and values through supported access to higher education. Moving from earning a GED to earning a PhD; developing and directing the ACCESS Project at Hamilton College (supporting other welfare eligible, single parent students); writing books and essays exploring the intersections of ideology, representation, public policy, and poor women; and creating the nationally recognized photo-narrative exhibit "The Missing Story of Ourselves; Poverty and the Promise of Higher Education" all became transformative, community-building and life-changing projects for me and for my colleagues. Together, we learned to both embrace and push against mainstream knowledge embedded in the stories that surrounded and indeed marked us—and from which we had often been made absent by design.

Photo 1: Vivyan Adair, PhD

In our nationally touring photo-narrative installation as poor single mother students, we dedicated ourselves to dismantling and then retelling our own stories, pushing back against those explanatory narratives that had devalued and ultimately harmed us. Ours were complex, first-person views of what poverty and resistance look like from the inside out. Our narratives allowed us to map our own lives and values as well as to offer insights into larger ethical questions of human value, the power of education, and community. In telling different stories of our value and in exposing the processes of ideology through which our value is traditionally determined and disseminated, we hoped to interrupt that closed circuit of desire that would otherwise mark and guarantee our place as dangerous "other" in cultural, social, legal, and policy matrices.

As we were diligently learning and constructing our own counter-stories and images in school, politicians and pundits continued to extol the perils of poor "children having children." Former Speaker of the U.S. House of Representatives, Newt Gingrich proposed that children of welfare mothers be placed in orphanages. He argued that out-of-home care would be better than the damage unmarried welfare mothers provide and insisted that cutting the emotional bonds and removing the damaging modelling that welfare dependent women inflict on their young would be good for the nation (Covert). Robert

Rector in "How Welfare Harms Kids," offered a similarly frantic warning:

> Overall welfare operates as a form of social toxin. The more of this toxin received by an aid-addicted mom, the less successful the child will be as an adult. If American children are to be saved [from their own mothers] the current welfare system must be replaced. Higher welfare payments do not help children, they increase dependency and illegitimacy, which have a devastating effect on the children's development. (3)

Rector went on to proclaim that any financial, housing, food, or medical assistance allows (indeed encourages) poor teen mothers to "have walking around money for cigarettes, booze and clothes" (adding that some of "these moms like to dress their kids up") and serves as a "disincentive to prohibiting indulgent poor teen moms from having children who threaten the lives and health of legitimate children and families" (O'Mara).

In "The Effects of Welfare Reform," Rector reiterates that "providing food, education and shelter to poor teen mothers rewards and encourages their immoral sexual choices," causes delinquency, school dropouts, criminality, and more out of wedlock children. He adds (without evidence) that "illegitimacy among teen moms is passed like a virus and illegitimacy is the major factor in America's rampant crime problem." Rector's crony Heather MacDonald agrees, insisting that poor single teen moms are "lazy due to years of government programming, illogical...out of control" and "crazed trying to meet [their] own self needs." In "The Real Welfare Problem is Illegitimacy," evoking suspect social science data, she adds the following:

> Illegitimacy dooms children to prisons, foster-care homes, and homeless shelters to failing at school, committing suicide, suffering child abuse.... 70 percent of long-term prisoners, 60 percent of rapists, and 75 percent of adolescents charged with murder grew up without fathers. The risks to children living outside a two-parent home go beyond social failure, as witness New York City's never-ending cortege of tiny coffins containing children beaten, suffocated, and scalded by their mothers' boyfriends. (MacDonald)

Fifteen years later, in 2013, while praising Mayor Bloomberg's million dollar ad campaign designed specifically to stigmatize pregnant teens, Staten Island Borough President James Molinare chided the state for having become a willing "sugar daddy" and advised instead to "turn off the welfare spigot" in order to "stop rewarding bad behavior," forcing poor teen mothers to take responsibility for their own "bad actions" (qtd. in Kriss). Molinare added that effective policy should "make them take responsibility and pay a price for their immoral actions and bad choices." Otherwise, Molinari argued, support for housing, medical care, and food not only imposes "a great cost and unfair burden to the taxpayers, but [also encourages] an incentive program for licentious teens to have children" (2013).

Molinare echoed journalist William Raspberry, who a decade earlier had framed poor teen mothers as selfish and immature. Raspberry submitted that "all of our other social ills—crime, drugs, violence, failing schools—are a direct result of the degradation of parenthood by emotionally immature, licentious teen mothers" (A31). Raspberry went on to assert that poor single teen mothers must be made visible reminders to the rest of the culture of the poor choices they have made. He claimed that rather than "coddling" a young single mother by providing her with even minimal welfare support, society has a responsibility to "shame and punish her" and to use her failure to teach other young women that it is "morally wrong for under-aged, unmarried women to bear children" in order to "cast young single motherhood as a pathological, selfish and immature act" (A31).

Rewriting the Narrative

Against these simple, reductive and pejorative images, in *The Missing Story of Ourselves*, poor single mother scholars present complex stories that refuse the iconography of the poor teen mother as law breaker, bad mother, incapable worker, or degenerate citizen. Claudia writes of surviving the stigma of welfare, leaving her family home, and having a child at age sixteen. Determined to change her life for the sake of her beloved child while enduring hunger, exhaustion and family alienation, Claudia is now a doctor of optometry with her own growing practice and a bright, happy and well-adjusted college-bound daughter:

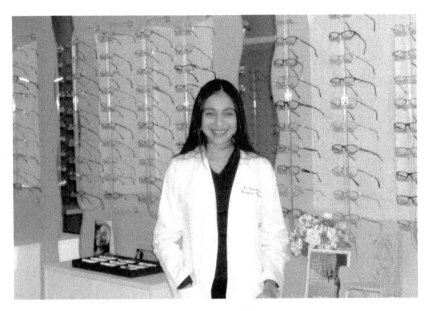

Photo 2: Claudia, Doctor of Optometry

Vision is important. When I was a child, my poor, immigrant parents could do little to advance my education goals because they spoke only Spanish and because no one in my family ever attended—or ever stepped foot in—a college. My father is a self-employed roofer, and my mother sells cosmetics. Yet I saw myself as a college graduate, and I held fast to that vision even when I fled my unstable, abusive, and alcoholic father with my boyfriend. I was only sixteen. I soon became pregnant, but the thought of giving up on college never crossed my mind.

My daughter was born, and I finished high school and began college while working full time. I sacrificed many college and social events because I had different priorities and responsibilities than my friends and peers. I studied, worked, and cared for my beloved daughter. I earned my bachelor's degree in four years and entered the College of Optometry. Now, I am a therapeutic doctor of optometry and business partner in a private optometry practice. I still struggle to balance the time I have to devote to my practice—which is open seven days a week—and to care for my daughter. That struggle is made easier because I understand the trust my patients and my daughter have for me.

The most important sight I have is seeing my daughter growing up in a household with a strong, educated, competent mother as a role model. My ultimate goal is that my daughter will learn through my experience that hard work, discipline, and motivation can help her attain her own vision and reach her own fullest potential. She is growing up in a household that values education. She attends a wonderful, nurturing school—not the neighbourhood school I attended that passed everyone without really caring if we knew the material. Carinna expects to attend college and knows that I will be behind her as she finds her own vision. Being a mother, a doctor, and a business partner can be exhausting. Yet I find the strength I need when I look at my daughter and see in her better opportunities because of the sacrifices I made for both of us. (Adair, The Missing Story 10)

Jamala was the daughter of a welfare recipient and a single mother herself at age fifteen in Chicago. Today, she remembers using higher education to "break the cycle of poverty," as she recalls in *The Missing Story of Ourselves:*

At the age of fifteen, and as I began my sophomore year of high school, I had a baby. My mother, a single parent to five children receiving aid from the state of Illinois, simply added my son to our family allotment. Growing up in inner-city Chicago in an environment of drugs, gangs, and a sense of helplessness, I had used school as an escape route. I believed education was the key to a better way of life. I completed high school near the top of my class and was accepted at the University of Illinois at Urbana-Champaign; my three-year-old son went along with me. I became solely responsible for my son. I was eighteen, a single parent to a toddler, away from home with no family or financial support, and a full-time college student at an educationally demanding university. The road ahead appeared daunting, but I was not deterred.

My son and I finished college in four years, before many of my peers who had little or no responsibilities. Not only did I earn my college degree, I was also active in several school organizations, co-founding a single-parent support group on campus. I graduated with high distinction in political science, achieving a 3.7 grade point average. I attended one of the top ten law schools in the country, clerked for a federal judge, and now practice law in a prestigious law firm. My son, now thirteen years old (and already discussing college), has been with me through it all. Welfare in no way held me back as a single teen mom, but it did make a difference in my life. Welfare made it easier for me to succeed and concentrate on what was important—my child and my education. For those who believe that welfare is cyclical and repeats throughout generations—for this family, the cycle is broken. By receiving aid that allowed me to focus on my responsibilities as a student and mother, I was able to show my son, younger siblings, my community, and particularly other teenage mothers that anything is possible (Adair, The Missing Story 34).

Photo 3: Jamala, Attorney at Law

Nolita earned her general education degree at a Native American academy, and in the same year, she became a single teen mother. In her narrative for *The Missing Story of Ourselves* collection, she recognizes that "the cultural text of my devaluation, as written and read through public policy and welfare reform, suggests that my being a young, unmarried and pregnant woman of color, would mark me as being a problem, as an undeserving human being and mother" (26). She goes on however, to counter that: "the truth of my pregnancy was that it changed my young life in remarkable and positive ways." She writes the following:

My beautiful daughter is caring, energetic, and a delight to be with. She loves me very much and looks up to me to provide her with the love and guidance she needs to be successful in life. I realize that I owe my daughter the best I can provide and want to be a successful mother. The life I had growing up was full of hardships and struggles; the fear that my daughter might have to experience the things I did at her age motivates me to get up every morning and continue on the pathway I began a few years ago.

When I was two years old, I was introduced to the world of violence, abuse, alcoholism, and drug addiction of my parents. My first memory of my mother was that she was drunk and broke my arm; the second was when I was beaten so badly that I was knocked unconscious. My older brother and I were eventually removed from my parents' home after years of torment. My other two siblings were sent back to the reservation with my mother. My father just disappeared, and to this day, I have no clue as to his whereabouts.

My life changed the day I was told that I was pregnant at eighteen I did not want to turn out like my own mother. I wanted to protect my child from abuse and foster care, and I knew I needed to get my life together and complete my education. In January 2001, I gave birth to a healthy baby girl and received my GED. Everything from that point on became increasingly better for my daughter and me (Adair, The Missing Story 26).

Photo 4: Nolita, Clerking for Judge Cook

In June of 2006, Nolita graduated with a degree in philosophy from Hamilton College. Her beautiful five-year-old daughter walked proudly by her side. Single mother student Stephanie graduated with Nolita. Today, she is a proud college graduate, homeowner, career professional, and mother. Stephanie recounts the following in *The Missing Story of Ourselves*:

Three years ago, I began my college career as a full scholarship student at Hobart and William Smith Colleges, where I studied for one semester and played on the field hockey team. I planned on being a successful college student, playing collegiate sports and getting to know and befriend other college students. I have always known that I wanted to graduate from college and assumed I would take the normal route. I was wrong, and I am happy that I was.

My life took an unexpected twist when I realized at the end of my first year at college that I was pregnant and had to drop out. Giving birth to my twin boys has helped my expand my dreams and goals, and has given me even more incentive to succeed in school. I am going to college not for myself, but for all three of us so that I can assure a stable future for my family.

Working and attending school full time and caring for the children I love so dearly is a challenge. I have learned to be proactive, organized, energized, and thorough. I have learned how to connect and how to care about knowledge, facts, and culture. Today, I make plans, calculate strategies, and carry through with attention to both detail and the larger picture. I am becoming a strong, capable worker, and student while remaining a loving, nurturing parent. My boys are with me, learning and loving life through it all (Adair, *The Missing Story* 32).

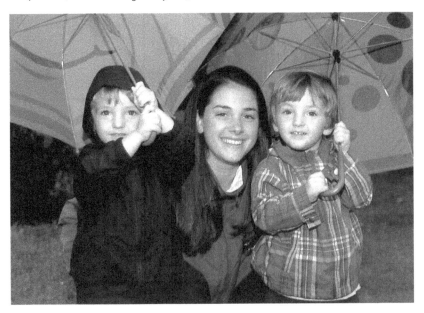

Photo 5: Stephanie and Family

In writing and curating *The Missing Story of Ourselves*, poor, single mothers as well as welfare scholars learned to both embrace and push against mainstream knowledge that surrounded and indeed marked us—and from which we had most often been made absent by design. Although we knew that the negotiation of privileged knowledge in academe could not erase the marks or the memories of our poverty, we came to understand that contestation and the deployment of different meanings could transform the ways in which we were able to interrogate and reformat the discursive structures that had fixed and framed us.

Noemy Vides and Victoria Steinitz, in "Together We are Getting Freedom," remind us that "by talking and writing about learned shame together [poor teen mothers] pursue their own liberation" (Vides and Steinitz 305). Vides adds that it is through this process that she learned to challenge the dominant explanations that decreed and assured her lack of value in the world, "provoking an awareness that the labels—ignorant peasant, abandoned woman, broken-English speaker, welfare cheat—have nothing to do with who one really is, but serve to keep women subjugated and divided." She goes on to say that "this consciousness gives poor single mothers the tools to understand the uses of power; it emboldens us to move beyond the imposed shame that silences, to speak out and join together in a common liberatory struggle" (305).

Because power is diffuse, heterogeneous, and contradictory, poor, single, teen mothers struggle against the marks of their degradation. Resistance swells in the gaps and interstices of productions of self. We become caught up in the contradiction between our body's meaning as a despised public sign and our shared sense of communal power. In struggling together, we contest the marks of our bodily inscription, disrupt the use of our bodies as signs, change the conditions of our lives, and survive. In the process, we come to understand that the shaping of our bodies is not coterminous with our beings or abilities as a whole. Contestation and the deployment of new truths cannot erase the marks of our poverty, but the process does transform the ways in which we can interrogate our lives and the systems of power that have branded them with infamy. As a result, these signs are rendered fragile, unstable, and ultimately malleable.

Works Cited

Adair, Vivyan. "Branded with Infamy: Inscriptions of Poverty and Class in the United States." *Signs; Journal of Women in Culture and Society.* vol. 27, no. 2, 2002, pp. 451-71.

Adair, Vivyan. *The Missing Story of Ourselves: Poverty and the Promise of Higher Education.* Canterbury Press, 2004.

Covert, Bryce. "That Time Newt Gingrich Tried to Take Kids Away from Welfare Recipients and Put Them in Orphanages." *Think Progress,* 2016, thinkprogress.org/that-time-newt-gingrich-tried-to-take-kids-away-from-welfare-recipients-and-put-them-in-orphanages-261e525ea22e/. Accessed 15 June 2019.

Kriss, Erik. "Ban Welfare for Teenage Mothers." *The New York Post,* 9 March 2013, nypost.com/2013/03/09/si-beep-ban-welfare-for-teenage-mothers/. Accessed 15 June 2019.

MacDonald, Heather. "The Real Welfare Problem is Illegitimacy." *The Social Order,* 1998, www.city-journal.org/html/real-welfare-problem-illegitimacy-12161.html. Accessed 15 June 2019.

O'Mara, Richard."Are Orphanages Better for Kids than Welfare?" *Baltimore Sun,* 27 Nov. 1994, www.baltimoresun.com/news/bs-xpm-1994-11-27-1994331010-story.html. Accessed 15 June 2019.

Raspberry, William. "Worse Than Welfare as We Know it?" *The Washington Post.* 8 August 1996, A31.

Rector, Robert. "How Welfare Harms Kids." *Backgrounder: The Heritage Foundation.* Washington DC. 5 June 1996.

Rector, Robert. "The Effects of Welfare Reform." *The Heritage Foundation.* 15 Mar. 2001, www.heritage.org/node/201682/. Accessed 15 June 2019.

Sparks, Holloway. "Welfare 'Reform' Debate Tainted By Racism, Sexism." *Penn State News,* 20 June 2003, pus.edu/ur/2003/welfare queens. Accessed 19 June 2019.

Vides, Naomi, and Victoria Steinitz. "Together We Are Getting Freedom." *For Crying Out Loud,* edited by Diane Dujon and Ann Withorn, South End Press, 1996, pp. 295-306.

Chapter Eight

Becoming "Yazzi": A Queer Story of Young Parenthood

Johanna Lewis

I was twenty-two years old when I became a parent—in the most accidental and also most intentional of ways. As a queer femme, and eventual parent of the child that my trans-masculine partner birthed just ten months after we started dating, neither my journey to parenthood nor my experience of parenthood fits into any neat boxes. Journeys and experiences, after all, rarely do. Because of this messiness—indeed, because of all the messiness and diversity and difficulty and beauty of young parents and our many truths—I feel compelled to share my story as an expert in my own life. I seek to offer with descriptions of particular moments and with situated reflections an account of grappling with my own set of intersecting identities and experiences. In the four years that have passed since my kid was born, I have often felt isolated. I don't only mean the isolation that can come with newborn life and the challenges that young kiddos can pose on maintaining relationships and communities. I mean feeling alone in a broader sense, in that I could never find stories that reflected my experience. I share my own in hope that other young parents may find something in it that resonates with them and that researchers, service providers, and advocates will be reminded to account for the many ways that young people come into parenthood.

***

My partner now, J, is a decade older than me and had wanted to have a kid for years. After various relationships and arrangements had fallen apart, they had decided to try to get pregnant with supports but as a single parent.[1] I knew this was the plan when we decided to go on a date, but who knew how long that would take. We had no idea where, if anywhere, our new relationship would take us. We could deal with that later, if the need even emerged. It felt very far away. But a month in, on their third insemination attempt, J got pregnant.

Our budding gay summer romance was full of making out in parks and talking about visionary science fiction. It was also unusually full of morning sickness and urgent conversations about where we thought this relationship may be going. After much agonizing and negotiating and dreaming, I decided that I wanted to be around for J and for this future baby. I stopped applying to grad schools outside of Toronto. For months, I went to the hospital checkups and ultrasounds, and we excitedly anticipated the arrival of Lentil (the fetus's name). Throughout J's pregnancy and the preparation leading up to the birth, I was a primary support and had intended to be part of the babe's unconventional queer family. A femme auntie, or something. But J and I were never planning to co-parent.

My journey to parenthood was, therefore, both unusual and unexpected. I offer four vignettes and a series of reflections to illustrate some of the aspects and contours of my particularly situated experience, of my becoming "Yazzi." I share one queer story of young parenthood in order to celebrate and honour all the others.

Moment One

The labour is a disaster. I support J through active contractions for almost twenty-four hours. Complication, complication, emergency C-Section. Also a disaster. J's body isn't responding to the meds, and they've been screaming in pain since the doctors started cutting into them. I sit by their head and try to whisper calm and encouraging words through the minutes that feel like hours, but I am just horrified by the whole process. The hospital gowns and masks lay like a slimy shrieking creature on a table. They wave me over and hand me scissors to cut the umbilical cord, or shorten it, really, where they show me to. It's already been cut of course, and I'm not sure if this is a necessity or just an attempt to involve me in the process. They bundle up her wrinkled body in a blanket and put a hat on her squishy head. They hand her to me and tell me to go show J, who is still on the operating table, arms in restraints, a sheet draped vertically at their chest. "Here," I say, lowering the baby to their face, "look." I feel empty, shocked. Is this how it happens? That's how babies are born?

J is still in agony, out of their mind with pain and medication; they can't look at me or their baby. "There's nothing more we can give you," says the anesthesiologist. "Knock me out," they demand, "Just knock me out." "At this point it's quite risky; some people don't wake up." "Just do it," they gasp. They won't remember this later. The OR nurses usher me away. If they are putting a patient under, no one other than the medical staff is allowed in the room. The staff members open the door and gently push me and the two-minute-old infant into the empty hallway. They shut the door. I hear J screaming inside. The baby is screaming in my arms.

When you hold your baby for the first time, you're supposed to feel love, I hear, or some kind of joy. But I hold this baby and feel nothingness and then panic, nothingness and then panic. In the forty-five minutes between being ejected into the hallway and J being wheeled into the recovery area, my mind lands on the worst-case scenario and gets stuck. Some people don't wake up. What if they never wake up? Panic. How will I take care of this tiny human? Panic. We hadn't prepared for this possibility. I hadn't considered that we would be separated during this process, even for an hour. I was just here to support them.

I have no fucking clue how to care for this baby that is screaming and needing and breathing for the first time. My body feels tense, awkward, unnatural. "Skin to skin is comforting," says a nurse, guiding me from the hallway into an empty recovery room. I unbutton my shirt and lay the baby on my chest. My breathing feels tight. My movements feel like someone else's. Is this how it happens? Nurses keep poking their heads in, asking if I need anything. I don't know how to reply. The babe is still crying. Singing is comforting, one of them says. So I stand with her and sing something and rock and wait and wait and wait. I feel dissociated from my own body and disconnected from this other body in my arms. We're both crying now. "Here's some formula," a nurse says, "maybe she's hungry." I take the hospital-issued bottle and put the nipple in her tiny mouth. It's a movement I will repeat thousands of times, but this is the first time, for both of us. She sucks and quiets. I take a deep breath. I sense this tiny body, so fragile, so strong, so close to mine.

I don't feel like a supportive partner anymore. These feelings—the panic, the tears, the visceral connection—this is me becoming a parent. I just didn't realize it yet.

My Journey to Parenthood: Ambivalence, Precarity, and Attachment

J did wake up from surgery, thankfully. And after we made it back to their apartment, I was there every day, every night. We made decisions together. Took turns with naps and feedings and burping. Split the night shift in half. We were anxious together, fell in love with this new human together, and supported each other through every step. This strange Pisces baby and I found each other. We chose each other. A month went by and I hadn't even been back to my apartment. J and I had to have some real conversations and talk about what this meant. In true Virgo-on-Virgo style, we made a chart, plotting our dreams and our fears, logistical and emotional, about moving in together, about parenting together, about jumping into a family and life together before we even had been dating for a year. But it felt like we were just putting a label, at that point, to what had already happened. I had—accidentally and intentionally—become a parent by parenting.

Both J and I struggle with anxiety at the best of times, and the postbirth trauma, profound sleep deprivation, and colicky baby of the first few months didn't help. I moved in, and we were negotiating a still quite new relationship, co-habiting for the first time, and simultaneously finding our feet (for me, unexpectedly) as parents. Most aspects of my life were suddenly, without even a nine-month prep period, turned upside down. Those early days, and especially those early nights, were pretty brutal. But I also feel such deep gratitude that my life took this dramatic and chaotic turn. What a gift, to get to fall in love with this baby, to fall in love with this baby with a playful brilliant babe of a co-parent. It feels strange to look back—now that I have been a loving and loved parent to this kid for years—on how easily things could have turned out differently.

Because of those possibilities, though, my early days as a parent were fraught with uneasiness about whether or not I was one. Not only was I not related to my child by genes or by birth, which caused its own internalized self-doubt, but also—unlike all the other queer non-bio-parents I knew—I had never been her intended parent. Surrounded by loving parents who had worked and planned and tried for years to have a baby together, it was hard not to feel like a last minute and incidental addition—a bit of a fraud. We had to navigate the expectations and puzzlement of our families, who didn't understand our ambiguousness and who struggled with our non-normative and last-minute family making. For months, I felt undercut and questioned by those around us, always having to be on the defensive. For months, too, anxious thoughts and internalized heteronormativity would sneak in at my most vulnerable moments. I would undercut and question myself: who was I to parent this baby? What was I doing? But these questions became quickly obsolete.

I was also worried about being seen as illegitimate and insignificant by the law. Worried that, should something happen to my partner, a family court would look at me—twenty-two, without stable income, without custody documents, without even common-law status—and not consider me the caregiver in the best interests of this kid, who was now so very much mine. (I am also painfully aware of how much higher the risk of Children's Aid intervention is for poorer parents, for younger parents, for Black, Indigenous, and other parents of colour.) Although the laws in Ontario have recently changed (so parentage for our next baby should be recognized by the state from birth), my still precarious legal position scares me. Now, at least, my very expressive four-year-old communicates loudly to the world about the things that are important to her. "I neeeeeed you foreeeeeever!" is her refrain these days, arms clamped around my neck.

My path to parenthood was unusual, hard (as is perhaps always the case), and profoundly connective. I had the chance to meet the baby to whom I had been whispering sweet words through my lover's body, and this small human and I held each other through our respective life transitions. We have done that ever since. And I will be her Yazzi forever. I am here to celebrate all the fucking magical ways that people become parents and caregivers—the strange, unexpected ways that kids arrive in our lives and change them forever. I want to celebrate the validity and strength of familial relationships of care and love—genetically linked, or not, legally recognized, or not, carefully planned, or not. We all deserve validation, celebration, and support.

Moment Two

The day after our baby was born, my partner's mom and sister come to visit. We are still at the hospital. Neither of us has slept in over forty-eight hours. We are still reeling. They come into our room. J's mom takes the babe out of my arms. They talk to J, ask them how they're doing, admire the baby.

Their mom finally speaks to me. "Could you step outside for a few minutes? Just so we can have some time alone ... as a family."

J is strung out on pain meds, after what was a disastrous labour, disastrous C-section. I am strung out on supporting them through the same process. Neither of us has recovered from the shock of suddenly being responsible for an infant. Neither of us has slept. Neither of us intervenes.

"Oh ... of course." I step outside.

I sit down beside the door to our room, staring at the nondescript walls of the maternity ward hallway. I read the posters about nursing and skin-to-skin contact and sanitizing your hands. I try to hold back the tears. They slip out anyway. I feel fragile, bits of me all barely held together. I try not to crumble.

Time alone. As a family.

The fluidity and indefinability and weirdness of our queer relationship render it illegible as "family." So I draw on queer legacies, on the strength of the many who have been pushed out of hospital rooms, too fabulous and too unexpected to be clearly understood. I draw on legacies of resilience in hard moments.

Young, Queer, Femme: Judgment, Identity, and Belonging

Having a baby strapped to your chest somehow elicits a particular degree of public scrutiny. Passersby seem to feel totally licensed to touch, comment, stare, engage, ask, and judge and judge and judge. "Where is that baby's mother?" J is scolded with these words two weeks after having birthed the baby by an older man in a neighbourhood bakery. "What are you doing out so late! Get that baby home!" A stranger practically yells at me while I'm attempting to soothe my baby, who has been inconsolable since she woke up two hours prior, with a walk around the block in a carrier. "You're an incompetent parent" is what I hear. Also, "what's wrong with you?" "You're way too young to have a child!" I am reprimanded by the woman ahead of me at a bus stop. The comments that are vocalized seeming to stand in for the judgement suppressed in glances and questions and unease and surprise.

I noticed another uneasy pattern, particularly when my kiddo was younger and when I was alone with her: that strangers in parks would assume that I was her caregiver or babysitter, sometimes even after I had indicated otherwise. I wondered what fed this stubborn assumption. Was my face too young? Was my hair too gay? My skirt too short and my neckline too low? Did the intersection of these not equal "parent" in the strangers' minds? I am always already crosscut by my whiteness, which changes how strangers read me and the im/possibility of my parenthood.

Becoming a parent launched me into new spaces and places, and led me to attempt to build connection with people who I never would have encountered in my life prior to the baby. This was a sometimes uneven and patchy process. Baby spaces are so often and so overwhelmingly straight—in culture, not just in the identities of many of the participants. I always felt like I was sticking out, like me and my presentation and my kid and her big feelings were forever too much. I was always navigating when and how and how much to disclose with well-meaning strangers about my kid, my partner, my family: when other mothers bonded over shared birth experiences and I had to shut up or out myself as lacking that history, when drop-in staff asked how my breastfeeding was going, when passing small talk took turns towards the cringe-inducing (about gender, most often), when, when, when. I couldn't find my politics, priorities, communities, and values in those parenting spaces; I couldn't find a place for my whole self. In queer parenting spaces, there were fewer assumptions about our story and more space for diverse ways to come into parentage. But I still struggled and struggle to find a peer group there. I am usually younger than many of the queer parents that I encountered often by a decade or two. And I was (relatedly, in part) less established—in my life, in my relationship, in my work—than many of those we encountered. Younger parenting may be more of a norm in many communities, but it was not a shared experience that I have ever had access to. (Once, I saw a poster advertising a support group for young moms. I eagerly read the details, but the dates had already passed. I was still within their target age bracket, but perhaps outside of their target expectations. I always seemed to be.)

Meanwhile, in many of my other community spaces and possibilities, parenthood seems either undesired or unthinkable or located in some distant future. None of my friends had babies when I had one, and none of them have had babies since. One friend came by and did laundry every week for the first few months of my baby's life; many others just fell off the map. Through my master's and now my PhD, it has been hard to form connections; I feel in such a different life place than my graduate school peers. While they bond over beers and late-night marking get-togethers, I am rushing off campus to pick up my toddler. While they can offer support and empathy for one another as crunch season approaches, none of them are doing it with a kiddo at home.

I also felt isolated from community spaces that used to feel like they nourished me. Though always circumscribed and elusive, a sense of a queer community had often congealed, for me, around events, per-formances, fundraisers, rallies, exhibits, meetings, and dance parties. But as is so often the case for parents of young kids, these spaces became inaccessible. Being suddenly unable to participate in events that once made me feel connected to something larger felt like a loss. Parenting is by far the most challenging thing that I have ever done, but it is also perhaps the most radical. I am forever frustrated by queer politics (so often those centring gay male experiences) that don't have space for kids, caregiving, and families (radically redefined! chosen and otherwise!) in their analysis or worldview. Although I have found ways to bring my family into community organizing spaces and have found people to organize with who try to be accommodating, my partner and I are still often the only parents in the meeting room—kid friendliness and accessibility so often falls on us to bring up again and again. I do sometimes encounter, of course, other weird rad queers with kids. These encounters don't always solidify into relationships (made that much more difficult by the tricky logistics and schedules of having young kids to begin with), but the flickers of recognition feel connective nonetheless.

Disclosing my queerness or my femmeness or my non-monogamous relationship with a nonbinary trans partner, may be at issue in the wider (and especially parenting) world. But among people who are in my life and communities, my biggest coming out moment is disclosing my age. This generates surprise more often than not, given that many of my friends and peers are much older than me and that many carry with them particular ideas about what being young and particularly being a queer in their early twenties means. For a long time, I felt ashamed of being young, afraid of not being taken seriously, and defensive towards people's shifted assessment of me when they found out. I would avoid talking about it openly and would push back internally. Age is just a number! It doesn't mean anything! (Read: It doesn't make me a less qualified parent! It doesn't make my perspectives less valuable!). This defensiveness and insistence on sameness, on my young age not mattering, led me to repress and ignore the ways that my experience of parenthood and of my partnership (with someone significantly older than me) actually were affected by my age. My youth wasn't an automatic liability, but it wasn't a nonfactor either. I want to have the space to reflect on how power works across gaps of age and experience, how my coming into my own as an adult was affected by already having a child, and how my parenting is affected and enriched by my being young without feeling like I am compromising myself. The truth is that I never had the twenties that so many of my older friends now look back on and moved on from. For better and for worse, I had a narrow window of adulthood without the responsibility of parenthood.

When I told my boss at the time, a doctor and researcher who I admired very much, that my partner was pregnant, she was a bit taken aback. Well, she said, you've always been responsible for your age. Maybe, I thought. Or maybe you need to check your assumptions about what young people are capable of. I have always been told that I seem older than I am, and maybe this is true in some ways—it is certainly a tempting narrative given the contempt widely directed towards young people (or, flippantly, by people towards their younger selves). But I don't want to position myself as better or as more equipped than other young parents or young people. I want all young parents' voices to be taken seriously and young people's wisdom to be acknowledged and celebrated. I want young parents to be offered support without judgement and to have our diverse struggles recognized and our many strengths validated. My mom was twenty-one when I was born, and I am grateful daily for the skills and care that she modelled—short generations are a family legacy. Being a young parent is a resource, which, for me, offers energy, strength, and creativity. It offers me an exciting proximity. When my kid becomes an adult, I'll barely be forty—a time when many are having kids for the first time. All these choices and circumstances are valid and beautiful, but my own early ones should not be deemed less-than. Coming into parenthood at a young age should not be assumed to have been a regrettable mistake that disrupted my education or career, that hijacked my life. Parenting certainly changed my life, but it made it more beautiful as well as more difficult, and made me so much stronger in the process.

Existing at an unusual overlap of identities and experiences has made my journey through parenthood sometimes feel like a lonely one. Of course, shared parenthood or shared queerness or shared youth or shared politics are not necessary for maintaining or forming relationships— but becoming a parent is certainly a life-altering, landscape-shifting, and thought-consuming change, and one inflected for me by the other, always interrelated parts of who I am. Although I haven't found anyone whose experiences and perspectives mirror mine in all the ways, I have found people whose experiences and perspectives complement mine in some of the ways. I have found support and belonging across different points of commonality and difference. There are queer dears who are not parents but are active involved caregivers and are also trying to navigate conversations about gender with the kiddos in their lives; the mom I befriended through collectivized care arrangements who got pregnant quite young and unexpectedly and is also trying to navigate her parenting, partnership, and holding on to her own sense of self and purpose; an old friend who has little experience or interest in babies but provides humour and support for other areas of my life; my femme lover who reminds me how to care for myself and not just those around me; the parent and kids we now live collectively with as we garden together, cook together, and have raucous toddler dance parties together; the classmate who I can have coffee with to talk about our supervisors or swap papers for feedback even though our lives are so profoundly different; and my own parents who do their best to respect our choices even when they don't understand them and provide immense grandparental supports through the mundane moments and the times of crisis. And through tears, laughter, and decisions big and small, there is my partner and co-parent, my collaborator and co-conspirator. I never found a community that fit, never found ready-made supports that met my needs, never found resources that were aimed towards someone in my position. So I have nurtured relationships to sustain myself and my family and my loved ones. I have nurtured care for myself and my family and my loved ones.

Moment Three

Our kiddo is nine months old, and we're looking ahead to the end of J's parental leave. We're trying to work our way into a neighbourhood home-based daycare collective. We pick a day over Facebook to meet with the organizers and some of the other families who are interested in participating. I'm planning to connect with J and the baby to head over together, but they are instead looping the block for a later-than-usual afternoon stroller nap. So I go to the house alone, walk up the stairs, navigate through the tangle of strollers on the porch, and knock on the door.

I go in and sit down in the living room with the other moms nursing their respective babies. They're all in jeans and ponytails, and I am suddenly acutely aware of my lack of maternal accouterments. My body tenses self-consciously. I'm wearing bright turquoise tights, a high-waisted black and white floral skirt, a crop top, and a denim vest with a "femme pride" patch stitched onto it with magenta embroidery thread. My head is half shaved, and my tattoos peek out. I have a backpack full of books from my MA classes instead of a baby wrap. No breastfeeding happening here. I don't even have a baby with me to justify my belonging in this club.

I feel simultaneously so gay and (I know, it's my own internalized crap) so nonparental. These moms are sweet, several of them activists; one would later become a close friend and a support. No one says anything to make me feel uncomfortable. But I feel uncomfortable anyway. Not ashamed. Just out of place.

Happily Queer: In/Visibility, In/Difference, and my Fraught Relationship with Motherhood

I wasn't very practiced at performing "parent" early on, much less "mother." I never really got more used to the early years centre and baby time circuits, and—especially early on when pregnancy and birth stories seem to dominate mom conversations—it was hard to connect. We have so little in common, I would realize, exhausted and harried and trying to make small talk with a mom in the park, except that we both have babies. Is that enough? I forever felt like an interloper in straight spaces, an undercover agent in an ineffective disguise. I was trying to find a place for myself but always already sticking out.

The unpleasant flipside of my frequent experiences of out-of-placeness, however, is experiences of being forced into a place I was assumed to fit and being crammed into boxes that were never made for me. Strangers and acquaintances would attempt to read me and my family according to the scripts most familiar to them. J and I are queer looking, after all, but—particularly in the strange ecosystem of child-rearing—straight passing. (People see what they want to see, and ignore what doesn't fit the narrative. Because they read J as male, no one ever saw them as pregnant, even days before they gave birth. It was too inconceivable. And I am told that my child looks like me on a weekly basis.) The sometimes humorous and sometimes gutting erasure that come from being coercively read as straight (when it is not how either of us identify or experience ourselves or our relationship) mean that we may avoid the more overt homophobia that we might otherwise encounter. But it also wraps us in a web of lies and untold stories and misreadings and assumptions. It initiates the challenges of disclosure (What do I share and how much? When do I intervene and in what way?). It enacts a cost—the cost of not being recognized for who we are.

I felt a push-pull, especially early on. I wanted so much for people to recognize me as a parent, yet I also felt invisible by people who saw me as a mom and then placed all their assumptions about what that meant onto me. I know many people who came to parenthood in many ways (including queers, including trans folks, including nonbirthing parents) and who find home in the words "mother" or "father" (or whatever derivative of those they land upon). I have endless respect for folks who have defined and redefined those words and their expansive possibilities. But "mother" never fit for me. My choice to adopt an alternative parental label was not more-radical-than-thou posturing—it felt personally necessary. People "mom" me on the street and I cringe; that word doesn't feel like home to me. My trans-masculine, non-binary, birthing-parent partner didn't identify with either trad-itional gendered parent titles. And neither did I. We didn't want to be Mom and Dad, and we didn't want to be Mom and Other. So we made up new ways of labelling our parental roles to mark ourselves in ways that felt good and that felt true. We've been "Yazzi" and "Zazz" ever since. This is not to say that I don't share much with rad mamas, queer parents, and other caregivers. I absolutely do. Using a different parenting title is not to place myself on an island of unique experience or to isolate myself from collective struggles. I align myself with motherhood when it makes sense to do so, politically, in terms of shared issues, or personally in terms of shared experiences. But I am much more comfortable defining myself as a parent, and as a co-parent; as my kid's Yazzi.

Sara Ahmed theorizes different ways of being queer in the world. "The unhappy queer is unhappy with the world that reads queers as unhappy," she argues; unhappiness can be an embodied critique of an oppressive world and a rejection of heteronormative scripts of happiness (105). The "happy queer," on the other hand, is imbued with hope that "reimagines the world as if there is no discrimination" (113); it is marked by the desire to be like and to approximate happy heterosexual reproductive family making, leaving behind the many for whom that script is not desirable, possible, or even proximate (114, 51). Embracing being "happily queer" however, makes it possible to find (or take) happiness without adopting conventional ideas of what that happiness looks like or how it is achieved (115). It means being defiant and undefeated but not erasing struggle and oppression: "characters who are happily queer in the face of a world that is unhappy with queer lives and loves can be energizing, can give us hope" (Ahmed 118).

Ahmed's work, in the context of my confrontational politics and familial realities, generates a question: is it possible to be unapologetically and happily queer while also engaging in reproductive family making? I think the answer is yes. Being happily queer means not shying away from struggle, not pretending that the world as it is accepts us in our diversity and not leaving behind those who are still deemed unacceptable, and not organizing around approximating heteronormative promises of happiness (Ahmed 115-19). I think all of these things are possible even in and through the act of having and raising babies. Our "alternative kinship stories" don't have to include reproduction—but they can (114). Reproductive family isn't inherently driven by "the promise of happiness as 'being like'" (114); we can raise our babies in queer ways, with queer politics, through queer community and in queer families. Some might appear nuclear, whereas others might not—especially for those of us who are more femme, more trans, more politicized, less wealthy, less white, less mono-gamous, and embody other identities and family structures that might make it harder to integrate into homonormative scripts. We can or even must make family on our own terms.

"Yazzi" and "Zazz" are home for us. They are also strategic: an opportunity to start a conversation with our daycare about our family's sometimes invisibilized truths and particular needs. It is a way to disrupt gendered assumptions from strangers or grandparents about what our roles are in our family and our relationship, and it is a tool as part of our larger set of conversations with our kid about her parents and family and origin story—a way to intervene in the incessantly heteronormative world of kid's literature and beyond. For me, coming to find home in Yazzi meant embracing being too much, rejecting absorption into stories that were written by and for other people, and disrupting people's easy and deeply misguided assumptions about me and my family. It marks our family as different in ways that are true to who we are and want to be. It means being able to define a parent role for myself and a way of parenting in partnership. And it means also drawing on the legacies of my own mother, my own very involved father, and the many mamas and other queer and gender diverse parents who inspire me daily. It is resistive, and it is celebratory. It is happily queer.

Moment Four

Just last week, I texted our donor frantically. I'm ovulating! He comes over that evening. We make brief small talk, and then he jerks off in our bathroom. We do a pass off in the hallway. "Good luck!" He says. And let's himself out.

My partner is downstairs entertaining our now three–year-old, they're reading books on the couch. I sit in bed, syringe in one hand, turquoise Dixie cup in the other. Here we go. I lie down, my hips propped up on some pillows, as fellow queer baby makers and my family doctor had instructed me. Gravity helps, right?

With a deep breath, I take the plunge. It's awkward, it's weird, it's quick. For all the waiting and deliberating, this part of the process is bizarrely unceremonious. I've been instructed to lie down with my pelvis elevated for an hour. I settle against my leopard print pillows and take a requisite #inseminationselfie, sending it immediately to lovers and friends. I don't feel private about this process.

From downstairs, my kiddo has noticed my absence and starts yelping, "YAZZI! YAZZI! I NEED YOUUUUU YAZZI!" My partner tries to dissuade her, but she knows I'm still in the house and is not to be turned away. "It's fine," I yell down, "she can come in!" I lie there slightly immobilized while my weirdo family traipses into the bedroom and clambers onto the bed. Yazzi! Yazzi!

One gorgeous strange frustrating beloved gayby climbs on my face while dreams of another make their way towards my cervix. Queer parenting at its finest.

Endnote

1. I use "they/them" when referring to my partner because those are J's current correct pronouns, but note—because it is relevant to the experiences I am sharing—that they used he/him pronouns at the time of these events and have been perceived/read as a man for many years.

Work Cited

Ahmed, Sara. *The Promise of Happiness*. Duke University Press, 2010.

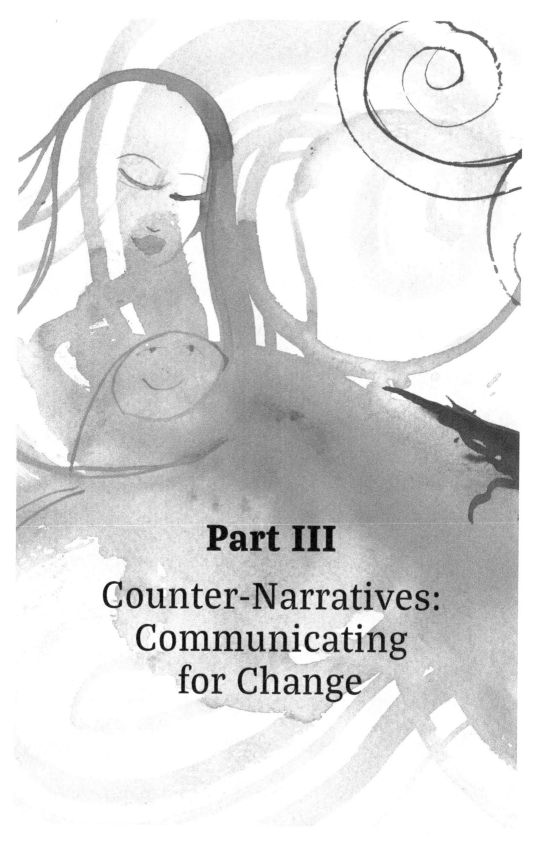

Part III

Counter-Narratives: Communicating for Change

Chapter Nine

"The Nurses Looked at Me As If I Had Two Heads— Because I Was So Young": Mothering in Suburban Melbourne between the 1960s and 1980s

Miranda Francis

Introduction

"The nurses looked at me as if I had two heads"—that is how, almost half a century later, Linda remembers her experience of giving birth at the age of seventeen. Attitudes towards young mothers have changed over the years, but the experiences of the young mothers themselves, at the time, were not consistent either. This chapter explores both these premises through the narratives of four Australian women: Linda, Lily, Rosemary, and Therese.[1] These women reflect, as older women, on the period in their life when they were, or were labelled by others, a young mother. These compelling family stories are illustrative rather than representative. They illuminate the continuities and changes surrounding social attitudes towards young mothers in postwar suburban Melbourne, Australia.

When Linda was two years old, her father deserted the family. Fifteen years later and faced with an adolescent pregnancy, Linda did not do the same. Born in 1954, Linda was brought up by her Catholic mother and grandmother. Both women encouraged her to finish school, and when she showed academic aptitude, they "strongly guided" her towards applying for a place at medical school. Linda studied hard and, at the age of sixteen, began a degree in medicine at the University of Melbourne where she felt "pretty lost" and especially isolated being one of only five students in her year from a working-class family. In 1971, at the end of her first year, Linda discovered the Billings method of contraception was not always effective. She was pregnant. Her mother called a family meeting to see what should be done about this unplanned pregnancy. Linda resisted family pressure to have an abortion but followed their advice to marry the father of her baby. Several months later, in the maternity wing of St. Vincent's Hospital, Linda became acutely conscious of her age. She felt that the nurses looked at her as if she "had two heads" because she was "so young." Pregnant at seventeen and a mother at eighteen, Linda did fit the category young mother. However, she was only a few years younger than her peers whose pregnancies were normative. Data from the Australian Bureau of Statistics (ABS) show that in 1970, the median age of mothers in Australia was the lowest on record. It gradually declined from twenty-eight in 1945 to twenty-five in 1970 and has steadily increased since then.[2]

Despite her youth, Linda does not remember her early mothering years as being difficult. Instead, she recalls feeling confident about her transition to motherhood. Other young mothers had quite different experiences. As has been noted by sociologists and historians for several decades, young mothers are not, and have never been, a homogenous group (Letherby et al.; Phoenix, Breheny and Stephens). Their lived experiences are diverse and complex. Ideas about mothering are also not fixed culturally or historically. One difficulty for interviewees is that they are remembering mothering experiences often from thirty to fifty years ago through the lens of the subsequent changes in society as well as their own lives. These decades saw new ideals of love, sex, and relationships, which fundamentally changed understandings of the Australian family (Bittman and Pixley; Gilding and Robinson). Social changes affect private lives unevenly, and this complicates the way these experiences play out in families and how they are remembered by individuals. As Ofra Koffman found in her study of young mothers in London, the problem in 1960s Melbourne was not being a young mother but being an unmarried one. The moral character of the mothers mattered more than age during this immediate postwar period. This began to change in the late 1960s and early 1970s when, as Shurlee Swain and Renate Howe have argued, shifts in attitudes to "sexuality, the family and the status of women enabled single mothers to move from a position of negotiation within the system to one of greater social and economic independence" (196). Around this time, teenage pregnancy became more problematic.

Mothering stories can highlight the interplay between social change and family lives. This interconnection is evident in two recent government investigations into historical forced family separations. In 1997, the Human Rights and Equal Opportunity Commission tabled the "Bringing Them Home: The 'Stolen Children'" report into the forced removal of children from Aboriginal and Torres Strait Islander communities (National Inquiry). The report included personal testimony from more than five hundred Indigenous Australians. In 2001, the Australian government investigation into forced child migration was completed, and its report "The Lost Innocents: Righting the Record—Report on Child Migration" also highlighted the importance of providing an opportunity for people to "tell their story, be heard and believed." The women interviewed for this study were not directly caught up in these forced removals but were telling their stories in the shadow of these reports. In volunteering to be interviewed for this project, these mothers also expressed their desire to tell their story and be heard and believed.

The chapter begins with Linda's and Lily's contrasting stories, which illustrate the differences between being a young, married mother and being a young, unmarried one in the early 1970s. These stories are followed by excerpts from Rosemary and Therese, whose family stories act as a bridge, as both women reflect on the differences between their own parenting experiences and their children's experiences. The generational differences point to the ways that families navigated and influenced shifting social mores surrounding lone and young mothering between the 1960s and the 1980s.

An "Awful Situation" Redeemed through Marriage (Linda, 1971)

Technically a teenager, Linda did not remember her family being worried about her becoming a young mother in 1971, but they were greatly concerned about her being an unmarried mother. She described the family meeting when this "awful situation" was discussed:

> There was a big family meeting [relaxed laugh] at which they discussed what they could do about this awful situation. I stepped out to the kitchen, and John's [Linda's boyfriend] father, who was a staunch Catholic, suggested abortion. But I'd been supported by my uncle, and he was Catholic as well, of course. But he had suggested that abortion would be difficult for me—as would adoption, in terms of the psychological aftermath. So, I listened to him. You know, I was, like seventeen [laughs]. So, yes, I didn't know what to do. But, I did listen to him. And it all seemed—you know, the prospect of a baby—they're cute, and cuddly, and all of that. I thought that was rather nice. So, yes, I was not making entirely logical decisions at the time.

Linda herself did not remember feeling too young to have a baby, and even when she was presented with the option of relinquishing her baby to adoption or abortion (which was made legally possible in the State of Victoria in 1969), she chose to continue with her pregnancy. Growing up in her grandmother's house with her mother who was a deserted wife, Linda knew she would have a financial struggle as a lone mother, as the Supporting Mother's Benefit[3] was not introduced in Australia until 1973. As a result, Linda bowed to her family's pressure and married her boyfriend.

Mothering itself, however, was not a challenge for Linda, who remembered coming home from the hospital and "just set about caring" for her son:

> I'd spent quite a lot of time with my cousins, a family of five, and I'd had experience with my youngest cousin, from the time she was six weeks old ... so I was not overwhelmed by the idea of handling a little baby. I was quite confident about that, yes. I know nowadays it's regarded as being extremely difficult. But, I remember the lack of sleep, walking the floor, lying in bed,

rocking him, trying to design something that would automatically rock him [laughter]. But, oh, I was not intimidated by that, no.

This fits with several recent studies that indicate many young mothers cope well with the demands of childrearing, once parents had accepted their daughter's pregnancy (Arai). Linda was not "doomed to poverty" (Byrd and Gallagher) and had a successful career as an occupational therapist. However, becoming a young mother at a time when formal childcare was limited did disrupt Linda's education. For two years, Linda struggled through her medical studies taking her infant son to lectures where he would babble at the back of neuro-anatomical classes. In her third year, she badly injured her hand and failed her exams. She decided studying with a young child was "just too hard," and, to use her words, she "left medicine behind." The regret about this was still evident in Linda's voice more than four decades later.

"One Day You Will Have a Child of Your Own"

The emotional wounds for other young mothers cut deeper—if pain can be measured. Lily also found out she was pregnant in 1971. She was fifteen. Lily's parents also called a family meeting to discuss what was to be done about her unplanned (but not unwelcome) pregnancy.[4] Despite coming from a working-class Catholic family like Linda, Lily's experience was quite different. Lily and her boyfriend wanted to marry, but both sets of parents objected, as there were religious and class differences between the families:

> We were happy to [marry], but phhh [deep sigh]! I remember that his parents and my parents had a meeting—when I was about seven months' pregnant. We weren't there! And so they must have come to some agreements. I don't know. Darryl [father of baby] and I had a really good relationship, we'd been together for more than a year by then, and he was the best thing that ever happened to me—when I was young. I was desperately in love, and he was gorgeous. He was working, and he was doing his apprenticeship. Yes, it was just my parents. Oh, and his. But, I mean their problem was that we were Catholics and my parents' problem was that he was a Proddie [Protestant]. Oh, my God! And he was a working-class boy, a tradie, dirty [in a whisper]. Oh, my God, can you believe that?

Being too young to be a mother was never mentioned by Lily's family. Lily was at high school and working part time in a nursing home for elderly people. She was "radiant with good health and beauty, in love, and having a baby." Her father insisted she move out of the house and claimed that Lily being unmarried and pregnant was not a good example for her younger siblings. Although her mother spoke about adoption, Lily "kind of assumed it would be all right." This continued right up until she went to hospital to give birth:

> As far as I was concerned, it was, it was seriously unresolved. Mum took me into hospital because I was induced. And, oh I remember it as crystally clear as ever. We walked up to the counter, and there's a matron with those wings, you know the hats? And Mum said: "This is my daughter, and she's placing her child for adoption." And I looked at her and went: "That's not agreed to, Mum." And the sister and Mum looked at each other, and the deal was done. Unbelievable! [deep intake of breath].

After giving birth to her son with the "brightest blue eyes like her father," Lily was pressured to give her consent to adoption. She explained the hospital social worker did not know how to deal with her as she was "really interesting mix of a person ... I was quite young and immature and naïve but I was strong." After ten days, Lily left the hospital without her baby but with a date to visit the Social Welfare Department to sign the adoption papers. The problem was Lily had nowhere to take her baby. She understands now she was young and naive:

> I didn't understand the world. I just didn't. I just, it just wasn't there for me. And it's like I'd been in a closet, all my life. But I was only fifteen. Yes, but like so young, inside my head I was—I didn't have the wherewithal to make the plans, to just put it in place and say: "Get fucked, that's what I'm doing." Even if I'd been three years older, would that have [long pause]? It might have made a difference. I could have perhaps had a better negotiation.

Lily kept the appointment and signed the papers to relinquish her son. Almost immediately, she changed her mind and tried to retract her permission:

And I rang them, the next day and said: "That's a terrible decision; it's the wrong decision, and I really want him back. So where is he?" And they said: "He's already gone; he's been placed with a family." And I said: "I don't believe you. I think you're lying. I only did this yesterday morning." It was nine o'clock the following day, and I was at a public phone box, and I rang them. And I went to see a solicitor and he said: "You haven't got a hope in hell; forget it, it's all over." And I said: "That can't be true," and he said: "It is. Go away. Get over it. Life will move on, you'll be right."

This attitude of telling relinquishing mothers "you'll be all right" and to get on with life was widespread in the late 1960s and early 1970s Australia (Quartly et al.). Another interviewee spoke to me about being pressured to give her baby up for adoption and being repeatedly told by family and friends rather curiously "one day you'll have a baby of *your own*" [my emphasis]. Lily did have four more children of her own, but the trauma of relinquishing her first child remains. It deeply affected her life, the baby's father, and Lily's subsequent children. As Daryl Higgins points out in his research on the impact of forced adoption practices, "time does not heal all wounds" (Higgins). Lily tried to put into words the effect of the loss on her other children:

I think behind all of it was this, a profound sense of loss, that I haven't really recovered from. I don't know that we ever do, really. You know, you can't get back what you didn't have. I would have happily had more children. But I think that that's because you can never have enough. It's like trying to get back the thing that you'll never get back. And so you have another one. So I think all of them [Lily's children] experienced, in their own way—in different ways, they experienced the sense of [long pause] my not-present-ness.

This loss has driven Lily's career advocating for the rights of relinquishing mothers and other disadvantaged groups, such as single mothers. Through her connection with women from the Council for the Single Mother and her Child (CSMC), Lily was pivotal in establishing the Australian Relinquishing Mothers Society (ARMS) in 1982 (Meggitt). Deeply committed to this work, she talked about being "on a mission" driven primarily by the loss of her son:

I wasn't present in the way that would have been much better for them. So I think there's loneliness for them, in that. They all love me, deeply, in a more attached way than I see other children with their parents. But I think it's laced with a sense of loss [pause]. I always had something else that was really important, and in a way it was [her relinquished son]. You know, in a sense he drove everything that I did, everything that I did was about repair. So I had all the rest of my children, at home, with a midwife, you know, I had my friends there. I'm sure it all stems from this one singular point, really. But I think that stemmed from all that had gone before, this intense aloneness, of child-hood, the not-being-loved-ness, because Darryl [father of her son] loved me. I felt loved. And then, I didn't. And then I didn't have my child. Then I had nothing—again [almost whisper]. Then there was nothing, and nothing mattered, nothing mattered as much. Oh, la-la. [drums her fingers]

Social attitudes towards adoption began to change in the 1970s, as there was a dramatic decline in the number of adoptions in Victoria and Australia more widely. In 1967, more than half of Victorian children born out of marriage were adopted. In 1975, this had fallen to only 10 percent. The number of adoptions in Australia peaked in 1971-1972, when 9,798 adoptions were recorded. Four years later, this number had halved (4,990 in 1975-1976); by 1979-1980, it had dropped to one third (3,337), and by 1995-1996, there were only 668 adoptions recorded in Australia.[5]

Families Bridging and Negotiating Social Change

These changing attitudes towards unmarried mothers and adoption are illustrated in another woman's life story. Lily met Rosemary through her work with CSMC. I interviewed Rosemary in 2016, and her story shows a shift in attitudes during the 1970s when the social opprobrium towards unmarried mothers began to move to teenage mothers. Rosemary was twenty-two and unmarried when her first daughter was born in 1961. Her daughter was the same age when she had her twins in 1984. Rosemary compared their hospital birth experiences at a major Melbourne maternity hospital twenty-five years apart:

In fact, it was quite interesting because nobody said I was too young, although a lot of people said I was immoral—I was aware that that was the prevailing view, you know. And when my daughter had her twins [in 1984], she was also twenty-one, coming on twenty-two, and nobody said she was immoral, but lots of people said she was too young! [relaxed laugh], and it was an interesting change of views.

Barbara Hanna's observation that contemporary teenage mothers live "publicly examined lives" applied to Rosemary as an unmarried mother in 1960s Melbourne (Hanna 460). So much so that Rosemary only felt able to begin her political activism for unmarried mothers after she married:

Not while I was single, while I was single I was up to there, busy, you know, just surviving. And so it was only after I got married, and I was kind of safe and it was, it felt like, just having, you know, two children and another one expected, and being safely married, felt really easy and secure, compared with, you know, being a single mother. I mean I remember when I was a single mother. I remember just thinking, feeling as though there was a cliff just over there, and I wasn't quite sure what'd happen when I got to the cliff, you know, so it was quite a scary time. And I remember also when I was pregnant, the feeling that I'd been surfing, and suddenly I'd got dumped, you know, yes, it was an interesting, you know.

"You Know It's a Young Mum These Days If You're Thirty!"

Rosemary and Lily worked tirelessly to remove the social and legal stigma associated with being an unmarried mother. However, social disapproval shifted to a new group: teenage mothers. This negative discourse that marginalizes and stigmatizes teenage mothers appears to be common throughout Western countries, as Helen Wilson and Annette Huntington have shown in their study of teenage motherhood in United States, United Kingdom and New Zealand. The constant theme among the countries has been a social concern with what Mary

Breheny and Christine Stephens identified in New Zealand as being "as much about the wrong sort of young women becoming mothers, as mothering too soon" (Breheny and Stephens 307). Young single parents (and especially mothers) remain one of the most socially disadvantaged groups in Australia, especially under the current "welfare to work policies," which Kay Cook demonstrates have affected single mothers disproportionately (Cook et al.; Cook and Noblet).

Young mothers comprise a large proportion of Australia's homeless population (Keys). Young, single mothers are particularly vulnerable and are often the focus of stigmatization, as Elizabeth Yardley has identified in Britain. A 2017 newspaper article on teenage parents reported a fifteen-year-old mother had "felt the pressure from some friends, family and doctors to have an abortion" (Lamperd 10). There is also political condemnation as Maggie Kirkman and her colleagues have identified. In her 2016 maiden speech to the Australian Senate, far-right politician Pauline Hanson specifically identified teenage single mothers as a drain on the Australian taxpayer and not deserving of welfare, unlike the aged and sick. She made a distinction between "single mums having more children just to maintain their welfare payments" and "wronged" mothers who had babies while married:

I am not speaking of women whose marriages breakdown and who then find themselves in the position of having to raise their children without the help of the father. My concern is for those who start young with children out of wedlock and then repeat the performance—in many cases with a different man... it is not in the real interests of the mothers or the children, especially when the mother is little more than a child herself. The cost to the taxpayer for teenage sole parents alone currently runs to over 120 million dollars a year.

The senator called on her "experience not only as a mum myself but also as a grandmother" to support her position. Interestingly, she did not identify herself a single mom, although she had mothered outside marriage for many years and first became a mother herself when a teenager. Senator Hanson's reticence about her own experience of lone motherhood and her harsh criticisms of young single mums suggests, as April Gallwey has shown in Britain, changes in attitudes to young mothers in the Australian context have also been complex and not necessarily linear.

Given that young mothers are not a homogenous group, it is not surprising that community attitudes towards young mothers are also not uniform. Therese was married at twenty in 1977 and had her first child three years later. In early 1980s Australia, she was not too young to be a mother. However, she recalled being perceived as young, as she was short and looked young: "Oh, I don't think I did feel young because we'd been going out together for four years. I think because I'm little, I know I looked very young, and people were a bit surprised, you know, that I was as old as I was. I think they thought I was really quite young, yes, so I got treated quite young." Melissa Kearney and Phillip Levine point out that an unplanned pregnancy does not equate with an unwanted pregnancy (162). The median age of first-time mothers was increasing in the 1980s, and this has trend continued. As Therese pointed out, "it's a young mum these days if you're thirty." Therese's son Gareth became a father in 2005, at the age of nineteen. This is considered young in twenty-first-century Australia. The median age for fathers has also been increasing since the 1970s. In 2005, it was 32.9 years. This means young parents are more conspicuous, especially in suburban Melbourne.

A recent newspaper article about a university Young Mums Program reports a woman saying, "I'd never seen a 14-year-old with a baby before. You can read about it but it's not the same" (Kermond). Therese's son and his partner met the challenge of becoming young parents, and, as several studies have also shown, this has strengthened wider family relationships (Shea et al.). Therese fondly remembered her son taking on the responsibility of being a father:

I think, because he was a dad so young. Oh, it was just beautiful, watching him being such a wonderful parent to those boys. I think we got a lot closer because he very quickly went from being a teenager, who didn't really know what he wanted, to being a responsible dad, which he was. And he took that responsibility very well; they both did. They've been brilliant parents. The best parents you can imagine. They're just amazing, so in tune with the children, and their activities, they spend so much time. It's just lovely to see, the way they're so involved.

Conclusion: Mothering out of Sequence with Social Norms

This chapter began by suggesting that attitudes in society towards mothering have changed over the past fifty years. As Rosemary's experience shows, the social expectations that influence families and within which they must function, also change. The criticism levelled at Rosemary as a young unmarried mother that she was immoral was not the same as that directed at her daughter that she was too young. Rosemary's family became the arena in which the social pressures were exhibited as well as shaped. By focusing closely on the lived experiences of mothers like Rosemary, this chapter has outlined not so much the process of change in social attitudes towards young mothers but how individual families have coped with these shifts and made decisions within these frameworks. It has captured the voices of women whose family lives have been affected by these shifting mores and shown their lasting impact across generations. Most importantly, it has also shown how mothers have been influential in modifying social attitudes surrounding mothering. Families matter, especially when mothering happens at a time that is out of sequence with current social norms.

Endnotes

1. As preferred by the interviewees, the real names of research participants have been used in this chapter.

2. In 2015, births to mothers aged nineteen years and under continued to decline both in number (8,574) and proportion of all births (2.8 percent). In comparison to other countries, the teenage fertility rate of 11.9 births per 1,000 women was very close to Canada (11.1), less than New Zealand (18.5) and less than England and Wales (14.5). For more details see The Australian Bureau of Statistics, "Births Registered."

3. The supporting mother's benefit was a government payment for single mothers not eligible for the widow's pension. It was introduced in 1973 following a campaign by the National Council for the Single Mother and Her Child (NSCMC), which evolved from the Victorian Based Council for the Single Mother and Her Child (CSMC).

4. There was a cooperative crèche on campus at the University of Melbourne (Melbourne University Family Club established in 1965), but it relied on parents putting in equivalent time, and Linda's medical degree was a fulltime course.

5. For more details see The Australian Bureau of Statistics, "Family Formation: Adoptions."

Works Cited

Arai, Lisa. "What a Difference a Decade Makes: Rethinking Teenage Pregnancy as a Problem." *Social Policy and Society,* vol. 8, no. 2, 2009, pp. 171-83.

Australia. Parliament. Senate. Community Affairs References Committee., Rosemary Crowley, Honourable, (speaker), and Australia. Parliament. Senate. Community Affairs Rewferences Committee. "Lost Innocents : Righting the Record: Report on Child Migration." Canberra Senate Community Affairs References Committee Secretariat, 2001.

Australian Bureau of Statistics. "Births Registered." *ABS,* 2018, www.abs.gov.au/ausstats/abs@.nsf/mf/3301.0. Accessed 18 June 2019.

Australian Bureau of Statistics. "The Number of Adoptions. "Family Formation: Adoptions," *ABS,* 2018, www.abs.gov.au/AUSSTATS/abs@.nsf/2f762f95845417aeca25706c00834efa/c14cbc586a02bfd7ca2570ec001909fc!OpenDocument. Accessed 18 June 2019.

Bittman, Michael, and Jocelyn F. Pixley. *The Double Life of the Family.* Allen & Unwin, 1997.

Breheny, Mary, and Christine Stephens. "Youth or Disadvantage? The Construction of Teenage Mothers in Medical Journals." *Culture, Health & Sexuality,* vol. 12, no.3, 2010, pp. 307-22.

Byrd, Deborah, and Rachel Gallagher. "Avoiding the "Doomed to Poverty" Narrative: Words of Wisdom from Teenage Single Mothers." *Journal of the Association for Research on Mothering,* vol. 11, no. 2, 2009, pp. 66-84.

Cook, Kay, et al. "The Quality of Life of Single Mothers Making the Transition from Welfare to Work." *Women & Health,* vol. 49, no. 6-7, 2009, pp. 475-90.

Cook, Kay, and Andrew Noblet. "Job Satisfaction and 'Welfare-to-Work': Is Any Job a Good Job for Australian Single Mothers?" *Australian Journal of Social Issues*, vol. 47, no. 2, 2012, pp. 203-19.

Gallwey, April. "Love Beyond the Frame: Stories of Maternal Love Outside Marriage in the 1950s and 1960s." *Love and Romance in Britain, 1918-1970*, edited by Alana Harris and Timothy Willem Jones, Palgrave Macmillan, 2014, pp. 100-23.

Gilding, Michael, and Peter Robinson. *Australian Families: A Comparative Perspective*. Addison Wesley Longman, 1997.

Hanna, Barbara. "Negotiating Motherhood: The Struggles of Teenage Mothers." *Journal of Advanced Nursing*, vol. 34, no. 4, 2001, pp. 456-64.

Hanson, Pauline, "First Speech." The Senate, 14 September 2016, Queensland, AUS, Senate First Speech, parlinfo.aph.gov.au/parlInfo/search/display/display.w3p;query=Id:%22chamber/hansards/16daad94-5c74-4641-a730-7f6d74312148/0139%22. Accessed 22 June 2019.

Higgins, Daryl. "Current Trauma: The Impact of Adoption Practices up Till the Early 1970s." *Family Relationships Quarterly*, vol. 19, 2011, aifs.gov.au/cfca/publications/family-relationships-quarterly-no-19/current-trauma-impact-adoption-practices-till. Accessed 22 June 2019.

Kearney, Melissa S., and Phillip B. Levine. "Why Is the Teen Birth Rate in the United States So High and Why Does It Matter?" *The Journal of Economic Perspectives*, vol. 26, no. 2, 2012, pp.141-66.

Kermond, Clare. "The Good Life: Lunch with Kerry Kornhauser Activist." *The Sydney Morning Herald*, May 2017, www.smh.com.au/entertainment/lunch-with-kerry-kornhauser-20170510-gwl5yr.html. Accessed 22 June 2019.

Keys, Deborah. "Opportunity for Change: Young Motherhood & Homelessness: A Report from the Becoming a Mother Project," *Family Access Network*, 2007, www.fan.org.au/files/Opportunity_for_change_young_motherhood_and_research_project.pdf. Accessed June 20 2018.

Kirkman, Maggie, et al. "'I Know I'm Doing a Good Job': Canonical and Autobiographical Narratives of Teenage Mothers." *Culture, Health & Sexuality,* vol. 3, no. 3, 2001, pp. 279-94.

Koffman, Ofra. "Children Having Children? Religion, Psychology and the Birth of the Teenage Pregnancy Problem." *History of the Human Sciences,* vol. 25, no. 1, 2011, pp. 119-34.

Lamperd, Ruth. "Mum at 14, Dad at 15...Not Your Typical Teen Dream." *Herald Sun,* 23 April 2017, p. 10.

Letherby, Gayle, et al. "Young Mothers." *Encyclopedia of Motherhood,* edited by Andrea O'Reilly, Sage Publications, 2010, pp. 1289-90.

Meggitt, Marie. "Take Arms ... Against a Sea of Troubles." *The Scarlet Letter,* vol. 4, 1982.

National Inquiry into the Separation of Aboriginal and Torres Strait Islander Children from their Families (Australia). Human Rights and Equal Opportunity Commission. "Bringing Them Home: Report of the National Inquiry into the Separation of Aboriginal and Torres Strait Islander Children from Their Families." Human Rights and Equal Opportunity Commission, 1997.

Phoenix, Ann. *Young Mothers?* Polity Press, 1990.

Quartly, Marian, et al. *The Market in Babies: Stories of Australian Adoption.* Monash University Publishing, 2013.

Shea, Rebecca, et al. "'Nappy Bags Instead of Handbags': Young Motherhood and Self-Identity." *Journal of Sociology,* vol. 52, no. 4, 2016, pp. 840-55.

Swain, Shurlee, and Renate Howe. *Single Mothers and Their Children: Disposal, Punishment and Survival in Australia.* Cambridge University Press, 1995.

Wilson, Helen, and Annette Huntington. "Deviant (M)Others: The Construction of Teenage Motherhood in Contemporary Discourse." *Journal of Social Policy,* vol. 35, no.1, 2005, pp. 59-76.

Yardley, Elizabeth. "Teenage Mothers' Experiences of Stigma." *Journal of Youth Studies,* vol. 11, no.6, 2008, pp. 671-84.

Chapter Ten

Reconceptualizing Vulnerability and Autonomy as a Way to Shift Dominant Narratives about Young Mothers

Erin Kuri

Introduction

As human beings, we are all inherently vulnerable to some degree. Some individuals and groups experience a higher degree of vulnerability than others. Situational factors such as young age, dependency on caregivers and services, and being a caregiver, all increase one's vulnerability. Traditional patriarchal and neoliberal notions surrounding the concept of vulnerability position those labelled vulnerable as weak, passive, and in need of protection. Critical feminist scholars have been working toward the goal of reconceptualizing vulnerability as entwined with autonomy (Butler; Fineman; Mackenzie). I argue that as a society, we have a moral obligation to support one another in building the capacities necessary to exercise autonomy. In support of this argument, I assert that instead of viewing vulnerability as a site of paternal oppression, in opposition to autonomy, we must understand vulnerability in relationship with resistance, as a necessary component of autonomy. The reconceptualization of vulnerability offers a counter-narrative to the way that the socially constructed identity group of young mothers is often portrayed in public discourse. Throughout this chapter, I will explore ways that traditional understandings of vulnerability are problematic for many young mothers and how a shift in the way we think about vulnerability could reshape the way society views them.

In support of my argument, I begin this chapter by providing an overview of vulnerability and autonomy. In the second section of the chapter, I demonstrate our moral obligation as a democratic society to respond to vulnerability and support capacity building towards autonomy. In the third section, I examine the tensions in feminist theory between the concepts of vulnerability and autonomy, making clear why the binary must be dissolved. Finally, I bridge these points of discussion with the discourse surrounding the needs of young mothers.

The themes of relational interdependence and trust will be highlighted throughout this work. The content of this chapter is heavily influenced by the works of Margaret Urban Walker, Catriona Mackenzie, and Judith Butler. These authors explore the topic of vulnerability and autonomy within a feminist theoretical context and within a feminist moral framework of ethics. I will also be drawing from contemporary feminist theory in motherhood studies with respect to discussions on the topic of young mothers. These areas of theory present commonalities with respect to their value of understanding relational dynamics in shaping the concepts of vulnerability and autonomy.

For the purpose of this chapter, young mothers are understood as those who give birth to their first child during their teenage years. This author acknowledges that not all young pregnant individuals identify as women with the female gender pronouns "she" and "her"; therefore, I will integrate the pronouns "they" and "them" throughout this chapter in an effort to be inclusive of youth who identify as genderqueer, trans*, or nonbinary. I acknowledge gender-based oppression that women in particular experience (Gladu) as well as particular forms of oppression, such as transphobia, experienced by pregnant youth who identify as queer (Trotzky-Sirr). Much of the literature I cite about pregnant and parenting youth refers specifically to youth who identify as women. This author recognizes a dearth of literature that focuses on the experiences of pregnant youth who identify as queer. Further research is needed in this area.

Young mothers are often portrayed in societal discourse as a homogenous group; however, they are diverse with respect to ethnicity, culture, sexual orientation, gender, class, age, ability, and life experience (Al-Sahab et al.; Byrd; Eni and Phillips-Beck; Trotzky-Sirr). In contemporary Western society, youth who give birth in their teenage years tend to experience stigma and stereotyping (Phoenix; Rock). The term "young mother" has become a socially constructed identity category shaped by powerful political and faith-based regimes that impose dominant values of capitalism, patriarchy, and white supremacy upon young women and trans* youth (Giles; Gore; McGrady; Trotzky-Sirr). These forces seek to control the moral conduct of society through the conservative ideals of childhood innocence and the nuclear family (Wilson).

Unrealistic ideals of motherhood are placed on youth by the state and members of society. False stereotypes depict teenage mothers as delinquent children and irresponsible caregivers (Darisi). Youth may also experience intersectional forms of oppression in addition to being labelled as young mothers, such as classism (Liegghio and Caragata; Phoenix), racism (Byrd; Clarke), ageism (Darisi), sexism (Gladu; McGrady; RedHalk and Richard), ableism (Savage, et al.), and sanism (Joseph). Such forms of oppression in the lives of young mothers can result in exposure to precarious living conditions (Fortin et al.; Keys), interpersonal violence (Crenshaw; Kennedy; Kulkarni, "The Relational Consequences"; Kulkarni, "Interpersonal Violence"; Leaman and Gee; McDonald-Harker; Young et al.; Willie et al.), and being labelled with mental illness (Meadows-Oliver and Sadler; Tseris). These factors contribute to a general lack of trust that many young mothers experience in relationships with authority figures and paternal institutions that aim to protect them (Kulkarni; Schrag and Schmidt-Tieszen).

Emerging feminist theory on the topic of vulnerability seeks to understand vulnerability as an ontological human experience, not as a derogatory state of weakness (Mackenzie). Many of these theorists, however, continue to situate the concept of vulnerability in opposition to discourses of autonomy, resistance, and agency (Mackenzie; Butler). Where does this binary leave marginalized groups such as pregnant and parenting youth? Butler states that resistance to the use of the concept of vulnerability is often grounded in political anxieties relating to the perceived risk of increased surveillance and discipline of particular marginalized groups. She also asserts that our desire to view ourselves as "agentic" (i.e., proactive and self-regulating), as opposed to dependent on others, may be in support of a belief that if we think this way, we will experience more desirable political consequences as a result (Butler 23). Butler states that such assumptions about vulnerability lead to "political misunderstandings about the importance of the term" (Butler 22). Walker brings attention to the concept of vulnerability within the context of particular interpersonal relationships, shared norms, and fields of responsibility, whereas Mackenzie asserts that "it is a mistake to theorize vulnerability and autonomy in opposition terms" (33). She insists that we must have a proper ethics of vulnerability that prioritizes autonomy as a means of ensuring that the concept is not abused by dominant paternalistic powers. In order to do this, Mackenzie claims that the way we currently understand vulnerability and autonomy must be reconceptualised (Mackenzie).

Overview of Vulnerability and Autonomy

Vulnerable can be defined as "capable of being physically or emotionally wounded; open to attack or damage" ("Vulnerable"). Mackenzie has theorized sources of vulnerability into three categories: inherent, situational, and pathogenic (Mackenzie). These categories are described in further detail below. Mackenzie asserts that this division is necessary in order to bring attention to our responsibility to one another as well as to ways that factors of inequality affect the distribution of resources that can support resilience for some while leaving others behind (Mackenzie). Resources may include physical, human, social, or environmental (Fineman qtd. in Mackenzie). Both Mackenzie and Walker remind us of the importance of considering vulnerability within the context of an individual's situation and personal relationships. Therefore, we cannot generalize among individuals, as they will have different contexts and their vulnerability will manifest in different ways (Mackenzie; Walker).

Mackenzie positions vulnerability to be both ontological in nature and situational (Mackenzie). She theorizes three sources of vulnerability. Inherent vulnerability refers to vulnerabilities that one is born with relating to "our embodiment, human needs, and inevitable dependence on others" (37). The degree to which we are inherently vulnerable depends on factors such as "age, gender, health status, and disability" (37). Here, we may consider the inherent vulnerabilities of a young person who is pregnant or the vulnerabilities of a young person who is postpartum and in relationship with their newborn infant. We also may consider the differences in context that may arise depending on housing stability, adequate health insurance, pregnancy or birth complications, infant health, or the presence of social supports to prepare food or take turns holding baby so the caregiver can sleep. Mackenzie asserts that in a just society, citizens should be able to rely on supportive infrastructure to mitigate the effects of inherent vulnerabilities and to attend to matters of inequality. Examples would include healthcare, financial aid, and childcare (Mackenzie).

Mackenzie's second source of vulnerability is situation vulnerability (39). This type of vulnerability relates to the context surrounding an individual (e.g., social, political, and environmental). These sources may be short term, intermittent, or enduring. An example for a pregnant youth may be the vulnerability they experience remaining on wait lists for priority housing in an effort to leave an abusive home environment, waiting for childcare so that they can seek employment, or struggling to make ends meet while trying to complete their high school diploma.

Mackenzie's third source of vulnerability is pathogenic vulnerability (Mackenzie 39). This category is identified as a subset of inherent and situational vulnerability. Pathogenic vulnerability is described as "arising from prejudice or abuse in interpersonal relationships and from social domination, oppression, or political violence" (Mackenzie 39). Understanding vulnerability in this way helps to identify how some interventions that aim to support individuals experiencing inherent or situational vulnerability may do more harm than good. An example of pathogenic vulnerability for pregnant youth may include experiences in which services that aim to support them are carried out by service providers holding racist, ageist, transphobic, or faith-based beliefs that result in conscious or unconscious judgment or poor-quality service provision.

Autonomy can be described as "self-directing freedom and especially moral independence" ("Autonomy"). Mackenzie argues that dominant discourse surrounding this term demonstrates a connection with individualist values that place increased responsibility onto individuals and minimize any responsibility that the state has for the welfare of its citizens (Mackenzie). Walker describes a mythical "autonomous man" who represents an ideal version of autonomy and the moral agent within moral philosophy (Walker). He is described as "disembodied, disembedded, unencumbered, affectless, isolated, detached, unpleasantly self-interested, defensively self-protective, abnormally self-reliant, and narcissistically self-reflective" (Walker 137). She calls upon members of society to apply a socially critical moral epistemology that requires a close examination of how this myth of autonomy shapes a society's moral understandings. Walker poses the challenge to critically analyze how and to whom moral understandings are made available within a society, how responsibility is enforced, who is enforcing, who is made invisible within this system, and what the costs are to all those involved (Walker).

Mackenzie understands autonomy as "both the *capacity* to lead a self-determining life and the *status* of being recognized as an autonomous agent by others" (Mackenzie 41). She views autonomy to be an imperative component to membership in a liberal democratic society. She expresses her concern that feminist vulnerability theorists who view autonomy to be connected with masculinist ideals of individuality make a mistake when they wholly reject the concept. Instead, she suggests looking to relational theories of autonomy that view capacity and status within a framework of interdependent relationships (Mackenzie). This view is aligned with Walker's expressive collaborative model that examines how members of a given moral community may come to know and understand what is expected of them morally, how to live respectfully and harmoniously among one another, and how to make amends when harm has been done (Walker). Within this feminist model, Walker considers relational facets of power, oppression, domination, corruption, transparency, and accountability.

Efforts to support increased autonomy for members of society (particularly those most vulnerable) require focusing on building particular skills and capacities (Mackenzie). Mackenzie identifies five areas of focus with respect to capacity building in alignment with values of relational autonomy. The first area relates to cognitive skills such as reasoning and information processing. The second area focuses on one's ability to critically reflect and question societal norms. The third area focuses on more introspective skills that allow one to engage the reflective practice of understanding oneself. The fourth area focuses on emotional capacities relating to attunement and empathy that support one's ability to sustain interpersonal relationships and engage with others in a cooperative manner, whereas the final area focuses on imaginative capacities that support one's ability to envision alternative narratives and ways of existing within the world. Such concrete suggestions lend supportive direction to community leaders, organizations, and individuals who wish to support one another in attending to matters of vulnerability. These areas of focus could be intentionally integrated by community agencies in collaboration with pregnant youth with respect to the focus of programing and the manner in which the service is provided.

Moral Obligation to Respond to Vulnerability

In the following section of this chapter, I demonstrate our moral obligation as a democratic society to respond to vulnerability and support capacity building towards autonomy. I draw from Walker's works focusing on moral understandings and moral repair (Walker). The three areas of focus will include the following: the need for shared moral understandings; failures of moral recognition; and how trust and autonomy may be rebuilt in situations of wrongdoing. I conclude the section by drawing parallels with the values of relational autonomy.

Walker's book titled *Moral Understandings* focuses on the topic of "moral epistemology, that is, the nature, source, and justification of moral knowledge" (Walker, *Moral Understandings* 4). Moral understandings encompass shared social norms, when and to whom standards apply, how norms are credibly invoked, and at what cost. From a feminist perspective, Walker seeks to situate dominant moral knowledge within the fluid context of social knowledge. She explores the ways that social phenomena influence how we understand moral obligations and how, in turn, such understandings then influence the way we make sense and carry out our moral obligations within our communities. The positions of those who create moral knowledge must be questioned, as such individuals are also complicit within complex social systems that influence their perceptions of right and wrong. Walker demonstrates the imperfections of human moral systems and asserts the need to attend to these dynamics if we are going to learn from them, reflect on them, and effectively critique them. Most importantly from the perspectives of those who experience vulnerability, one must be able to understand when one can place trust in another, who will take responsibility, and how accountability will be managed (Walker, *Moral Understandings*).

As a democratic society, we have a moral obligation to determine whose voices are not being heard, which groups or individuals become rendered invisible, and whose vulnerabilities and needs for autonomy go unrecognized. Walker highlights the common tendency of humans to treat those viewed as "different" or "other" with indifference, fear, disrespect, and hatred (Walker, *Moral Understandings*). This tendency can lead to dominant groups devising erroneous common sense belief systems about marginalized groups as well as creating perceived moral justification for abuse, neglect, and erasure. Walker asserts that we are morally obligated to examine the mechanisms involved in how unjust standards of treatment are upheld—for example, identifying when certain knowledge is concealed and when questions go unasked. By making transparent ways that vulnerabilities of some groups are masked by those in power, space can be created to challenge such systems, which is necessary to work towards moral recognition, repair, and, ultimately, a more respectful and harmonious shared moral order (Walker, *Moral Understandings*).

A final step in responding to vulnerability is the rebuilding of trust and autonomy for groups and individuals who have been wronged. As members of a democratic society, we have a moral obligation to acknowledge one another's vulnerability, to care and advocate for one another, to ensure efforts are made to repair harm done, and to create measures to ensure that harm will not reoccur. Walker describes moral repair as "the task of restoring or stabilizing—and in some cases creating—the basic elements that sustain human beings in a recognizably moral relationship" (Walker, *Moral Repair* 23). Walker goes onto demonstrate how democratic societies around the globe have been attending to matters of moral repair as a means of healing historical wounds and moving forward as more harmonious communities. Moral repair can be sought through means of retributive justice (such as court hearings and prison sentencing), redistributive justice (such as victim compensation), and restorative justice (such as truth and reconciliation commissions) (Walker, "Moral Repair"). These ongoing efforts have resulted in mixed experiences of justice and continue to evolve with the inclusion of marginalized voices. Through efforts of moral repair, trust and autonomy can be re-established. Recognition of one's membership status in society can be granted or regained. Those experiencing vulnerability can be empowered through relationships with the capacities to mobilize and exercise resistance.

In this previous section, I have demonstrated the moral obligation to respond to vulnerability experienced by members of society. The three areas discussed included the need for shared moral under-standings, failures of moral recognition, and the need to rebuild (or create) trust and autonomy when harm has been done. These three areas relate to values of relational autonomy, as they all must occur with the cooperation of a complex social network. No one individual can achieve any of these three aims in isolation from one's community. In each of these areas, higher numbers of supportive allies will strengthen the recognition of marginalized individuals and groups in the face of dominant societal forces. It would make sense then that vulnerability and autonomy are interconnected. Vulnerability occurs in relation to one another, as do moral repair, the rebuilding of trust, and the development of capacities for autonomy.

Tensions between Concepts of Vulnerability and Autonomy

Despite connections that can be made between vulnerability and autonomy, a history of tension exists between the two concepts within feminist theory (Butler; Mackenzie). The following section of this chapter examines these tensions and present arguments demonstrating that the binary between vulnerability and autonomy does a disservice to feminism and to individuals and groups who experience vulnerability.

The first area of tension I describe within the discourse of vulner-ability and autonomy has to do with differing conceptions of autonomy. Many feminists aligning with dominant models of autonomy have worked tirelessly to shift away from degrading socially constructed perceptions of women and other oppressed groups as helplessly de-pendent victims. Dominant (i.e., white-Eurocentric-patriarchal) conceptualizations of autonomy tend to centre the notion that one can freely make choices and govern oneself accordingly. Mackenzie draws attention to the argument made by relational theorists that our choices and actions, however, are always shaped within the context of our social relationships and environment (Mackenzie).

Butler focuses her theorizing of vulnerability on embodiment and performativity. She identifies the human body in relationship with the social and political infrastructure that supports it. Butler argues that if we cannot conceptualize the body with an understanding of its surrounding context, then we place ourselves at a disadvantage by not being able to create the strongest and most relevant platform for social justice advocacy efforts.

Butler also examines the effect of internalized language: how we "act through speech" and how "speech acts on us" (Butler 17). This description of linguistic vulnerability helps us to understand how some pregnant youth come to internalize negative discourses, socially constructed identity categories, and stereotypes placed on them by society, which potentially robs them of the self-confidence and sense of agency required in their role as a new parent. Butler encourages feminist theorists to be critical of the desire to distance oneself from vulnerability, as this desire may illuminate one's internalized masculinist ideals of strength over weakness and individualism over relational dependence (Butler).

Another major tension within feminist discourse on vulnerability and autonomy surrounds concerns of paternalistic abuse of power. Paternalism can be defined as "coercive interference with individual liberty to protect or promote the person's welfare, goods, happiness, needs, interests, or values" (Mackenzie 47). Butler acknowledges that from a political perspective within the context of human rights and legal institutions, when a group is defined as "vulnerable," their power tends to transfer to governing regimes tasked with the duty to protect them. As this transfer of power is a justified concern in a society where extensive inequality and oppression exist, Mackenzie asserts that responses to vulnerability must be guided by values of relational autonomy, and justifiable, nonpatriarchal forms of protection (Mackenzie). She identifies that such responses are necessary to empower those who experience vulnerability and that such empowerment is necessary to counter the risk of being subjected to paternalistic interventions. Butler agrees that it is necessary to understand the relationship between relational vulnerability and resistance within the context of resistance to paternalistic models of intervention.

A third and final tension to be discussed relates to the belief that the concept of vulnerability has an opposite meaning from agency and resistance. Butler challenges feminist theorists to reconceptualize vulnerability. She expresses that vulnerability must not be viewed as an essentialist identity that may weaken the political position of women but should be "understood as a deliberate exposure to power" (Butler 22) and as engaged and embodied forms of resistance. Butler troubles the assumption that only those in positions of oppression are vulnerable. She recognizes that dominant regimes also have vulnerabilities and that they can be dismantled by oppressed collectives who form acts of resistance. Therefore, it is possible to mobilize vulnerability as a means of exercising power (Butler). From this perspective, Butler demonstrates that vulnerability and resistance are not in opposition to one another but are together necessary in order to achieve political social justice aims.

Discussion

I am going to return now to the topic of young mothers. Due to factors such as age, gender, and state of pregnancy, we could identify these young people as experiencing some inherent vulnerability (Mackenzie). They require supportive infrastructure such as shelter, financial support, sustenance, and pre- and postnatal care. Some may have support of their families, intimate partner, or communities. In a capitalist, white-supremacist, patriarchal, and transphobic society, many pregnant youth will not be able to trust that a supportive infrastructure will be available for them.

This chapter has demonstrated the moral obligation that both the state and members of a democratic society have towards groups such as young parents. Pregnant youth are socially excluded from dominant ideologies of motherhood in Western society. Walker's attention to the consequences of failures of moral recognition can be applied to young parents (Walker, *Moral Understandings*). Young mothers are homogenized, othered, and stereotyped through the influence of dominant political and faith-based groups. Such behaviour results in the perceived moral justification to shame, punish, and position young parents as needing to be saved or rehabilitated. This group, politically labelled as vulnerable, becomes subjected to paternalistic forms of intervention, as identified by both Butler and Mackenzie. Forms of paternalism may include harsh child protection and family court systems that deem young people as deviant children and incompetent parents; maternity homes that subject youth to restrictions and surveillance; medical services that offer little to no options; or social services that focus more on risks to society than fostering capacities for autonomy.

Although there are risks that this group will be subjected to paternalism if labelled as vulnerable, I would argue that it is still imperative that the inherent vulnerabilities mentioned along with situational and pathogenic vulnerabilities must be understood in relation to supporting capacities for autonomy. Mackenzie states the need to understand how issues of inequality factor into the ways that opportunities are socially distributed (Mackenzie). Vulnerability relating to poverty, food insecurity, inappropriate medical care, gender-based violence, racism, and transphobia are not challenges that anyone can overcome on one's own. As a society, we have a moral obligation to dismantle forms of oppression that force young people to be exposed to precarity.

The vulnerabilities that pregnant and parenting youth experience have also been documented to mobilize them to resist negative socially constructed stereotypes associated with young mothers (Kelly; Trotzky-Sirr). Many young parents battle public transit everyday to get their toddlers to daycare and to get themselves to work and school. They fight societal stigma and shield each other from judgmental comments. They collaborate in building personal and political collectives and in offering advocacy and public education. Many engage in collaborative social programs that commit to supporting their ongoing development of capacities to exercise autonomy and agency within a social infrastructure that cannot always be trusted to support their needs or the needs of their children.

Conclusion

Butler beautifully describes vulnerability as "a kind of relationship that belongs to that ambiguous region in which receptivity and responsiveness are not clearly separable from one another" (25). Throughout this chapter, I have argued that as a democratic society, we have a moral obligation to recognize vulnerability and to support one another in building the capacities necessary to exercise autonomy. This obligation is particularly relevant in the lives of young mothers who are situationally vulnerable because they are young and, therefore, more dependent on caregivers and services and because they are also caregivers themselves. I have drawn from feminist theories of moral ethics, vulnerability, and relational autonomy to present perspectives demonstrating the need to dissolve the oppositional binary between vulnerability and autonomy. These areas of theory were illustrated with examples from the lives of young mothers—a socially constructed identity group that experiences a great deal of inequality with respect to the social distribution of life chances and supportive infrastructure. By reshaping the way that the concept of vulnerability has traditionally been understood in a patriarchal, white-supremacist, ableist, and capitalist culture, we may then also shift the way we think about young mothers, their needs, and society's obligation to respond to those needs in a manner that supports their autonomy.

The first section of this chapter provided an overview of the socially constructed identity category of young mothers and then described the concepts of vulnerability and autonomy. The second section then drew on Margaret Urban Walker's argument that as a democratic society, we have a moral obligation to care for one another, to prevent social injustice, and to repair wrongdoing. The final section then attended to tensions within feminist theory relating to the existing binary between the concepts of vulnerability and autonomy.

The works of Catriona Mackenzie and Judith Butler were combined to contribute to the claim that vulnerability and autonomy must be understood in relationship to one another, instead of being viewed in opposition (Butler; Mackenzie). Butler identifies this reconceptualizing as a significant feminist project that aims to increase understanding of how "vulnerability enters into agency" (Butler 25). For pregnant and parenting youth, it is imperative to understand the complex history and relationships between powerful societal forces that either impose or fail to recognize vulnerability in this group. Through increased societal understanding of the layered relational complexities of vulnerability, young parents and allied members of society can mobilize to create stronger platforms of resistance towards lasting social change.

Work Cited

Al-Sahab, B., et al. "Prevalence and Characteristics of Teen Motherhood in Canada." *Maternal and Child Health*, vol. 16, no, 1, 2012, pp. 228-34.

"Autonomy." *Merriam-Webster Dictionary*, www.merriam-webster.com/dictionary/autonomy. Accessed 19 June 2019.

Butler, Judith. "Rethinking Vulnerability and Resistance." *Vulnerability in Resistance*, edited by Judith Butler et al., Duke University Press, 2016, pp. 12-27.

Byrd, D.L. "Young Mothers and the Age-Old Problems of Sexism, Racism, Classism, Family Dysfunction and Violence." *Mothers, Mothering and Motherhood across Cultural Differences: A Reader*, edited by Andrea O'Reilly, Demeter Press, 2014, pp. 487-505.

Clarke, J. "The Challenges of Child Welfare Involvement for Afro-Caribbean Families in Toronto." *Children and Youth Services Review*, vol. 33, 2011, pp. 274-83.

Crenshaw, K. "Mapping the Margins: Intersectionality, Identity Politics, and Violence against Women." *Stanford Law Review*, vol. 43, no. 6, 1991, pp. 1241-99.

Darisi, T. "It Doesn't Matter If You're 15 or 45, Having a Child Is a Difficult Experience": Reflexivity and Resistance in Young Mothers' Constructions of Identity." *Journal of the Association for Research on Mothering*, 9(1), 2007, pp. 29-41.

Eni, R., and W. Phillips-Beck. "Teenage Pregnancy and Parenthood Perspectives of First Nations Women." *The International Indigenous Policy Journal*, vol. 4, no. 1, 2013, pp. 1-22.

Fortin, R., et al. "I Was Here: Young Mothers Who Have Experienced Homelessness Use Photovoice and Participatory Qualitative Analysis to Demonstrate Strengths and Assets." *Global Health Promotion*, vol. 22, no. 1, 2015, pp. 8-20.

Giles, M.V. "From 'Need' to 'Risk': The Neoliberal Construction of the 'Bad' Mother." *Journal of the Motherhood Initiative*, vol. 3, no. 1, 2012, pp. 112-33.

Gladu, M. *Taking Action to End Violence against Young Women and Girls in Canada: Report of the Standing Committee on the Status of Women.* Seventh Report, 42nd Parliament, 1st session. *House of Commons/ Chambre Des Communes*, 2017, www.ourcommons.ca/Content/ Committee/421/FEWO/Reports/RP8823562/feworp07/feworp 07-e.pdf. Accessed 19 June 2019.

Gore, A. "High Risk: Who a Mother Should Be." *Maternal Theory: Essential Readings*, edited by Andrea O'Reilly, Demeter Press, 2007, pp. 756-60.

Joseph, A.J. "The Necessity of an Attention to Eurocentrism and Colonial Technologies: An Addition to Critical Mental Health Literature." *Disability & Society*, vol. 30, no. 7, 2015, pp. 1021-41.

Kelly, D.M. "Young Mothers, Agency and Collective Action: Issues and Challenges." *Journal of the Association on Mothering,* vol. 9, 1, 2007, pp. 9-19.

Kennedy, A.C. "Resilience among Urban Adolescent Mothers Living with Violence: Listening to Their Stories." *Violence against Women,* vol. 11, no. 12, 2005, pp. 1490-1514.

Keys, D. "Complex Lives: Young Motherhood, Homelessness, and Partner Relationships." *Journal of the Association for Research on Mothering,* vol. 9, no. 1, 2007, pp. 101-10.

Kulkarni, S. "Interpersonal Violence at the Crossroads between Adolescence and Adulthood: Learning about Partner Violence from Young Women." *Violence against Women*, vol. 12 no, 2, 2006, pp. 187-207.

Kulkarni, S. "The Relational Consequences of Interpersonal Violence (IPV) for Adolescent Mothers." *Youth & Society*, vol. 41, no. 1, 2009, pp. 100-23.

Leaman, S.C., and C.B. Gee. "Intimate Partner Violence among Adolescents and Young Adult Mothers." *Journal of Family Violence*, vol. 23, 2008, pp. 519-28.

Liegghio, M., and L. Caragata. "'Why Are You Talking to Me Like I'm Stupid?': The Micro-Aggressions Committed with the Social Welfare System against Lone Mothers." *Affilia: Journal of Women & Social Work*, vol. 31, no. 1, 2016, pp. 7-23.

Mackenzie, Catriona. "The Importance of Relational Autonomy and Capabilities for an Ethics of Vulnerability." *Vulnerability: New Essays in Ethics and Feminist Philosophy*, edited by Catriona Mackenzie et al., Oxford, 2014, pp. 33-59.

McDonald-Harker, C. *Mothering in Marginalized Contexts: Narratives of Women Who Mother in and through Domestic Violence.* Demeter Press, 2016.

McGrady, S. "The Authentic Lived Experiences of Young Mothers." *Journal of the Motherhood Initiative*, vol. 3, no. 1, 2014, pp. 66-83.

Meadows-Oliver, M., and L.S. Sadler. "Depression among Adolescent Mothers Enrolled in a High-School Parenting Program." *Journal of Psychosocial Nursing*, vol. 48, no. 12, 2010, pp. 34-41.

Phoenix, A. *Young Mothers?* Polity Press, 1991.

RedHalk, S.L., and T.N. Richard. "An Exploratory Investigation of Adolescent Intimate Partner Violence among African American Youth: A Gendered Analysis." *Journal of Interpersonal Violence*, vol. 28, no. 17, 2013, pp. 3342-66.

Rock, L. "The 'Good Mother' vs the 'Other Mother': The Girl Mom." *Journal of the Association on Mothering*, vol. 9, no. 1), 2007, pp. 9-19.

Savage, A., et al. "Disability-Based Inequity in Youth Subjective Well-Being: Current Findings and Future Directions." *Disability & Society*, vol. 29, no. 6, 2014, pp. 877-892.

Schrag, A., and A. Schmidt-Tieszen. "Social Support Networks of Single Young Mothers." *Child and Adolescent Social Work Journal*, vol. 31, no. 4, 2014, pp. 15-27.

Tseris, E.J. "Trauma Theory without Feminism? Evaluating Contemporary Understandings of Traumatized Women." *Affilia: Journal of Women & Social Work*, vol. 28, no. 2, 2013, pp. 153-64.

Trotzky-Sirr, Rebecca. "The Revolutionary Artist Mom and Baby League: Putting Young Queer Parents on the Map." *Who's Your Daddy? And Other Writings on Queer Parenting*, edited by Rachel Epstein, Sumach Press, 2009, pp. 133-138.

"Vulnerable." *Merriam-Webster Dictionary*, www.merriam webster.com /dictionary/vulnerable. Accesseed 19 June 2019.

Walker, M.U. *Moral Repair: Reconstructing Moral Relations after Wrong-doing.* Cambridge, 2006.

Walker, M.U. *Moral Understandings: A Feminist Study in Ethics.* 2nd ed. Oxford University Press, 2007.

Willie, T.C., et al. "Stress in the City: Influence of Urban Social Stress and Violence on Pregnancy and Postpartum Quality of Life among Adolescent and Young Mothers." *Journal of Urban Health*, vol. 93, 2016, pp. 9-35.

Wilson, C. "An Inappropriate Transition to adulthood? Teenage pregnancy and the discourses of childhood in the UK." *Journal of the Association on Mothering*, vol. 9, no. 1, 2007, pp. 9-19.

Young, M. E. D. et al. "Sexual Abuse in Childhood and Adolescence and the Risk of Early Pregnancy among Women Ages 18-22." *Journal of Adolescent Health*, vol. 49, 2011, pp. 287-93.

Chapter Eleven

Destabilizing Self-Destruction: For the Sake of Young M/others

Sunahtah Jones

Introduction

As a Black lesbian feminist scholar, who was raised by a single Black mother (who was also raised by a young, single Black mother), the pervasiveness of taboos surrounding single mothers and young mothers has always been conspicuous and inescapable. Within these ubiquitous spaces, I witnessed the ways in which young mothers struggled against the tides of generational poverty, systematic racism, gender-based violence, capitalism, misogynoir, and countless other institutions while continuing to work feverishly to ensure the prosperity of both themselves and their families. It was also within these spaces that I became aware of the immense weight of blame and dehumanization strapped to the backs of young mothers, especially young Black mothers. I came to understand the hypocrisy of failing to acknowledge the violent and systematic nature of oppressive institutions that ensure the layered destruction of marginalized communities while also shaming young mothers of colour forced to survive within such systems.

It is both dishonest and detrimental to essentialize dichotomous and cis-heteronormative notions of mothering that inherently demonize young mothers and single mothers. However, it is productive and beneficial to both think of mothering as an inclusive and dynamic act and to acknowledge the destructive impact of institutions of oppression that shape, and scapegoat, the experiences of young mothers and single mothers. Through these poems, I honour young mothers and single mothers of colour. I listen to them and denounce stereotypical notions that aim to violently strip away the humanity of young mothers and single mothers. I challenge our communities to recognize the ways in which we perpetuate our own destruction by choosing to ignore the experiences of young mothers and single mothers as well as the ubiquitous nature of systematic oppressions. I challenge our communities to do better and be better for the sake of young mothers and single mothers and for the sake of ourselves.

Reality See, Reality Me

I remember holding you in my arms for the first time,
encapsulated with fear and anxiety,
how am I to raise a human being with feelings of pure inadequacy
festering inside of me?
spreading like cool morning dew,
dripping off of the tips of iridescent fescue.

Underaged.
unprepared.
welfare queen.
another teen mom.
etched into my Black skin,
invading the minds of strangers that I will encounter,
hovering over me regardless of where I go,
never letting me out of their sight,
"Just another Black teen mom"
I am caste by strangers who know absolutely nothing about my life,
nothing about my determination to excel in all of my endeavours,
for the sake of my child and for the sake of myself,
despite the world's predetermined fate of young Black mothers in
my position.

In the face of the white supremacy,
patriarchy,
classism,
and misogynoir,
stereotypical opinions of Black people make you think that you
already know *who* we are,
or who we'll *become*.
I wonder if your preconceived notions will ever be jolted by my reality,
the reality of my forced assimilation into a society that refuses to view
me as human,
the reality that Black babies are labelled undesirable,
perceived as criminals and jezebels from their conception.

Less likely to be adopted,
doomed to age out of foster care,
condemned to the streets,
predestined to the violence,
gunshots and police brutality drowned out by the sirens.

I wonder if the compulsive stigmatization will ever lift its cloak,
forcing open your eyes,
making visible the unjust markers of "less than" ascribed to us,
note that none of us subscribed to this,
to systematic racism and generational poverty,
that treat my body like a commodity,
A simple means of production,
that is to be abused and deployed.

But when I look down into my arms,
and gaze into your chestnut eyes,
I am overwhelmed by waves of emotion,
through life we will row together,
protecting each other,
for I am your sanctuary,
and you are my ocean.

Young Mother of Colour

A young mother,
and a woman of colour,
forced to manoeuvre in societies socialized to prey on my destruction,
to such institutions, I function as a mere tool,
a human bar stool to pounce on and conquer,
but who cries for me?
who cries for my children?
who weeps for the Black mothers stripped of their kin for the
inability to completely function within racist capitalist institutions
that strip us "others" of our humanity?
who sobs for immigrant mothers?
forced to provide slave labour in factories owned by executives who
view them as nothing more than "illegals,"
armed with institutional xenophobia and hateful tongues,
such wrath is lethal,
who sheds tears for the mothers in Middle Eastern and African
countries?
forced to bury loved ones in soil still stained from detonated mines,
soil that is no longer home,
filled with drones that surveil the area,
cutting down human beings as if they were trees,
the same earth engraved with the footprints of soldiers of imperialism
who serve the west,
brown earth gutted from the excavation of resources,
oil, gold, knowledge, and human beings stolen,
countries misshapen,
who whimpers for the mothers subjected to forced sterilization,
invaded and abused all in the name of cold iron bars?
slaves to the industry,
dehumanization,
And prison windows barely big enough to allow a glance at the sky,
if any windows at all,
who cries for us all?

Chapter Twelve

Matrifocality, Maternal Empowerment, and Maternal Nurturance: Conceiving Empowered Young Motherhood in Miriam Toews's *Summer of My Amazing Luck*

Andrea O'Reilly

Introduction

Motherhood scholar Deborah Byrd argues that young mothers are "rarely invited to tell their own stories" (496). Indeed, what we know about young mothers has been narrated and constructed by dominant discourses, which in the words of Tanya Darisi, position young motherhood "as a social problem in need of remedy" (29). Young mothers, as studied in research or portrayed in popular media, are represented "as either unworthy choice makers or as passive victims: either fully in charge of their lives or without any agency" (Kelly 10). A major challenge for young mothers, Byrd argues, "is resisting the cultural pressure to internalize the negative stereotypes of young mothers as unambitious, irresponsible, immature, immoral, and as incapable of adequately nurturing a child's cognitive, physical, emotional development" (497). In this chapter, I consider how Miriam Toews's novel *Summer of My Amazing Luck,* a story about single young mothers living in public housing in Winnipeg Canada, counters these normative discourses by situating young motherhood as a resistant and redemptive maternal space wherein young mothers are empowered to define and live their own meanings and practices of mothering. More specifically, I explore how the young mothers create a matrifocal space at the residence they humorously name Half-a-Life and how through this community the women are able to achieve maternal empowerment through an empowered mothering and an empowered maternalism. Finally, I consider how the matrifocal space, particularly as it is enacted in Lish's maternal nurturance, gives rise to Lucy's quest of rebirth through which Lucy achieves self-integration within a self-created community to secure an empowered maternal subjectivity as a young mother.

Empowered Mothering: "Reclaiming the Power Stolen from Us"

In *Of Woman Born*, Adrienne Rich writes, "we do not think of the power stolen from us and the power withheld from us in the name of the institution of motherhood" (275). The aim of empowered mothering is to reclaim that power for mothers and to imagine and implement a mode of mothering that mitigates the many ways patriarchal mother-hood, both discursively and materially, regulates and restrains mothers and their mothering. More specifically, the overarching aim of em-powered mothering is to confer to mothers the agency, authority, authenticity, autonomy, and advocacy-activism that are denied to them in patriarchal motherhood. "Maternal agency," as Lynn O'Brien Hall-stein explains in her encyclopedia entry on the topic, "draws on the idea of agency—the ability to influence one's life, to have a power to control one's life—and explores how women have agency via mothering" (698). A theory of maternal agency focuses on, as O'Brien Hallstein continues, "mothering practices that facilitate women's authority and power and is revealed in mothers' efforts to challenge and act against aspects of institutionalized motherhood that constrain and limit women's lives and power as mothers" (698). "Authenticity," as explained in Elizabeth Butterfield's encyclopedia entry, "is an ethical term that denotes being true to oneself, as in making decisions that are consistent with one's own beliefs and values [whereas] inauthenticity is generally understood to be an abdication of one's own authority and a loss of integrity." In the context of empowered mothering, maternal authenticity draws on Sara Ruddick's concept of the "conscientious mother" (701) and my model of the "authentic feminist mother," and it refers to "independence of mind and the courage to stand up to dominant values" and to "being truthful about motherhood and remaining true to oneself in motherhood" (Butterfield 701). Similarly, maternal authority and maternal autonomy refer to having confidence and conviction in oneself, holding power in the household, and possessing the ability to define and determine one's life and practices of mothering, which means the refusal, in Ruddick's words, to "relinquish or repudiate one's own perceptions and values" (112). Finally, the topic of maternal advocacy-activism foregrounds the political and social dimensions of mother work, whether such is expressed in antisexist childrearing or maternal activism.

Overall, empowered mothering allows mothers to effect real and lasting change in their lives, in the lives of their children, and in the larger society. However, even as feminist researchers concur that empowered mothering is good for mothers and their children, discussion continues on how empowered mothering, as both practice and politic, may be achieved and sustained (Green; O'Reilly). In other words, how do mothers individually and collectively refuse and resist the ideology and institution of patriarchal motherhood? What makes this possible? Although researchers agree that "the process of resistance entails making different choices about how one wants to practice mothering" (Horwitz 58), the larger question remains: what is needed at both the individual and cultural level to empower women to engage in this process of resistance?

In *Summer of My Amazing Luck*, the mothers, I argue, can resist and refuse patriarchal motherhood and realize empowered mothering in and through the matrifocal community they create at Half-a-Life. By way of empowered mothering and empowered maternalism (discussed below), the mothers secure maternal empowerment to conceive, create, and envision their lives as strong and independent women. And for the main character Lucy specifically, an empowered maternal subjectivity is achieved by way of a spiritual quest of self-transformation that is delivered and directed through her best friend Lish's maternal mentoring and healing.

Matrifocality and Empowered Mothering: "Mothers You Can Be Sure Of"

Matrifocality, as explained in Kinitra D. Brooks's encyclopedia entry, "means mother-centred [and] describes a mother focused kinship system that is female headed" (735). Matrifocality, as Brooks emphasizes, "challenges the Western normality of the nuclear family" and reconstructs family "as a site of power and independence for women" (736). Cultures that allow for matrifocality," Brooks continues, "tend to be much more communal in nature and view childrearing as a communal effort, rather than the primary occupation of the individual family unit" (736). Matrifocality, as enacted in families or communities, affords women the "power, strength and independence" denied to them in patriarchal motherhood and thus makes empowered mothering possible. In *Of Women Born*, Rich, when describing a vacation one summer without her husband, details how empowered mothering arises from matrifocality. She writes the following:

> I remember one summer, living in a friend's house in Vermont. My husband was working abroad for several weeks and my three sons—nine, seven, and five years old—and I dwelt for most of that time by ourselves. Without a male adult in the house, without any reason for schedules, naps, regular mealtimes, or early bedtimes so the two parents could talk, we fell into what I felt to be a delicious and sinful rhythm.... We lived like castaways on some island of mothers and children. At night they fell asleep without murmur and I stayed up reading and writing as I had when a student, till the early morning hours. I remember thinking: This is what living with children could be—without school hours, fixed routines, naps, the conflict of being both mother and wife with no room for being simply, myself. Driving home once after midnight from a late drive-in movie ... with three sleeping children in the back of the car, I felt wide awake, elated; we had broken together all the rules of bedtime, the night

rules, rules I myself thought I had to observe in the city or become a "bad mother." We were conspirators, outlaws from the institution of motherhood; I felt enormously in charge of my life. (194-95)

In this matrifocal space, Rich is able to "break all the rules," "be herself," and "feel enormously in charge of her life." "Without a male adult in the house," Rich becomes an outlaw from the institution of motherhood and acquires the autonomy, authenticity, agency, and authority of empowered mothering.

The young mothers of Half-a-Life, I would suggest, are similarly "castaways on some island of mothers and children," and "without a male adult in the house," they too create the matrifocal space that gives rise to empowered mothering. Significantly, in this first-person-narrated novel, the women who reside in the public housing apartment are introduced before Lucy, the narrator, is. There is Sarah, who becomes mute as a result of a rape and who fights to keep custody of her son, and there is "the trio of women who practice witchcraft and treat each other's various infections and rashes with rare herbs and potions" (16). Naomi arrives at Half-a-Life after her first husband choked to death on his own vomit while drunk and her second husband sexually molested her daughter. And there's beautiful Teresa "with poor grammar and nails chewed down to almost nothing" (24), who discovers that her boyfriend impregnated her the same week he impregnated her neighbour Marjorie. Mercy, an uptight mother, reads books by feminist authors and is the only woman at Half-a-Life who works outside the home. The mothers at Half-a-Life "marvel at her routine. The truth was most of us were afraid of jobs, so our feelings for Mercy were a combination of jealousy and disgust" (116). There is also, most importantly, the eccentric Lish, Lucy's best friend, who is "the *de facto* mother hen of the block" (28).

"These women," as Lucy explains, "had escaped from horrible lives and had come to seek solace in Half-a-Life" (58). And although there are certainly complaints between the women and gossip among them, the women at Half-a-Life form a community of care and support. They are, to use Lucy's words, "one big rollicking, happy, impoverished family" (7). Referring to their designation as "single welfare mothers," Lucy says, "I was proud to be something finally, to belong to a group of people that had a name and purpose" (8). Lucy writes, "Half-a-Life and the women in it [was] a kind of shrine I worshipped. I had to, it was all I had. I really wanted it to be a good thing. I wanted the women in it to laugh all the time. I wanted them to be tough" (58). Although their lives are difficult as poor single mothers, most of the mothers, as Lucy comments, "are far more afraid of men than they are of poverty" (39). Some of the mothers are, on occasion, romantically involved with men, yet the women live their lives and raise their children in a community of women separate and independent from men. Thinking about her father, Lucy comments, "I get this image in my head of thousands of fathers rubbing small peepholes on frosty windows and standing in snow and looking into warm houses, watching their families inside" (21). During the day, as Lucy writes, some of the mothers "would laugh at the bleak humour of our situations" and "roll [their] eyes at the thought of trying to parent with some fumbling man and pity women who had to" (29). Lucy often wonders "even if [the] kids had their dads around, would it make any difference?" (9).

Later in the text, Lucy asks Lish why she does not ask one of her boyfriends to drive her for one of her co-op errands, and Lish responds: "Men are a nighttime indoors thing.' Going outside with them during the day with kids and bread and problems to solve would ruin it for her. She'd rather do it on her own" (70-71). And when Lucy hears the mothers' stories about their ex-husbands, she thinks "I was glad I didn't know who Dill's [her son] dad was" (22), and when she worries that she wasn't giving Dill a chance to know his father, she concludes, "but what difference does it make? At the very least, I knew I was his mother" (147). Later when she meets a man at a party, Lucy remarks, "I didn't know if he had a wife or kids, but I was sure he'd had a mother. Mothers you can be sure of, fathers, well ... they're the kind of people whose head always get chopped off in a picture" (127). The women at Half-a-Life—in their independence from men and through the female community they develop to support and sustain one another—create a matrifocal space in which, to borrow from Rich's words above, "they are in charge of their lives."

Rich argues that the goddess Demeter bespeaks "every mother's [longing] for the power Demeter [and] the efficacy of her anger" (240). In patriarchal culture, in which there are so few examples in either life or literature of maternal empowerment, Demeter's triumphant achievement in having her daughter Persephone returned to her models to women their power to enact resistance and effect change. In the novel, Lish can be likened to Demeter: as a mother outlaw, she embodies and exemplifies the autonomy, authenticity, authority, agency, and advocacy-activism of empowered mothering. Lucy tell the reader that Lish:

> had an attitude towards life that I wish I had. She did her own thing and she never noticed when people stared at her stupid spider hat or her long square-toed shoes ... [and she] let [her kids] do their own thing because she knew how much she needed to be able to do hers. She had successfully separated her identity from her kids' identities and so she could really enjoy them. She wasn't afraid to be alone, as I suspected a lot of us at Half-a-Life were. (56)

As autonomous as she is in her sense of self, Lish is also authentic in the way she mothers. Lucy writes, "She just let the kids fall asleep where they felt like and let the experts go to hell" (11). Moreover, Lish "never thought having the baby was the problem. She just wasn't sure she could handle having the man" (156). One particularly significant and memorable example that typifies the agency, authenticity, and activism of Lish's empowered mothering occurs when she and Lucy have dinner at a restaurant. At the restaurant, as Lish burps a couple times and laughs too loudly and her daughters "teetered, around the restaurant pretending their apple juice was beer" (77), the manager informs Lish that patrons have complained about the children's behaviour. In response, as narrated by Lucy, Lish pushes back her black hat, stares up at him, takes another sip of wine, and responds: "This is a public restaurant, isn't it? ... My kids are people right? ... If they're people, then they're part of the public ... [so what] you're saying is that your establishment discriminates against the young. You'd rather put them on a spit and sprinkle them with curry, wouldn't you? (77). Lish does not stop there:

> You people remind me of those other people who put signs up in their store windows that say "No strollers." Basically they're saying no women and children. Especially no poor women who have to cart their kids and everything else around in strollers. I'd like to see a sign in a window that said "No Suits" or "No Toupees" or "No Body Odour" for a change. (78)

As she leaves the restaurant, Lish takes out "a little bread bag from her Safeway bag [and] dump[s] all the quarters, forty-eight dollars and seventy-five cents' worth, onto the red carpet" (79). "It was," Lucy comments, "quite a beautiful thing to see" (79).

Lish's feisty and fearless defiance of normative motherhood inspires Lucy to enact her own. When Lucy is standing in line at the bank to cash her welfare cheque, she breastfeeds Dill and remembers Lish's words: "Feeding your child was nothing to be ashamed of and if people didn't like it they shouldn't look" (41). She lets Dill drink away, and when the receptionist tells her that breastfeeding is not allowed in the building, Lucy comments that she feels "like ripping off my shirt and shaking my milky tits in her face" (41). Lucy's most memorable moment of outlaw mothering occurs in a mall when her broken stroller crashes to the floor as the bank machine simultaneously withholds her deposit, and she screams: "I CAN'T FUCKING STAND THIS FUCKING FUCKING PIECE OF FUCKING SHIT NO FUCKING MORE!" (42). Lucy then throws the stroller into the fountain and walks into a Sears store, puts Dill into the first model she sees, and walks out of the store (43). Another significant enactment of maternal resistance occurs when Mercy, on behalf of the mothers at Half-a-Life, successfully blackmails Minister Bunnie Hutchison after she threatens to cancel the child tax credit by exposing the minister's bogus flood claim to the Disaster Board (98, 141, 213). Indeed, in their agency, autonomy, authenticity, authority, and advocacy-activism, the mothers at Half-a-Life achieve empowered mothering and realize the maternal power of the Demeter archetype.

Being young and poor, the mothers at Half-a-Life cannot be the good mothers of patriarchal motherhood; thus, they must imagine and implement nonpatriarchal mothering practices that, in their very otherness, open up new possibilities for mothering. Dawn M. Lavell-Harvard and Jeanette Corbiere Lavell conclude the introduction to their book *"Until Our Hearts Are on the Ground": Aboriginal Mothering, Oppression, Resistance, and Rebirth* with these words: "We, as Aboriginals, have always been different, we have always existed on the margins of the dominant patriarchal culture, and as mothers, we have operated outside of, if not in actual opposition to, their definition of acceptability ... we are, to use the words of Adrienne Rich, the original mother outlaw" (6). I would suggest that these words are equally applicable to the mothers at Half-a-Life. In creating their matrifocal community of women and through their transgressive mothering, the young mothers operate outside of and in opposition to normative motherhood and in their very unacceptability, they enact more empowering ways to mother and be mothered.

Significantly, Lucy's family of origin, while nuclear in formation, was also matrifocal in practice, as Lucy's mother was also an empowered mother. Remembering her father, Lucy says, "My dad was human when he was outside of our house. He talked a bit and smiled.... Inside the house he was dead, terrifying. He sat in the chair and silently shook his head at me when I made a lot of noise or ran around too much. On weekends when he wasn't working, he stayed in bed. We'd forget about him" (49). Lucy's mother, as will be discussed in more detail below, was a woman who "had always done what she wanted to do" (74). Recalling her parents' relationship, Lucy articulates the following:

> My mom did her best to ignore [my dad]. When it got to be too much she'd wake me in the middle of the night and off we'd go on the train to my cousins in Vancouver for a week or two. If that was impossible she'd run to the piano and play songs ... as loud as she could over and over until my dad left the house.... Once she spit into every pot and dish and cup he had washed and then threw them out the back door into the yard for all to see. (73)

The first full reference to Lucy's mother occurs after Lucy's resistant act of tossing the stroller into the water fountain, which Lucy connects to her own mother's rebellion: "I remembered my mother getting pissed off at an umbrella that wouldn't close.... The rain was coming down so hard it hurt.... I looked out the window and there was the umbrella tumbling through sky.... It was beautiful. My mom had thrown it away, let it go. I was impressed" (42-43). However, although Lucy's transgressive act recalls one enacted by her mother, she cannot yet fully appreciate her mother's legacy of maternal empowerment. Only through a spiritual quest of rebirth, delivered and directed by Lish's maternal mentoring and nurturance, is Lucy able to reconnect with her mother and reclaim her lineage of empowered mothering.

Maternal Mentoring and Nurturance

Theologian Carol Christ distinguishes between the social quest and the spiritual quest. She defines the social quest as "a search for self in which the protagonist begins in alienation and seeks integration into a human community where he or she can develop more fully" and the spiritual quest as "the self's journey in relation to cosmic power or powers. Often interior, it may also have communal dimensions" (317). Annis Pratt, elaborating further in *Archetypal Patterns in Women's Fiction*, writes "the purpose of the social quest is social integration while the goal of the spiritual quest is for the protagonist to integrate herself with herself to achieve selfhood" (136). I argue that because Lucy in *Summer of My Amazing Luck* is both a teenager and a mother, she embarks on the social and spiritual quest simultaneously to achieve integration into a female-created and female-centred community through which she acquires self-integration to secure an empowered maternal subjectivity.

The first stage of the journey inwards, Pratt explains, involves a "turning away from societal norms that the author graphically and specifically details" (139). With Lucy, her departure from expected societal norms occurs when she becomes pregnant as a teenager. As Lucy comments, "I should tell you right now how I got to where I am: single mother on the dole, public housing, all that. It wasn't a goal of mine certainly. As a child I never once dreamed, 'I will be a poor mother'" (3). Later in the novel, Lucy writes, "I thought about my friends from high school. What would they be doing now? ... Once in a while I'd meet one of them somewhere and they were always really friendly, promising to call to get together. But that never happened" (82). As a daughter from a middle-class family—her father being a professor and her mother a therapist—the expectation was for Lucy to attend university, secure professional employment, and later become a mother in marriage. However, the tragic murder of Lucy's mother derails her progress along the expected path; she seeks to cope with her loss by having sex with many men, which ultimately results in pregnancy and teen motherhood. As Lucy explains, "They said I hadn't grieved properly over my mother's death. That was the reason I became promiscuous, they said. They said I snuck out of my bedroom window every night because I needed to forget. I needed to forget, they said, because I couldn't bear the sadness of remembering" (3).

Significantly, as Deborah Byrd explains, young women who experience severe childhood trauma are "at a greater risk than other females of becoming teen moms—especially if they have experienced multiple forms of violence or family dysfunction" (491). When Lucy is barely a teenager, her mother is brutally murdered by a hitchhiker in a botched robbery attempt, and she "never got to see [her] mother's dead body on account of its being all beat up" (100). At her mother's funeral, she tells us that her "dad, all two hundred and fifty pounds of him, leaned against me in the front row and cried" (75). "I wondered," Lucy writes, "what was he going to do without her? What was I going to do with him?" (75). Lucy's father, devastated by the death of his wife and never having been an involved father in Lucy's life, does not provide the love and care Lucy needed after her mother's death and later when she becomes a young mother. Her father financially supported Lucy until she was eighteen years old but only because he did not want her to become a ward of the state, but Lucy never saw him and only received his cheques by mail. Lucy's father sees Lucy and meets his grandson for the first time only at the conclusion of the novel and only after Lucy's phone call to him (discussed in detail below). With the death of her mother, her estrangement from her father, and her unplanned pregnancy, Lucy becomes separated not only from her family but also from the life that she was supposed to have.

Another stage of the spiritual quest as discussed by Pratt, and one that is crucial for Lucy's journey towards a self-integrated empowered maternity, occurs when "an ideal, nonpatriarchal lover (either an actual figure or a revery one) appears as an initiatory guide and aids at difficult points in the quest" (140). "This Green World Lover," Pratt continues, "leads the hero away from society and towards her unconscious depths" (140). In this novel, because Lucy's physical and psychic spaces are matrifocal, her initiatory guide is not a lover, as Pratt theorizes, but is what Megan Rogers terms, a "maternal mentor." Drawing on the work of literary critic Maureen Murdock, Rogers argues that "the most important element for a protagonist to begin her ascent is a positive feminine individual. The fictional heroine needs a friend or mentor she can trust to help her cross the return threshold" (158). Rogers argues further that "by sharing her experience and knowledge with the protagonist, the maternal mentor, or 'wise old woman,' imparts the 'gift' of authority ... [and] understands, accepts and acknowledges the protagonist's new identity and role within society [which] allows the protagonist to learn from an experienced guide and develop her own authority" (148). However, for the maternal mentor to fulfill this role, she must exude an empowered maternalism: "the ability to employ care, nurturance and morality to effect change in one's own life and in one's community" (Rogers 142). To achieve an empowered maternalism, a woman must "assimilate elements of her private and public life so that they are integrated and so that both halves are as important and respected as the other" (142). Empowered maternalism also requires, as Rogers explains, "a transference of allegiance from a heterosexual relationship to one of intimacy between women" (142). Empowered mothering, as noted above, bestows agency, authority, autonomy, authenticity, and advocacy-activism to women, whereas empowered maternalism enacts self-integration and identification with women. Together, they form maternal empowerment to counter, as Rogers explains, "not only patriarchal motherhood but also patriarchal notions of how women occupy private and public spheres in general" (168).

As Lucy's mentor, Lish embodies and exemplifies the self-integration and allegiance to women that Rogers argues is necessary for empowered maternalism. Lish, to use Roger's words, "assimilates elements of her private and public life so that they are integrated and so that both halves are as important and respected as the other" (142). Lish has successfully separated her identity from her kids' identities, the two dimensions of Lish—woman and mother—are of equal importance and value in her life (36). Lucy tells us that when Lish "had one of her lovers over she'd lead him to the kitchen or bathroom or some room without children sleeping in it" (11) or "she would sit around burning incense and drinking tea and talking all night while her children lay sleeping in little heaps around her" (10-11). Lish honours and expresses both her sexual and maternal selves; moreover, although Lish is a devoted mother to her four daughters, she also has a full life outside motherhood. Lucy tells us how happy Lish is and how she listens to her music, cooks her garlic dishes, has fun with her kids, goes to the library, wears goofy pink dresses, and plays in the sunlight (161-62). Just as Lish integrates and values all dimensions of her identity, she also creates and expresses this identity in and through intimacy between women, as evidenced by the matrifocal community at Half-a-Life and her role as "the *de facto* mother hen of the block" (28). And in this commitment to herself and to the women at Half-a-Life, Lish fully enacts the demands of empowered maternalism as defined by Rogers: "the ability to employ care, nurturance and morality to effect change in one's own life and in one's community" (142). However, before Lish can fully impart maternal empowerment—empowered mothering and empowered maternalism—to Lucy, another task is required of her, which is maternal healing.

Maternal nurturance, I argue, may be read as a reactive or restorative practice: it seeks to repair women, whose selfhoods have been displaced or damaged by the hurts of a patriarchal culture, and it centres upon the recovery of a displaced selfhood for those women. Lucy simultaneously seeks to forget and to find the mother she lost through her many sexual partnerships with men. However, in repressing the pain of her mother's loss and in attempting to replace the mother through sexual relationships, Lucy moves further from her own original self. Only when Lucy mourns the loss of her mother is the recovery of adult selfhood made possible. To acquire self-love and achieve selfhood, Lucy must begin by being remothered, which is achieved by way of a spiritual or physic reconnection with a lost mother and by way of a reclamation of a lost or displaced daughterhood. Healing occurs when the daughter is able to remember the mother, mourn her loss, reconnect with her, and recreate for herself an identity as a mothered child. This connection, however, is not with an actual flesh and blood mother but with the spirit or memory of the lost mother. This psychic journey of return, reconnection, and reclamation, though directed to a spirit of a lost mother, is initiated and overseen by an actual mother figure, a close female friend of the troubled woman who serves as an othermother for her. In *Summer of My Amazing Luck*, Lish functions as this othermother for Lucy and provides the maternal nurturance that enables Lucy to heal and take the journey of remembering and reconnection to achieve the reclamation of the selfhood that she lost with her mother died.

Lucy arrives at Half-a-Life unable "to bear the sadness of remembering" (3). Half-a-Life is a place of refuge, a safe haven for Lucy, or as she describes it, "a shrine" (58). Lish's apartment, in particular, signifies a place of maternal nurturance. Lucy describes Lish's apartment as "a real home," and Lish would spend "entire days curled up in her big brown chair.... People would come and go and she would hold court from her brown chair" (30-31). Lucy marvels at Lish's apartment:

> It was full of junk mostly, secondhand furniture that she or the kids had painted, art from a lot of her boyfriends, kids' art, plants, old books, records, jars of organic food stuff, boxes of leather bits and material the kids could use to make things with, lamps with big fringy shades and two or three old-fashioned typewriters, photographs of her kids and her family, her great-grandparents, her friends. She almost always had music playing in the background and incense burning and big vats of soup or vegetables boiling on the stove. Mint and dill where her favourite smells, and she put huge amounts of garlic into everything she cooked. She had transformed her standard issue public housing suite into a marvelous home. I loved going over there. (47-48)

Lish's home—with its plants, jars of food, artwork, craft items, music and cooking—creates a sanctuary for Lucy and a space where maternal healing can occur.

Lish's maternal nurturance becomes central to and critical for the next stage of Lucy's quest: "a confrontation with parental figures in memory and from the past" (Pratt 40). Healing occurs for Lucy when she can remember her mother, mourn her loss, reconnect with her, and reclaim the legacy of her mother's empowered and empowering love. And it is Lish who delivers and directs Lucy's remembering to make possible Lucy's healing. Significantly, Lucy says, "Lish reminded me of my mother" (20). After making this comment, Lucy remembers her mother pulling her out of school to take one of their trips together to Vancouver and comments that "her mother was indifferent to school ... and never showed any interest in it whatsoever" (20). Lucy two pages earlier tells the reader that Lish "didn't trust schools and knew that she could do a much better job teaching her kids herself" (18). Lucy's mother had been a family therapist who counsels abused women; Lish, as the matriarch at Half-a-Life, serves as the counsellor for the women there. They are also both keepers of women's stories: Lucy's mother is killed protecting her briefcase containing the tapes and files of her female clients, and Lish protects the confidentiality of the tales related to her by the mothers residing at Half a Life.

Lucy's mother, also like Lish, embodies and exemplifies maternal empowerment as both empowered mothering and empowered maternalism through her rebellious mothering and in her integrated selfhood and commitment to women.

The novel's structure also emphasizes Lish's role as the conduit for Lucy's memories of her mother. An incident between Lucy and Lish often triggers a memory of Lucy's mother. For example, immediately after Lish receives a letter from the father of her twins, Lucy remembers and retells the circumstances of her mother's death (72). The most significant moment when Lish's presence prompts Lucy's remembering is on their trip to Colorado when Lucy sees the billboard where her mother's body was found. As they leave for their journey, Lucy comments, "All it meant was that we had decided to do something adventurous and then we had done it. If it didn't it work out the way we had hoped it to, fine. Who cares how it all ends? We had taken the steps toward something. Anything" (159). Less than an hour later and just as they are about to cross the border into the United States, Lucy sees the sign where her mother was killed, begins to cry, and asks Lish if they have the time to stop, to which Lish replies "Time is what we have" (166). This moment marks the final stage in Lucy's spiritual quest of rebirth—"the plunge into the unconscious" (Pratt 141)—wherein she reconciles with her father and reconnects with the memory of her mother.

Standing by the billboard, Lucy realizes that she was "spending so much time remembering my dead mother, I was forgetting to remember my father, who was alive. My mother may have been what I needed, but my father was what I had" (169). At this moment, Lucy experiences an epiphany of her father's life: "I think it made him sad. My mom, me, Dill, everything in his life hadn't turned out the way he had thought it would. I think he thought I wanted him to leave me alone" (174). She also wonders if her dad was "trying to slow his life down to somehow make up for the fast and furious pace mom lived life at" (175). At the border, she calls her father and gives him her number and address and a plan to meet upon her return.

The moment of Lucy's reconnection with her mother awakens Lucy to the importance of mothers' lives, however they may be lived. Lucy's mother "was desperate to keep [the records of her clients' lives], to preserve them and protect them" (167). And Lucy's mother dies while trying to protect them, telling the man about to rob her: "Look, you can have the car, you can have my money, just give me my bag" (74). However, when she reaches into the car to get the briefcase, the man, "freaked out [and] smashed her over the head with his gun ... dragged her out to the ditch, threw her briefcase on top of her and took off. A while later she died in the ditch" (74). Remembering this, Lucy asks "Why did he give her the files? The files of all those women trying to escape their lives, trying to find something better, trying to find happiness" (167-68). And the answer is her epiphany:

> Course they [the files] wouldn't have all the details, like whether or not they played in squares of sunlight on their walls, if they wore spiders on their hats, if they ate hamburger every other day, if they had ever made love in a yellow canola field tenderly or passionately or awkwardly. If they preferred dresses or pants, if they shaved their legs or didn't, or they preferred red peppers to green. Stuff was happening. Even in Half-a-Life. Little things, but it all added up to something big. To our lives. It was happening all along. These were our lives. This was it. My mom was hanging on to the lives, the recorded lives of these women. We might escape, but what if we didn't? What if we lived in Half-a-Life all our lives, poor, lonely, proud and happy? If we did, we did. These were our lives. If we couldn't escape them, we'd have to live them. (168)

Her mother's preservation and protection of women's stories reveals to Lucy that women's lives matter and that her own life, however it may be lived—poor, lonely, proud, or happy—is to be appreciated and honoured. Through her remembering of and reconnection to her mother, Lucy reclaims her maternal legacy—that women, their lives and their stories, are important. From this, Lucy secures a self-defined and integrated subjectivity of maternal empowerment as enacted in both empowered mothering and as empowered maternalism. In her study of the spiritual quest of rebirth, Pratt argues that the transformed hero "is unlikely to be able to reintegrate herself fully into 'normal' society" (143). I argue that in this novel, Lucy is able to reintegrate with her society precisely because it is a matrifocal one, which represents and expresses the values of maternal empowerment— namely, an intimate community of strong self-identified and self-integrated women. And it is Lish, as Lucy's maternal mentor and through her maternal healing, who delivers this new naming of Lucy's self and world.

Conclusion: "She Would Have Seen My Life, and ... Spoken the Words ...'Very Good'"

The novel concludes with Mercy's birth of a daughter, symbolizing the rebirth of Lucy and her realization of the importance of women's lives. We are also told that "since working for the Disaster Board, Mercy had a new life philosophy: to name what you fear, to look it in the eye and embrace it. And so she named her new daughter Mayhem" (212). Mercy's new found philosophy echoes and affirms the wisdom bequeathed to Lucy through her reconnection with her mother. Lucy's father and Hart, the man Lucy earlier met at a party and slept with, are present for Mercy's birth—her father because his home had been flooded and Hart to give legal advice to the landlord—and it is Lucy's father who Mercy insists be the midwife for her birth and who, in Lucy's words, softly "coax[ed] the new life out of Mercy" (211). Although the presence of men at Half-a-Life —in particular Hart who, it seems, will become Lucy's partner—may suggest an encroach-ment on its matrifocal space and its maternal empowerment, these men, I argue, confirm rather than contest the value and power of this very space. It is Hart and Lucy's father who clean the bathtub for the birth and do so wearing sanitary napkins on their knees, which symbolizes their attentiveness to and respect for the feminine and maternal (208). As Mercy births her baby, Lucy sees Lish "make a shadow puppet with her hand in the square of sunlight on Mercy's wall" (211), an image conveying contentment with self and life. And at this moment Lucy thinks that if her mother were still alive, she would have seen her life and, along with her father, spoken the words: "Very good, very good, very good" (211).

The novel ends with an image of Lish "in a square of sunlight" on the balcony wearing "a t-shirt that read[s] 'I'm with her'" (220). This image conveys and affirms the sanctity of their matrifocal community and represents the wisdom that Lucy acquires through her spiritual quest of rebirth—namely, that although she may be a poor, single young mother, her life matters and is of value. As well, the image represents and honours the maternal empowerment achieved and now enacted by Lucy. As Lucy remarks in the final sentence of the novel, "Half-a-Life. Winnipeg, Manitoba, city with the most hours of sunshine, the centre of the universe [was] home... And [her son] Dillinger Geoffrey Van Alstyne was a lucky boy" (22). In its affirmation of maternal empowerment and renewal, *Summer of My Amazing Luck* conceives, as both to create and to envision, young motherhood as an identity of both strength and promise.

Works Cited

Brooks, Kinitra D. "Matrifocality." *Encyclopedia of Motherhood*, edited by Andrea O'Reilly, Sage Press, 2010, pp. 735-36.

Butterfield, Elizabeth. "Maternal Authenticity." *Encyclopedia of Motherhood*, edited by Andrea O'Reilly, Sage Press, 2010, pp. 700-1.

Christ, Carol. "Spiritual Quest and Women's Experience." *Anima*, vol. 1, no. 2, 1975, pp. 4-14.

Byrd, Deborah. "Young Mothers and the Age-Old Problems of Sexism, Classism, Family Dysfunction and Violence." *Mothers, Mothering and Motherhood across Cultural Difference: A Reader*, edited by Andrea O'Reilly. Demeter Press, 2014, pp. 487-506.

Darisi, Tanya. "It Doesn't Matter if You're 15 or 45, Having a Child is a Difficult Experience: Reflexivity and Resistance in Young Mothers' Constructions of Identity." *Journal of the Association for Research on Mothering*, vol. 9, no. 1, 2007, pp. 29-41.

Green, Fiona. "Developing a Feminist Motherline: Reflections on a Decade of Feminist Parenting." *Journal of the Association for Research on Mothering*, vol. 8, no. 1-2, 2006, pp. 9-19.

Horwitz, Erika. "Resistance as a Site of Empowerment: The Journey Away from Maternal Sacrifice." *Mother Outlaws: Theories and Practices of Empowered Mothering*, edited by Andrea O'Reilly, Women's Press, 2004, pp. 43-58.

Lavell-Harvard, Dawn Memee, and Jeanette Corbiere Lavell. "Thunder Spirits: Reclaiming the Power of Our Grandmothers." *"Until Our Hearts are on the Ground": Aboriginal Mothering, Oppression, Resistance and Rebirth*, edited by Dawn Memee Lavell-Harvard and Jeanette Corbiere Lavell, Demeter Press, 2006, pp. 1-10.

Pratt, Annis. *Archetypal Patterns in Women's Fiction.* Indiana University Press, 1981.

O'Reilly, Andrea. *Rocking the Cradle: Thoughts on Motherhood, Feminism and the Possibility of Empowered Mothering.* Demeter Press, 2006.

O'Brien Hallstein. "Maternal Agency." *Encyclopedia of Motherhood.* Ed. Andrea O'Reilly. Sage Press, 2010, 997-699.

Rogers. Megan. *Resolving the Madwoman: Unlocking the Narrative Attic by Writing the Maternal Journey.* Dissertation, RMIT University, Melbourne, Australia, 2014.

Rich, Adrienne. *Of Woman Born: Motherhood as Experience and Institution.* W.W. Norton, 1986.

Ruddick, Sarah. *Maternal Thinking: Toward A Politics of Peace.* Ballantine Books, 1989.

Toews, Miriam. *Summer of My Amazing Luck.* Random, House, 1996.

Chapter Thirteen

Young Motherhood Lost and Found

Stephenie White

I've come from a past
Not many others could last
Fought through trauma and pain
From that I have gained
Courage, strength, and hope
I put down the alcohol and dope
So I can be a mother
An experience like no other
Like a flower I grow
My story I'd like to show
Inspire other to change their lives
Hard work and healthy risks make me thrive

I've been given a second chance
Two beautiful children, I glance
I'm giving them the live I never had
Most grateful, they have the best dad
My partner and I, we have broken a cycle
No intergenerational trauma, stories of survival
Because of all this I lack some skills
We both work hard but hugs don't pay bills
Despite the struggle, we both stay
Because Harmony and Leo just need us today
I can't find the words for the sacrifices I've made

Seeing my babies smile is all that it takes
The motivation I need to get through the week
To make their lives better is all that I seek
I teach my kids to love and be kind
Success and survival is what I hope they find

Afterword: Becoming and Unbecoming

Joanne Minaker

Courage, strength, and hope are three qualities I have always seen in Stephenie. When our paths first crossed several years ago, I saw sparks of her becoming Stephenie, yet she was also struggling to unbecome. When I asked Stephenie to contribute to our collection she humbly agreed, referring to the above powerful piece as "just a simple poem, rhyme, rap—whatever you would like to call it." I suggested we name it "Young Motherhood Lost and Found." Again, Stephenie agreed and said thank you so much for this opportunity. Young mothers like Stephenie need more opportunities for care and to care. They need platforms to share their stories. They need social support networks to soften their falls. They need friends and family to celebrate their rising. But most of all, we need to listen to, and learn from, young mothers. Two of the most important gifts I have received in studying young mothering and learning from young moms who find themselves mothering at the margins is the importance of listening with the intent to understand and the power of empathy.

For almost two decades I've taught a course on youth, crime, and society. One of the things that matters deeply for me in my teaching is that students learn not only academic discourse on the subject but hear and honour the voices of the young people whose lives we are attempting to understand. Several years ago, one of my friends who worked at a youth agency was coming to give a guest lecture for my students. That fateful day she chose to bring a guest, Stephenie. I recall that Stephenie didn't say very much that day, but her presence in the classroom itself made an impact. I met Stephenie again at a program called Woven Journey, created by iHuman Youth Society for socially and economically vulnerable and predominantly Indigenous young mothers. Months later, we were sharing the stage on a panel on youth and human rights. Stephenie later returned to present her own guest lectures to my classes and shared her story of her struggles with the child welfare and justice systems and the way motherhood had transformed her life. These have been few of the moments of connection where our paths working for justice for young mothers have aligned, and how delighted I was to recently receive this message from Stephenie: "Good morning! I wanted to share some good news. I just got a job at iHuman. I will be running the Mothers Program." Stephenie leads a support group for young, marginalized mothers, many of whom are Indigenous—a place where she herself healed from the trauma of loss, abuse, and oppression. She is giving back by offering resources and care to young mothers struggling with the same issues and concerns she battled during her youth and early motherhood.

Stephenie's story reminds us that as much as the young women whose lives and experiences inform this book are becoming, they too are unbecoming. They are letting go of expectations and barriers to agency and autonomy. They are pushing past their own perceived and socially constructed assumptions about who they are and where they belong. Stephenie's journey is one of losing motherhood as a site of pain, loss, and stigma, and finding motherhood as a source of power, healing, and empowerment; her story, like all of ours, continues to unfold. And I am so grateful to have been if even a small part of her journey. I believe that all young mothers deserve to flourish and become who they aspire to be. It is a challenging undertaking for us all, which involves taking off the masks, working through the myths, and resisting social expectations so readily placed upon mothers. It's important to remember that the issues revealed in this poem and discussed in this book are not something about "them" for "us" to read about. Rather, the matters at the core of this book are about all of us and what it means to be in the world caring together. As stated in the introduction to this collection, "young mothers, when truly supported, are empowered to take the lead mobilizing to create more supportive spaces from which to become—and raise—the people they desire to be." Cared for people care for people.

Notes on Contributors

Vivyan Adair, after earning her PhD in English Literature as a single mother on welfare, began teaching women's and gender studies and literature courses at Hamilton College, where she continues to teach and publish books and essays with a focus on representations of poor mothers and the impact of welfare reform on the lives of poor women and children and on education, law, and public policy.

Valerie Andrews is an adoption activist and a PhD student in gender, feminist, and women's Studies at York University. Her research focus is critical adoption studies. Valerie is the author of *White Unwed Mother: The Adoption Mandate in Postwar Canada*, and the executive director of Origins Canada, a national nonprofit organization supporting those separated by adoption.

Deborah Byrd is professor of English and women's and gender studies at Lafayette College, where she teaches literature and women's and gender studies courses from an intersectional feminist perspective and was the inaugural director of the Center for Community Engagement. Byrd has published books and articles on young and low-income mothers and on feminist, maternal, and community-based learning pedagogy.

Karen Felstead is a lecturer in literacy at Federation University Australia and is currently completing her PhD, which focuses on young mothers and early parenting. Karen's research interests revolve around young children and their acquisition of language and literacy; education and literacy for all; and transformative pedagogies in teacher education programs.

Miranda Francis is a PhD candidate at La Trobe University in Australia. Her research is an oral history of mothering in suburban Melbourne post-1945. It is based on interviews with women over sixty, focusing on their memories of mothering. She has published in such peer-reviewed journals as *Oral History, Provenance,* and *Oral History Australia Journal.*

Melinda Vandenbeld Giles is an anthropology PhD candidate at the University of Toronto and lecturer at Lakehead University. Her research focuses on neoliberalism, public policy, and homelessness (particularly for mothers) in Ontario. Melinda's publications include her Demeter Press edited volume *Mothering in the Age of Neoliberalism,* her co-edited volume *The Routledge Companion to Motherhood,* and her Inanna feminist fiction novel *Clara Awake.*

Heather Jackson, a former teen mom, is now a thirty-something single mom of a teen. She is a former site producer of girl-mom.com and currently works as a birth doula, childbirth educator, and trauma-based mental health therapist. She is co-editor of *Feminist Parenting* and *Motherhood and Social Exclusion* and co-editor on a forthcoming collection on mothering and abortion. She has also two zine series on eating disorder recovery and motherhood and anarchism (etsy shop: ramonegirl) and has published her work in such venues as thepushback. org, hipmama.com, girl-mom.com, and muthamagazine.com.

Sunahtah Jones is a second year master's student, pursuing a degree in women's and gender studies with a deep research focus on the complex marginalization of Black women and Black LGBTQ+. Through intersections of her research and artistry as a poet and writer, Sunahtah articulates the intersectional oppression of mothers globally.

Erin Kuri is a PhD candidate in social work/gender studies and feminist research at McMaster University. Her research and practice interests include arts-based research, critical feminist perspectives on vulnerability and autonomy, intersectionality, young mothers, infant/maternal wellness, and gender-based violence. Erin is a registered psychotherapist and registered art therapist in Toronto, ON.

Johanna Lewis is a queer femme parent, a community organizer, and a doctoral candidate in history at York University. She has engaged in community-based research with mothers and women living with HIV, and currently focuses her scholarship on histories of empire, colonial memories and legacies, and critical methodologies.

Joanne Minaker, PhD, is associate professor and associate dean in the Faculty of Arts and Science at MacEwan University. Joanne is an inspired mother of three and social scientist whose body of work centres around care, human connection, and social (in)justice. Her writing includes *Youth, Crime and Society: Issues of Power and Justice* (2009), *Criminalized Mothers, Criminalized Mothering* (2015) co-authored/edited with Bryan Hogeveen. Joanne's scholarship problematizes marginalizing processes that exclude, silence, and dehumanize young women, criminalized youth, and survivors of sexual violence.

Andrea O'Reilly, PhD, is professor in the School of Gender, Sexuality and Women's Studies at York University. O'Reilly is founder and director of the Motherhood Initiative for Research and Community Involvement, founder and editor-in-chief of the *Journal of the Motherhood Initiative*, and founder and publisher of Demeter Press. She is editor/author of twenty-one books, including *Matricentric Feminism: Theory, Activism, and Practice* (2016).

Jenni Sullivan is a midwifery student who is completing the final year of the midwifery education program. Jenni had her first child at the age of twenty-two and experienced poverty and hardship but also great joy and reward. She has had the opportunity to work with young parents in a mentoring role and continues to be inspired by their strength and dedication.

Stephenie White is a Métis mother of two, from Edmonton, Alberta. She is passionate about sharing her story. She is currently working with Woven Journey, a mothering support program at iHuman Youth Society. Stephenie has been involved with that organization for fourteen years, from youth to worker. Learning from her past experiences with homelessness, addiction to crystal meth, and getting sober, she inspires others to turn their lives around.